THEOLOGICAL
TRANSITION
IN AMERICAN
METHODISM: 1790-1935

THEOLOGICAL TRANSITION IN AMERICAN METHODISM

1790-1935

Robert E. Chiles

UNIVERSITY
PRESS OF
AMERICA

LANHAM • NEW YORK • LONDON

Library of Congress Cataloging in Publication Data

Chiles, Robert Eugene.
    Theological transition in American Methodism,
1790–1935.

    Reprint. Originally published: New York : Abingdon
Press, c1965.
    Bibliography: p.
    Includes index.
    1. Methodist Church–Doctrines–History. I. Title.
BX8331.2C5   1983   230'.7'09   83–16666
ISBN 0–8191–3551–8 (pbk. : alk. paper)

For DORIS

CONTENTS

INTRODUCTION 13

CHAPTER I. METHODISM'S THEOLOGICAL
             HERITAGE 21
             Doctrinal Standards 22
             Fundamental Doctrines 26
             Theologians in the "Course
             of Study" 32

CHAPTER II. METHODISM'S THEOLOGICAL
             HISTORY 37
             From Wesley to Watson,
             1790–1840 38
                 *Scholastic Statement and Indigenous
                 Growth*
                 *Wesleyan Orthodoxy in Richard
                 Watson*
             From Watson to Miley,
             1840–1890 49
                 *Moralistic Revision and Systematic
                 Integration*
                 Ethical Arminianism in John Miley

From Miley to Knudson,
1890–1935 61
*Cultural Impact and Liberal
Reconstruction*
Personal Idealism in Albert Knudson

CHAPTER III. FROM REVELATION TO REASON 76
Wesleyan "Scriptural, Experimental
Religion" 77
Revelation Through Scripture
Experience and Reason
Wesley's Theological Method
Watson on "The Divine Authority
of Scripture" 87
Scripture as Revelation
Evidence of Divine Authority
Authority and Method in Theology
Miley on "Theological Science" 95
Sources of Theology
Scientific Certitude
Systematization of Theology
Knudson's "Rational Justification of
Faith" 104
Religion and Theology
Epistemology and the Right to Believe
Metaphysics and Personalism
Method and Authority

CHAPTER IV. FROM SINFUL MAN TO
MORAL MAN 115
Man as Sinner in Wesley 116
Adam and Original Sin
Original Guilt and Depravity
Sinful Man

Watson on Man's Fallen Condition.....123
Man's Primitive Condition and Fall
Results of the Fall

Miley on Man's Need for Redemption...129
Primitive Man and the Fall
Native Depravity and Native Demerit
Definition of Sin

Knudson's "Presuppositions of
Redemption" 136
Man's Worth and Freedom
Suffering and Sin

CHAPTER V. FROM FREE GRACE TO FREE WILL..144

Wesleyan Free Grace 145
God's Atoning Grace
Prevenient Grace
Justifying Grace
Sanctifying Grace

Watson on "The Atonement and Its
Benefits" 158
Universal Atonement
Grace and Freedom
Salvation by Grace

Miley on the Divine Activity in
Redemption 165
"The Atonement in Christ"
Gracious Motives Freely Chosen
Justification and Regeneration

Knudson on Christ and Redemption 175
God in Christ
Metaphysical Freedom and Divine
Grace
The Christian Life

CHAPTER VI. TOWARD A PRACTICAL
APPLICATION 184
A Profile of Transition 185
The Sequence of Transition 188
The Dynamics of Transition 190
The Inevitability of
Transition 196
The Eternal Constancy 204

APPENDIX: Methodist Theological Literature 209

BIBLIOGRAPHY 215

INDEX 227

THEOLOGICAL
TRANSITION
IN AMERICAN
METHODISM: 1790-1935

INTRODUCTION

Is the history of Methodist theology the story of a fall from the perfection of a Wesleyan Eden into a world of theological defection? It is easy for a member of a generation recently concerned for orthodoxy to think so, and tempting for him to display his superior theological wisdom in interpreting this history, often indignant in his protest, caustic and sardonic in his language. In this study I have experienced these temptations firsthand. Through the years, however, for several reasons, they have become much less attractive. Not the least important among these reasons is the realization, on occasion dearly won, that polemics prompted by such feelings are far more successful in alienating than in illuminating the audience to which they are addressed.

But there are other reasons. I have become more appreciative of the complexity of the historical and spiritual processes involved in theological transition. There is reason to believe that the swing away from a period of theological vitality, such as the Wesleyan Revival, is unwittingly accomplished. The loss of theological truth through willful distortion or deliberate desertion is comparatively rare; it does not reflect intellectual obtuseness or spiritual perversity as much as it does the committed effort of the theologian to speak a language meaningful for his day, enhancing thereby the impact of the spiritual tradition out of which he works. It is commendable that in each generation there are men who take seriously the apologetic task of theology. Yet, struggling to maintain the relevance of theology and its respectability in a new world of science and philosophy, the theologian may lose his way. His theology may become so altered that it forfeits some of its power to speak God's word decisively to the very world it is concerned to save. Thus is Christ made to capitulate to culture. When the disposing cause of this theological captivity is the desire to gain relevance for a timeless faith in a changing world, however, I now find it awkward to maintain a critical superiority.

Another factor has increasingly impressed me with its significance for theological transition. It is based on the assumption that great periods of revival do in fact renew the lives of men, releasing them from old ties and necessities and opening them to new demands and possibilities. Revival does achieve a new liberty for the Christian man. This new state of things seems both too good to be true and too good to be lost. As it confronts these threatening possibilities, man's liberty may become an onerous burden which drives him to seek some external support. He may find this support in a sacred book, or a moral maxim, or, perhaps, in a reasoned view of life. Then he clings to his new security and cannot really be expected to surrender it, simply on being informed that his misplaced dependence distorts the original faith of his tradition. Life on the stream created where freedom and finitude flow together is often tempestuous and risky. It solicits compassion for those who have felt driven to seek shelter.

At best the perspective of history offers ambiguous evidence about the possibility of arresting the tendency of freedom to take refuge in more manageable securities. In every age there are men who apprehend the processes of religious decline and struggle to regain the faith of their fathers. But the tide that fearfully recedes from freedom can be arrested only by making freedom safer, and this requires a divine security which is beyond man's power to produce or control. Indeed, man's very inability to arrest the decay or to arrange the renewal of religion bears indirect witness to the sovereignty of God. The fact of his radical dependence on God may also help explain man's reluctance to acknowledge the impoverishment of his tradition; how can he do so if the power for its renewal is not subject to his command?

Thus I see a certain inevitability about the compromises in a theological tradition, an inevitability involving powerful and universal spiritual dynamics which are not alien to any one of us. Therefore, it seems to me that the study of theological transition is best carried on in an atmosphere of sympathetic understanding free from arrogant condescension. Theological transition, in its diversion of noble purposes to temporal accommodations, in its anxiety about the retention of God's good gifts, and in its inevitability and universality, surely is something of a fall. But it is a fall in which each theologian participates. He is well advised, then, to maintain his charity.

The mood of sympathetic understanding, however, does not require a denial of the critical theological changes which have taken place or the assurance that they are unimportant. Nothing is gained by blinking the truth; indeed, the unwillingness to see the truth, though understandable, may be the first great obstacle in the way of renewal. Therefore I have been straightforward and unapologetic in identifying the modifications that have taken place in American Methodism and in contrasting them with Wesley's theology. Charity hesitates long before it obscures the truth.

Honesty prompts a further admission. I prefer the orthodoxy of Wesley to the theology produced by his heirs. Now, much more than I once did, I understand and respect them, appreciate their efforts and acknowledge the importance of their apologetic purposes. Still, I renounce their theology in favor of Wesley's because, quite simply, I feel that his theology points more steadily and knowingly than theirs does at ultimate divine and human realities. This is not to deny that Wesley's theology is dated and has unresolved internal problems. In basic ways it failed to come to terms with the newer scientific and philosophical developments of its day; it bequeathed to the future somewhat uncertain com-

Sanctification

promises with regard to guilt, freedom, assurance, and sanctifica-tion. Therefore, in view of these shortcomings, it would be a lamentable mistake to attempt to force on Wesley's heirs an artificial conformity with his theology.

Not only lamentable but futile. I have a further conviction which is most firmly entrenched. I believe that theology is the mind's service to man's total being; it is the rational expression of a deeper, more enveloping religious reality. Though theology has some power to shape and confirm this reality, much more sig-nificantly it depends on and gives expression to this reality. It is difficult for me to sustain the proposition that bad theology critically corrupts living. In a more complex and mysterious way, an anxious, unresolved, or assertive response to life produces bad theology. If these considerations hold, then, it seems clear that a particular theological formulation cannot be imposed successfully on a religious disposition to which it is essentially alien. To their dismay, apostles of a return to orthodoxy sometimes make this discovery.

This belief about the derivative character of theology has further implications. First, the compromises of orthodoxy are serious, not for intellectual reasons, but because they tend to betray the prior depletion of viable redemptive reality. The quality of human life is at issue, not merely the propriety of theological propositions or the conformity of the theologian. Second, the belief that theology essentially mirrors a deeper reality implies that the power of the theologian to shape history, to stem the flood of decline or to stir the fires of renewal, is quite limited. The theologian's work is partial, confined, and transitory. Thus it becomes him to admit the modesty of his theological task. If man is not saved by reason, neither is he saved by theology. This assertion I take to be simply an expression of New Testament and classical Christianity: Man is justified by grace through faith alone. This same belief is intended to dominate this study of the theology of Wesley and his heirs.

These then are the basic convictions that have informed my

presentation. There are additional intimate relationships between my life and it. For the study has a distinct history inseparably related to my own. My history began in a Methodist parsonage in a family which has produced five ordained Methodist ministers in three generations. Thus Methodism was for me not only a way of living but, even more deeply and pervasively than I knew, a way of thinking.

In the middle of my seminary days at Garrett, in a prescribed course on Methodism, I was introduced to the theology of John Wesley and was fascinated by it. My interest, shared by an enthusiastic friend, led to extensive research in Wesleyan sources resulting in a collection of his statements on theology, subsequently, and to our unabashed delight, published as *A Compend of Wesley's Theology*. The more I learned of Wesley's thought, the more heightened seemed the contrast between it and the Methodist theology of my acquaintance. A persistent question clamored for an answer: What had happened between Wesley's day and mine? Thus when my doctoral program required a thesis for investigation, my subject was never in doubt.

The intermittent search for an answer to this basic question covered more than a dozen years and received invaluable assistance from many persons. I am particularly grateful to my former professors at Garrett Theological Seminary who stimulated this interest and to those at Union Theological Seminary and Columbia University who guided the research on which this book is based. In addition, my colleagues in Wesley studies through discussions and research have placed me in a debt which it is a pleasure to acknowledge. Finally, comments on this material by participants in ministers' conferences, Wesley Society meetings, laymen's classes in theology, and a seminary course have most certainly improved the presentation.

As the study developed several significant revisions seemed necessary. Two doctrines (the atonement and Christian perfection) were reduced to subordinate status, and a fourth successor of Wesley (Sheldon) was dropped from the list of primary figures.

To bring the theological transitions into sharper focus, a systematic order of presentation was adopted rather than one indecisively historical. Thus the answer to my question finally assumed the form in which it is given here.

The reader should note in advance some things not to expect in the pages which follow. First, this study is more an investigation in systematic theology than it is in the history of Christian thought. Both investigations are needed and have received recent attention, as indicated in the appendix on literature. The special interest here, however, is in the systematic comparison of doctrinal changes, not in a chronology of the successive contributions to theological development in American Methodism. Though the outline of history which is provided lays no claim to depth or breadth, as background for the doctrinal analyses and in view of the scarcity of other materials, it may prove useful.

Second, though some of the cultural and intellectual forces in American history which helped shape certain "fundamental doctrines" are suggested, principal interest is in what has taken place, not how or why. Perhaps virtue will be found in arriving first at some broad consensus on the *description* of what has happened before devoting primary attention to the more exacting and problematical task posed by the *explanation* of these happenings. For the illumination they cast on the Methodist tradition, a number of the studies listed in the Bibliography which interpret and explain theological transition in American Protestantism may be consulted by those interested. Admittedly modest, the description of doctrinal development may be able, in a small way, to help modern Methodism gain a clearer sense of identity by countering its chronic disregard for antecedents.

Third, it is neither assumed nor required, for the purposes of this study, that the three primary men had direct and decisive bearing on the development of Methodist theology. Such influence did exist and often will be demonstrated. But Watson, Miley, and Knudson have been selected chiefly as representative figures, and only secondarily for the lines of influence which can be traced to them (for which Butler, perhaps, and certainly Whedon and Bowne are more significant). Still, the relationships among various men are often acknowledged, and references to parallel discussions by other important Methodist theologians are frequently given, particularly in the notes.

Fourth, the presentation of Wesley's theology which is made normative here will disappoint those who desire a comprehensive justification for each view adopted, as well as those who desire only an impartial review of major interpretative positions. Both the limits of space and the nature of the study preclude the former. The latter demand is renounced for an evident preference. Wesley's theology is viewed here as essentially and distinctively Protestant; it is a legitimate heir to Reformed and classical Christianity; it is not simply evangelical Arminianism or Anglicanism in earnest. These convictions, which may represent a minority point of view, have survived repeated contests with their opposing possibilities. It is hoped that they are not blatantly arbitrary, however, or unduly skewed by polemical interests. Still, honesty requires me to acknowledge that personal existence and pastoral experience have significantly influenced my understanding and presentation of Wesley's theology.

Repeatedly, the issues with which this study deals have proved themselves timely and important, to me personally, and to Methodist students, clergymen, and laymen as well. The interest we have shared, I believe, reflects an awareness of a first necessity for the church in each generation: It must recover, from the time of its original vitality, the proud and painful memory of its conquests and capitulations. I offer this study as a modest contribution toward such a recovery, fully aware that it is faith, not knowledge, which saves man and renews the church.

CHAPTER I
METHODISM'S
THEOLOGICAL HERITAGE

John Wesley's busy pen occasionally notes his conviction that in the people called Methodists God had raised up a distinctive witness. Half a dozen general tracts contain his efforts to identify these people.[1] They are to be a sanctuary for sinners desiring to flee from the wrath to come. They are to be loving members of the New Testament fellowship come to life in the eighteenth century. They are to be distinguished not by particular opinions or modes of worship but by their confidence in God's grace to meet fully every need. They are to spread scriptural holiness throughout the land. Not a revision of Christianity but its renewal—this is Wesley's chief contribution to history.

[1] These tracts appear in *The Works of the Rev. John Wesley, A.M.*, ed. Thomas Jackson, in Vol. VIII: "The Principles of a Methodist," pp. 359-74; "The Character of a Methodist," pp. 339-46; "A Plain Account of the People Called Methodist," pp. 248-68; "A Short History of Methodism," pp. 347-50; and "Advice to the People Called Methodist," pp. 351-58.

Serving the Evangelical Revival for more than fifty years, he confronted the compromises which help stem the initial tides of evangelical passion. Knowingly, he counseled his successors to remain steadfast. "I am not afraid that the people called Methodists should ever cease to exist either in Europe or America," he writes. "But I am afraid lest they should only exist as a dead sect, having the form of religion without the power. And this undoubtedly will be the case, unless they hold fast both the doctrine, spirit, and discipline with which they first set out." He believes that a Methodism faithful to its heritage can endure permanently within Protestant Christianity. Thus he labored unsparingly, he says, to "fix [Methodists] upon such a foundation as is likely to stand as long as the sun and moon endure. That is, if they continue to walk by faith and to show forth their faith by works; otherwise, I pray God to root out the memorial of them from the earth." [2]

On many occasions through many years Wesley expressed the historic faith in an identifiable idiom. Together his statements constitute a worthy theological heritage for the Methodist community. In brief, it is the purpose of this study to examine essential aspects of this heritage and their reception and expression by successive generations in America. In particular, the study will note the elements of traditional conservation and transitional adaptation as Methodists have built on this foundation.

DOCTRINAL STANDARDS

If theology is not Wesley's ultimate concern, neither did he regard it as optional or irrelevant for Christian life. For several generations modern Methodism took satisfaction in proclaiming itself to be "nontheological," insisting that it was practical and

---

[2] The first familiar quotation is from "Thoughts Upon Methodism," published in the *Arminian Magazine* in 1787, quoted in Luke Tyerman, *The Life and Times of the Rev. John Wesley, M.A.*, III, 519; the second quotation is from "Thoughts Upon Some Late Occurrences," *Works*, XIII, 217.

evangelical instead. Usually it attempted to ground its indifference to theology in Wesley himself. However, since the general Protestant renewal of theological interest in orthodox sources, reflected in Methodism by the publication of George Croft Cell's *The Rediscovery of John Wesley* in 1935, this attitude has noticeably declined. There is now little inclination in scholarly circles to dispute that Wesley was theologically informed and deeply concerned to maintain a sound foundation for the Methodist movement. Though his catholicity of spirit and his stress on the experiential aspects of Christianity made it easier for later Methodism to relegate theology to a secondary role, such a devaluation is widely recognized to be untrue both to Wesley's intention and to his practice.[3]

From the sizable body of evidence supporting Wesley's insistence on the importance of theology, two points are especially relevant: his determination of doctrinal standards for the Methodist societies and his practice of distinguishing between "grand, fundamental doctrines" and "mere opinions."

In 1763 Wesley drafted a Model Deed stipulating that the pulpits of Methodist chapels were to be used only by persons who "preach no other doctrine than is contained in Mr. Wesley's 'Notes Upon the New Testament' and four volumes of 'sermons.'"[4] Thus a legal standard for Methodist doctrine was introduced which has prevailed within British Methodism to the present, having been reaffirmed in the Deed of Union in 1932.

After the Revolutionary War, when it appeared inevitable that Methodists in America would form a separate church, Wesley

[3] S. Paul Schilling reviews the evidence on both sides of this controversy in the first chapter of his *Methodism and Society in Theological Perspective*, Vol. III of *Methodism and Society*, pp. 23-43; see also Umphrey Lee's essay "Freedom from Rigid Creed," in *Methodism*, ed. William K. Anderson, pp. 128-38, and Colin Williams, *John Wesley's Theology Today*, pp. 13-22.

[4] *The Journal of the Rev. John Wesley, A.M.*, ed. Nehemiah Curnock, VIII, 335-41; the Deed and its place in British Methodism is discussed by Henry Carter in *The Methodist Heritage*, pp. 236 f.

addressed this plea to his American preachers: "Let all of you be determined to abide by the Methodist doctrine and discipline published in the four volumes of *Sermons* and the *Notes upon the New Testament* together with the *Large Minutes* of the Conference." [5] He also prepared an abridgment of the Thirty-Nine Articles of the Anglican Church, which he sent to America along with a revised *Sunday Service* and other orders from the *Book of Common Prayer*. With one article added on the "rulers of the United States," the Christmas Conference of 1784 adopted the Twenty-Five Articles of Religion as a basic statement of doctrine for the Methodist Episcopal Church in America and accepted the other doctrinal standards Wesley had proposed.

American Methodism gave further prominence and constitutional status to these standards at the 1808 General Conference. The first "Restrictive Rule" there adopted provided that "the general conference shall not revoke, alter, or change our articles of religion, nor establish any new standards or rules of doctrine contrary to our present existing and established standards of doctrine." Of the General Rules, this is the only one requiring a three-fourths majority of the annual conferences for its modification. In fact, this first rule has never been seriously challenged and stands unchanged in paragraph 9 of the current *Discipline*. According to reputable scholars, it can be historically demonstrated that the standards referred to in this Restrictive Rule are the Twenty-Five Articles of Religion, Wesley's *Standard Sermons*, and the *Notes upon the New Testament*. "These are the standards assumed when it is enjoined that neither clergy nor laity shall teach

[5] *The Letters of the Rev. John Wesley, A.M.*, ed. John Telford, VII, 191, "To the Preachers in America," October 3, 1783. Norman W. Spellmann in an illuminating discussion of "The Christmas Conference" describes the actions taken with regard to doctrine, discipline, and ritual, in *The History of American Methodism*, ed. Emory S. Bucke, I, 213-23. Helpful accounts of these formative years and events are found in Wade Crawford Barclay, *History of Methodists Missions*, Vol. I, *Missionary Motivation and Expansion*; Paul S. Sanders, "An Appraisal of John Wesley's Sacramentalism in the Evolution of Early American Methodism," unpublished Ph.D. dissertation, Union, 1954, pp. 187-234, 338-89; and William Warren Sweet, *Methodism in American History*, chaps. I-X, and *Religion on the American Frontier, 1783-1840*, Vol. IV, *The Methodists*.

contrary to 'established standards of doctrine' (Paragraphs 944, 962, 969)." [6]

It would be quite mistaken, however, to conclude that American Methodism generally has conformed to these doctrinal standards, or even that it has felt an obligation to do so. From the first, Methodism has sustained a continuing debate between those who find its theological reason for being in the Wesleyan heritage and those who locate it in the theological expression of its current religious life. The growing interest in Methodism's relation to the ecumenical movement has given renewed urgency to this controversy. While some Methodists who participate in the ecumenical discussion feel it is most important to reappropriate their Wesleyan heritage, others vigorously denounce attempts to invoke the Wesleyan standards, asserting that "the locus of reality in The Methodist Church is not John Wesley, or even the demonstrated tradition of being connected with him, but The Methodist Church as it actually worships, lives, and seeks to serve its Lord today." [7] Without intending to prejudge this debate, we may fairly say that twentieth-century American Methodism has been much more concerned with contemporary problems and issues than it has with preserving the integrity of a doctrinal heritage which, in some abstract, historical way, is still legally binding upon it. In any event, the investigation of transitions in Methodist theology should

---

[6] John Deschner, *Wesley's Christology*, pp. 9, 13; he quotes a private paper in which Albert C. Outler makes the same point. See also Franz Hildebrandt, "Is Methodist Emphasis Rooted in the New Testament?" *London Quarterly and Holborn Review*, 28 (1959), 232. In this context it bears mention also that between 1784 and 1808 the various editions of the *Doctrines and Discipline of the Methodist Episcopal Church* printed half a dozen doctrinal tracts, mostly by Wesley. Since they occupied considerable space, for purely practical reasons they were ordered removed from the *Discipline* and published separately from 1812 on. They did not appear independently, however, until 1832. Since 1808, doctrine has had but little place in the Methodist *Discipline*. All that remains in the current edition is the statement of the "Twenty-Five Articles," constituting only 7 of more than 700 pages. See Schilling, *Methodism and Society in Theological Perspective*, pp. 28 f., and John L. Peters, *Christian Perfection and American Methodism*, p. 98. For a discussion of the General Conference of 1808, which adopted a constitution for American Methodism along with its Restrictive Rules, see Frederick A. Norwood, *The History of American Methodism*, I, 474-80.

[7] Harold Bosley in a review of Colin William's *John Wesley's Theology Today*, in *Religion in Life*, 29 (1960), 616.

be of value if it offers evidence on the points at issue in this debate. Perhaps it need not also argue conclusions and propose solutions. Therefore, in the definition of changes, in order to show clearly *what* has happened, Wesley's views will be regarded as normative. The three major chapters on revelation, sin, and grace will each begin with a summary of Wesley's position which will serve as a continuing frame of reference as later developments are traced. The critical evaluation of the transitions thus identified, however, is quite another undertaking. Some suggestions about their meaning and consequences will be given in the concluding chapter. But what should be done about them, if anything, is one of the critical issues currently facing the recipients of the Wesleyan heritage.

FUNDAMENTAL DOCTRINES

The picture of a Methodist as a man with a warm heart and an outstretched hand may be a caricature, but it is not without some basis in fact. Wesley refused to do battle over "opinions (feathers, mere trifles not worth mentioning)" and was typically willing to go as far as he could to find common ground with those who differed with him. With remarkable fidelity he embodies the universal brotherhood or catholic spirit for which he habitually contends. And he is always clear in his judgment that the reality of the saving encounter with God is infinitely more important than any theological description of it. At the same time, he scornfully rejects "indifference to all opinions," as "the spawn of hell," and asserts that the man of truly catholic spirit "is fixed as the sun in his judgment concerning the main branches of Christian doctrine." [8]

He distinguishes, not always consistently or clearly, between "opinions" and "fundamental doctrines." Respecting divergencies in Christian belief, worship, and polity, "which do not strike at the root of Christianity," he acknowledges, "We think and let think." But when particular doctrinal interpretations seem to him to com-

[8] *Letters*, VI, 61; and *Wesley's Standard Sermons*, ed. Edward H. Sugden, II, 143.

promise or contradict Christian reality, he promptly corrects them.[9] In one context, he speaks of "three grand, scriptural doctrines—Original Sin, Justification by Faith, and Holiness"; in another, of "our main doctrines" repentance, faith, and holiness; in still another, of "the grand fundamental doctrines . . . the New Birth and Justification by Faith." In his careful review of this matter, Colin Williams compiles a list of doctrines which Wesley variously insists on as essential: original sin, the deity of Christ, the atonement, justification by faith alone, the work of the Holy Spirit (including new birth and holiness) and the Trinity.[10]

Not only does Wesley stress certain fundamental doctrines, and permit latitude with respect to more peripheral opinions, but he is also most unwilling to concede that Methodism is basically constituted of "singularities," "innovations," or "strange opinions." Rather, he says, it is a true rendering of the faith of the Church of England, the Reformation, and the New Testament. This faith has been so long forgotten that, when it is revived, it is suspected and opposed as though new.[11] Generally, such charges of heresy were leveled at the Methodist insistence on assurance and Christian perfection. But often these accusations reflect no more than the inability of the eighteenth century to reckon with the possibility that God's grace continues to be efficacious in human life and history.

Which of the "fundamental doctrines" are properly central in a critical review of Wesleyan theology? Though Wesley and the Methodists stand out in Christian history for their stress on the witness of the Spirit and the life of holiness, it is not obvious that the essence of Methodism is caught up in these doctrines.[12] Rather,

---

[9] *Works*, VIII, 341.

[10] *Letters*, IV, 146; II, 268; V, 224 f.; and Williams, *John Wesley's Theology Today*, pp. 16 f.

[11] *Letters*, II, 49; IV, 131; III, 291.

[12] On this point, John Deschner offers some cogent observations in his article on "Methodism" in a *A Handbook of Christian Theology*, eds. M. Halverson and A. A. Cohen. (New York: Living Age Books, 1958), pp. 232 f.: "Methodism in this country has a Wesleyan heart but an American head. Its characteristic emphases remain those of the core of the Wesleyan preaching—'heart religion' and moral renewal. Its theo-

they may themselves depend on and reflect the ebb and flow of vitality in other critical doctrines. It is proposed here that Wesley usually has in mind more elemental and common Christian realities when he speaks of "fundamental doctrines." Three of these—revelation, sin, and grace—have been selected for closer study.

Theology is unitary and circular in the sense that each doctrine presupposes and implies the whole body of doctrine. Thus it is ultimately impossible to study one doctrine in isolation from all the rest. But within the totality of theological concern, some doctrines may more surely and readily reveal the true tenor of a particular position or its essential modification. Perhaps revelation, sin, and grace possess such determinative character for Wesleyan, if not for all, theology.[13]

In the doctrine of *revelation*, broadly conceived, the foundation is laid and direction set for the elaboration of systematic theology. Theology's point of departure, the sources it uses, and the ultimate authority it respects are critical for the development of various doctrines and for the statement of a system as a whole. Thus to ignore this area would be to pass up one of the most sensitive guides to shifting theological currents.

Several essentials of Wesleyan theology are involved in the doctrine of revelation. In Wesley's world, deism had shunted aside God's saving self-disclosure, making the Christian drama of salvation seem implausible and reactionary. The practical effect of

---

logical articulation of this central emphasis has tended to lack stability and continuity, and to be unusually open to stimulus and influence from without. In part this situation roots in a characteristic Methodist attitude toward theology as subordinate to experience. . . . At a deeper level, this Methodist theological eclecticism bears witness to the fact that Methodism was born not as a church but as a movement and emphasis within Anglicanism, and that the Wesleyan heart needs again and again to reach beyond the 'Methodist doctrines' and renew its living contact, first of all, with the scriptural revelation, which Wesley emphasized, but also with the ecumenical theological tradition in which, through the Anglicanism which Wesley presupposed, it originally learned to know its own mind."

[18] David C. Shipley's illuminating study, "Methodist Arminianism in the Theology of John Fletcher," unpublished Ph.D. dissertation, Yale, 1942, focuses on the same three areas, theological method, anthropology, and soteriology. The "theological circle" presupposed in this statement is elaborated by Paul Tillich in his *Systematic Theology*, I, 8–11.

Wesley's work was to reverse this trend by showing God decisively active in the world as sovereign Lord and gracious Father. It made a place for evangelical experience, which could no longer be shrugged off as mere enthusiasm, and it denied that the life of faith could be regulated by the calm dictates of reason. Renewed openness to revelation also presupposed and promoted the recovery of the Bible as its chief deposit and medium. Finally, it supported sympathetic and independent expression of the doctrines of the Holy Spirit, assurance, and the witness of the Spirit. The fate of most of these concerns among Wesley's successors is one important part of this study.[14]

The doctrine of *sin* is significant also, for tracing theological affinities and alterations. In important ways it has supporting relationships with other doctrinal emphases, which inevitably respond to modifications in it. In Methodist theology the doctrine of sin is particularly sensitive to changes in theological climate because it joins an Augustinian-Calvinist understanding of man's corruption and helplessness to a Wesleyan stress on the universal influence of prevenient grace. Because its view of man is such a dialectical composite of sin and grace, Methodism must perennially resist the inviting temptation prematurely to cover the scourge of sin with the solace of grace and, further, to attribute to man a capacity which properly belongs to grace. Either concession produces a radically different picture of man's posture before God. Wesley's doctrine of sin is not distinctive. But the way it is kept in balance with grace is, and the balance is precarious. Therefore, our second primary concern will be the doctrine of sin. To assess transitional adaptations in Wesley's heirs, the nature of depravity, the ground of guilt, and the transmission of both from generation to generation will be examined.

The doctrine of *grace* is the third area for emphasis. Wesley

[14] Only brief attention will be given to the doctrines of assurance and the witness and fruits of the Spirit, for which see Lycurgus M. Starkey, Jr., *The Work of the Holy Spirit: A Study in Wesleyan Theology*, and Arthur S. Yates, *The Doctrine of Assurance*.

uses the phrase "the entire work of God" to catch up his twofold conviction that grace, both inclusively and exclusively, is God's work.[15] First, it expresses the distinctive Methodist accent on the inclusive nature of grace—it is the *whole* work of God. It thus denotes the characteristic prominence which Wesley gives to prevenient grace and to Christian perfection—to grace reaching back into man's life prior to salvation and forward to bring salvation to fulfillment. Both of these doctrines reflect his consistent refusal to limit God's operation in human life.

The decisive role given to prevenient grace prior to salvation expresses Wesley's conviction that before man thinks to turn to God, God seeks him. Through such universal grace Wesley relates divine initiative and human response, making salvation wholly of God, yet not without man's participation. In this connection Wesleyan theology may well have a creative word to speak in the more general theological conversation within Christianity.

The power of grace to accomplish perfection represents the forward projection of "the entire work of God." Wesley's "optimism of grace" is nowhere more clearly embodied than in his expectation that Methodists will go on to perfection.[16] This stress on sanctification and perfection gives to Methodism a singular place and voice among the major Protestant traditions. In these pages, however, it will be accorded only summary treatment. The place of perfection in American Methodist history already has been surveyed in detail by John Peters, whose book helps correct an important lapse in Methodism's theological memory.[17] As his in-

[15] *Sermons*, II, 444-60; Henry Carter's balanced survey of Wesley's theology uses this phrase as a key to its interpretation, *The Methodist Heritage*, pp. 162-87.

[16] Gordon Rupp, *Principalities and Powers*, pp. 77 ff., has a helpful essay on Methodist theology which suggestively contrasts the "optimism of grace" and the "pessimism of nature" and argues that Wesley's chief legacy is to be found in the fullness of his conception of grace. See also Rupp's "The Future of the Methodist Tradition," *London Quarterly and Holborn Review*, 28 (1959), 264-74.

[17] In addition to Peters' comprehensive study, Edward M. Fortney in "The Literature of the History of Methodism," *Religion in Life*, 24 (1955), 443-51, records no less than five unpublished doctoral studies on Christian perfection completed between 1946 and 1950: Robert B. Clark (Temple, 1946); George A. Turner (Harvard, 1946); Orrin A. Manifold (Boston, 1946); Claude Thompson (Drew, 1949); and James

vestigation shows, by itself perfection can be an exhaustive subject. Thus reasons of economy also urge setting this doctrine to one side. The final reason for doing so rests on the assumption that something else, perhaps more important, needs to be done.

The doctrine of grace has a second critical dimension. Historically and systematically, Wesleyan theology understands "the entire work of God" to be an assertion of salvation by grace alone —it is the *sole* work of God. Important as the *inclusive* character of grace is for Wesley, its *exclusive* agency is even more basic. In its emphasis on *sola gratia,* Wesleyanism represents "the Revival of the Reformation," to use Franz Hildebrandt's felicitous phrase.[18] It is in this historical reaffirmation, not in a unique theological thrust, that the dynamic of the Wesleyan Revival is to be found. Through the years, by their polemical and apologetic interests, Methodists have often suggested as much concern for Methodist "peculiarities" as for Christian verities. Or, preoccupied with the ethical application of Wesley's doctrine, they have forgotten that it is salvation which makes a good life possible. But at either turning Methodists embark on a perilous adventure.

An interpretation of Methodist theology which may seem to disparage or discount its handling of the fullness of the work of grace must be stated carefully, even reluctantly. Yet a different, perhaps deeper, demand can be met only by the central emphasis which Methodism shares with Protestantism and classical Christianity. Therefore the treatment of grace deliberately focuses on the plain fact of salvation by grace through faith alone. More specifically, it will fix on the point of meeting between God's grace and man's

---

Coggin (Southwestern Baptist, 1950). The last three give explicit attention to the place of Christian perfection in American Methodism. Timothy L. Smith has also written authoritatively in this area; see "The Holiness Crusade," in *The History of American Methodism,* II, 608-27, and *Revivalism and Social Reform in Mid-Nineteenth-Century America,* pp. 114-47.

[18] *From Luther to Wesley,* pp. 110-57. For further support given to the essential compatibility of Wesleyan and Reformation theology see the works listed above by Shipley, Williams, and Deschner, and also George Croft Cell, *The Rediscovery of John Wesley.*

sin as the most sensitive index to Methodism's fidelity to Wesley's deepest insights.

THEOLOGIANS IN THE "COURSE OF STUDY"

Methodist theological literature, beginning with Wesley and continuing to 1935, composes a formidable mass of material. In order to reveal the tendencies toward transitional adaptation in this literature several representative theologians have been selected for examination to secure, as it were, successive cross sections of dominant theological expression. By this means, more easily and perhaps more clearly, it will be possible to trace the developments in each "fundamental doctrine" and to compare them with the Wesleyan standard. Termination of the analysis at 1935 is indicated by the need for perspective and, more significantly, by the appearance at that time of a new interest in theological orthodoxy which coincided with a reappraisal of the original Wesleyan theology.

Not only is the literature produced by Methodists through this 150-year period sizable and varied; it is also largely unknown and unworked, even within Methodism. Thus the identity of the representative Methodist theologians in American history is not a matter of common knowledge or general agreement. In his search for representative theologians the student finds guidance for and confirmation of his own conclusions on two sides. A ready key to the most significant theologians, particularly in the nineteenth century, is the Conference Course of Study. A second helpful body of material is available in the occasional but significant investigations recently made in the history of Methodist theology.

In 1816 the General Conference of the Methodist Church authorized a Course of Study for Methodist preachers lacking formal theological training. Candidates studied selected texts and were examined on them. Since 1848 the books for this course have been listed quadrennially in the Methodist *Discipline*. Prior to the publication of such lists, Conference journals and publishers' notices indicate the books in use. Occasional references in the writings of Methodist leaders prior to 1848 also help identify the leading authors.[19] Since the vast majority of Methodist preachers through three-quarters of the nineteenth century were trained, not in seminaries, but in the Course of Study, its effect was widespread. By careful examination of the Course of Study, a roster of more than a dozen of the most influential Methodist theologians can be compiled: Clarke, Watson, Whedon, Raymond, Pope, Summers, Warren, Miley, Sheldon, Tillett, Curtis, Rall, Lewis, and Knudson. From this list three men have been chosen to represent successive periods in the history of American Methodist theology.

Richard Watson (1781-1833) is the first important systematic theologian among Wesley's heirs. An Englishman who made a signal contribution to British Methodism, he was also most influential in America through his writings, particularly his *Theological Institutes*.[20] The first part of this opus became a standard text in 1825 (before the last part was completed); the finished

---

[19] Nathan Bangs wrote an informative series of articles outlining a course of study which was published as *Letters to Young Ministers of the Gospel on the Importance and Method of Study* (New York: N. Bangs and J. Emory, 1826). By 1827 the Illinois Conference recommended, among others, the following books for the acquisition of theological knowledge: the Bible, Wesley's *Notes* and *Sermons*, Benson's, Coke's and Clarke's *Commentaries*, Fletcher's *Checks to Antinomianism*, Watson's *Institutes of Theology*, Locke's *On the Understanding*, Paley's *Philosophy*, Watt's *Logic*, *The Methodist Discipline*, and the *Methodist Magazine*—listed in Sweet, *Religion on the American Frontier*, Vol. IV, *The Methodists*, p. 304. The course which Bishops Hedding and Emory presented to the Philadelphia Conference in 1833 included Watson, *Biblical and Theological Dictionary*, Porteus, *Evidences of Christianity*, Watson, *Theological Institutes*, and Wesley, *Sermons;* also included, but not required, were Fletcher, *Works,* Baxter, *Reformed Pastor*, and Paley, *View of the Evidences of Christianity* and *Natural Theology and Moral Philosophy*—cited in Barclay, *History of Methodist Missions*, Part One, *Early American Methodism 1769-1844*, Vol. II, *To Reform the Nation*, p. 406 n. See also James R. Joy, *The Teachers of Drew*, 1867-1942, pp. 9-13, for a discussion of "The Standard Curriculum" at the founding of Drew, which Joy says "differed very little from the formula of all the early seminaries." Gerald O. McCulloh writes helpfully on the Course of Study and includes several lists of books in use around 1880 in *The History of American Methodism*, II, 650-55; see also comments by Cannon, I, 565-71, and Chandler, I, 669-72.

[20] Information on each work, as well as representative volumes for each man, is given in the Bibliography.

work continued on the Course of Study through 1876. Watson has no serious rival for theological leadership in the first half of the nineteenth century. Adam Clarke and Joseph Benson were known in America for their commentaries on the Bible and other writings. But neither of them produced a systematic theology, nor did their writings attain nearly the circulation of Watson's. Although Nathan Bangs and Wilbur Fisk played decisive roles in American Methodism in the early period, their chief theological contribution was limited to the controversy with the Calvinists.

 John Miley (1813-1895) is the second representative American Methodist theologian. Miley was professor of theology at Drew Theological Seminary for twenty-two years, from 1873 until his death. There he taught hundreds of students and reached thousands more through his writings, which were on the study lists from 1880 until 1904. His two-volume *Systematic Theology* was his most noted work. It is a careful, comprehensive presentation of Wesleyan Arminianism drawing into systematic form the emergent tendencies of nineteenth-century Methodism. In this second period the works of some other men are also important. Miner Raymond at Garrett Biblical Institute wrote a systematics in 1877, but his work is more dependent on Watson than is Miley's and also less sensitive to newer currents. The monumental three-volume theology by the Englishman W. B. Pope was listed on the Course of Study from 1880 until 1888. Since Pope did not teach in this country, and since his theological position was much more compatible with that of Wesley than with that of nineteenth-century American Methodism, he is not representative, as is Miley.[21] T. O. Summers' theology was well known in the southern church but on the whole not as widely heeded or as characteristic as Miley's. Daniel D. Whedon was by all odds the single most important Methodist the-

---

[21] Pope stands out as one of the towering figures in all of Methodist theology who with remarkable fidelity recaptured the essence of Wesley's theology. Recognition of his importance in this country has been aided significantly by the comprehensive study of his theology by E. Dale Dunlap, "Methodist Theology in Great Britain in the Nineteenth Century," unpublished Ph.D. dissertation, Yale, 1956.

ological figure in the second half of the nineteenth century. He did not write a systematic theology, however, and the full implications of his position were not drawn till later, most completely by Miley.

Albert Knudson (1873-1953) is the theological representative for the first third of the twentieth century, during which American Methodist thought put its most distinctive emphasis on personal idealism. The decisive figure in this development was Borden Parker Bowne, but since Bowne worked as a philosopher, not a theologian, it remained for his pupil, Knudson, to draw the implications of personalist philosophy into a theological system. Knudson had a long and distinguished career as a teacher at Boston and wrote extensively, some of his works appearing on the study lists from 1916 to 1948. His treatment of systematic theology in *The Doctrine of God* and *The Doctrine of Redemption* is his most noteworthy contribution. In the years between Miley and Knudson, other theologians might be considered. Henry C. Sheldon and Olin Curtis made a significant impact on Methodism through their teaching and writing, but their theology is transitional, agreeing in principle, if not in substance, with Knudson's. Harris Franklin Rall was more widely known than Knudson and was perhaps related at more vital points to developments in Methodism's life and thought. His systematic statements are not as comprehensively drawn as those of Knudson, however, and he reflects only indirectly the pervasive influence of personal idealism.

An investigation of the most *influential* figures in American Methodist theology (rather than of the most *representative* theologians) would deal with different men and materials. A plausible case can be made for the assertion that three men were most determinative: Joseph Butler, through his celebrated and widely used *Analogy;* Daniel D. Whedon, through his decisive work *The Freedom of the Will;* and Borden Parker Bowne, whose *Theism* is representative of his several influential books. While Butler's effect was indirect and may not have exceeded that of Watson, the impact of

Whedon and Bowne on Methodist theology seems clearly greater than that of Miley and Knudson.

All of these men will be appropriately placed in Methodist theological history in the survey in Chapter II. But the detailed account of the changes to which the Wesleyan doctrines of revelation, sin, and grace were subject in later Methodism will be largely confined to the views of Watson, Miley, and Knudson.

CHAPTER II
METHODISM'S
THEOLOGICAL HISTORY

It is perhaps more apt to say that John Wesley made history than to say that he recorded it. Yet he did both. Consuming more than 4000 pages in the standard edition, his *Journal* spans some sixty-five years of his remarkably active and productive life. It chronicles the rise and spread of the Evangelical Revival which now bears his name and provides a wealth of material for students of the movement. Repeatedly Wesley speaks of the Revival as "the work of God" and describes it in ecstatic terms as "amazing," "wondrous," "marvelous," and "glorious." Early in the *Journal* he proposes "to declare to all mankind what it is that the Methodists (so-called) have done and are now doing—or, rather, what it is that God hath done, and is still doing, in our land. For it is not the work of man which hath lately appeared. All who calmly observe it must say, 'This is the Lord's doing, and it is marvelous in our eyes.' " The Revival, he feels, does not depend on human strategies but demands sensitive response to God's "providential openings." [1]

[1] Cited from Wesley's *Journal*, II, 67 and 476; see further II, 65, 386-89; and IV, 27, 174, 331, 477, 519.

Thus Wesley knows God to be at work, himself to be a dutiful servant, and the Revival to be the rich harvest of Spirit-empowered labor. In his understanding of the Revival, as in his understanding of theology, he gives priority to God, whose grace alone can renew men and the church. Our concern is with the history of the people called Methodists, and especially with the grace-centered theology which Wesley bequeathed to them. A crucial consideration in the survey of the faith of each passing generation will be the clarity with which it sounds the authentic Wesleyan note concerning God's gracious action.

FROM WESLEY TO WATSON, 1790-1840

In New York and Baltimore, societies were begun by laymen who brought Methodism to the New World. Soon after their founding, in 1769, John Wesley sent the first official missionaries to America. After the Revolutionary War, the noteworthy Christmas Conference of 1784 launched the Methodist Episcopal Church as an independent religious group, and it was not long before Methodism's rapid spread made it one of the most popular religious bodies in this burgeoning country. In the early years Wesley was regarded as the spiritual father of the church, and his writings, along with those of John Fletcher and the hymns of Charles Wesley, supplied the standards for theological judgment and belief. But as time wore on, the legal separation of American from British Methodism, its isolation from England, its lack of a major theologian of its own, and its hurried reading of Wesley and Fletcher for polemical purposes tended to produce modifications within American Methodism. To these modifying forces the American setting added its own demands and needs, producing a Wesleyan theology with an identifiably American cast.[2]

[2] Leland H. Scott, "Methodist Theology in America in the Nineteenth Century," unpublished Ph.D. dissertation, Yale, 1954, pp. 21-24. Scott's study will continue indefinitely as an indispensable reference for all investigation of American Methodist theology. Frequent references acknowledge the indebtedness of this chapter to it. It will be identified subsequently as "Methodist Theology." References to a digest of its

Scholastic Statement and Indigenous Growth

Two theological characteristics of the first fifty years in the life of the new church in America are readily apparent. The earlier is a systematic and reasoned endeavor to present and defend the Wesleyan theology, drawing on the British "scholastic theologians," Richard Watson, Adam Clarke, and Joseph Benson, in addition to Wesley and Fletcher. These second-generation interpreters tend to find a place for natural theology and to emphasize the role of reason, especially in establishing Christian "evidences." [3]

The second characteristic of the period is the rise of a theological literature more independent of the original Wesleyan sources and more open to the influences of the frontier, revivalism, and Calvinism in the American environment. Though essentially Wesleyan, this indigenous theology exposes the roots of later modifications in the statement of original sin, the atonement, and the gracious foundation of man's freedom.

The history of Methodist theology from 1790 to 1840 is most simply reviewed, therefore, by summarizing first British "scholastic theology" and then the American theology, which began to develop its own distinctive issues and emphases.

In the formative years of the Evangelical Revival John Wesley

---

major conclusions, published under the same title in *Religion in Life,* will be identified in full. Significant related material by Scott appears in *The History of American Methodism:* an account of the period to 1845 under the title "The Message of Early American Methodism," I, 291-359; and a review of "The Concern for Systematic Theology, 1840-70," II, 380-90. See also Paul S. Sanders, "An Appraisal of John Wesley's Sacramentalism in the Evolution of Early American Methodism," pp. 202, 367.

[3] E. Dale Dunlap, "Methodist Theology in Great Britain in the Nineteenth Century," unpublished Ph.D. dissertation, Yale, 1956, pp. 212-18, "The Health of a Heritage." "The difference between John Wesley and his early successors was not so much one of clear-cut distinction as it was a subtle shift of spirit. As a result of this subtle shift of spirit, the theological enterprise of Clarke and Watson was more 'scholastic' and less dynamic than the theology of Wesley. However, . . . it must be acknowledged that in general both Adam Clarke and Richard Watson were faithful to the essential emphases of John Wesley's theology" (p. 218). The theology of the preachers in the period from 1834 to 1867, Dunlap further observes, "Was an uncreative patterning of the emphases of Clarke and Watson for the most part. The scholastic methodology discovered in the earlier period was, if anything, deepening" (p. 263; see also pp. 239 ff.).

was supported by and received significant theological assistance from his brother Charles. However, his most important theological aid came from John Fletcher (1729-1785). A devout and humble man, Fletcher long has been recognized as the saint of the early Methodist movement. He was a man of considerable theological accomplishments whose ability as an apologist came to the fore in the Calvinist controversies of the 1770's in an able, convincing, finely argued series of writings, the *Checks to Antinomianism.* Wesley published Fletcher's work and held it in high regard. Through its convincing power and irenic spirit it proved a potent force in the Calvinist struggle. Fletcher's writings continued to occupy a place of honor in later Methodism, appearing on the Course of Study down to 1880.[4]

The second generation of British Methodists worked in an environment which was in many ways the same as Wesley's. The impact of Newtonian science and Cartesian philosophy encouraged the development of deism, a religion based on nature, interpreted by reason. Though Wesley occasionally entered the lists against deism, the second-generation "scholastics" were much more deliberate in their attention to it. They appealed more frequently to nature and reason and to miracles and prophecy as evidences for the authenticity of scriptural revelation. By their uncritical attitude and use of reason, however, they contributed to the further extension of rationalism.

The general character of their rationalistic tendencies is illustrated in the *Analogy* of Joseph Butler (1692-1752), to which American Methodism gave an important place in the Course of Study down to 1892, a longevity exceeded only by the writings of Wesley himself! In his celebrated *Analogy* Butler sought to stem the erosion of the Christian faith by the tides of critical deism. In brief, he argues that both natural and revealed religion are

---

[4] A noteworthy service was rendered Wesleyan theology by Shipley's comprehensive, historically oriented study of John Fletcher. Not only is Fletcher's theology admirably presented but illuminating comparisons are drawn between it and Wesley's theology and that of broader Protestantism. See also Luke Tyerman, *Wesley's Designated Successor,* for details on Fletcher's life and work.

analogous to nature in that they share with it common uncertainties and mysteries which defy understanding and explanation. Therefore, since they have common problems, natural and revealed religion stand or fall together. In the development of this argument Butler makes use of the same natural evidences for God as do the earlier deists.[5] But if natural religion (the stronghold of the deists) can claim grounds no less precarious than those of revealed religion, many skeptically concluded that both should be cast aside, not kept as Butler had intended.

Methodist apologists, however, widely regarded the argument of the *Analogy* as a valid support for their Wesleyan faith as well as for the natural theology which increasingly found a place among them. Still more important, they believed that it exempted the vitals of evangelical revelation from the destructive consequences of philosophical criticism. Thus, uncritically, they endorsed and extended the rationalistic tendencies represented by Butler and the British scholastics.

Among these writers, three stand out for special mention. Joseph Benson (1749-1821) served under Wesley, was a close friend of Fletcher's, and actively championed Methodism, writing prolifically in his later years. His most important work was his commentary *Notes, Critical, Explanatory and Practical* (1811-1818), published in five volumes. It was brought out in an American edition in 1820 and widely used by Methodists.

A second and even more important British interpreter of Wesley was Adam Clarke (1762-1832), one of the best educated and most highly respected of the early Methodists. A scholar of note, he wrote, translated, and edited numerous books. His most influential work was an eight-volume commentary on the Bible (1810-1826). It was marked by independent and at times controversial insights. Publication of the commentary in America began shortly after its announcement in 1810. Along with his *Discourses,* the

[5] Joseph Butler, *The Analogy of Religion, Natural and Revealed, to the Constitution and Course of Nature,* Pt. II, chap. VII. See also E. C. Mossner, *Bishop Butler and the Age of Reason,* pp. 45 ff., 98 ff.; 155, and John Herman Randall, *Making of the Modern Mind,* chaps. 12 and 16.

commentary made Clarke an important figure in American Methodism in the period from 1810 to 1840.[6]

Both in Britain and in America Richard Watson (1781-1833) was easily the single most determinative of the early Methodist theologians. So pervasive was his impact and so characteristic was his theological formulation that he is the obvious choice in this early period as the representative theologian whose work must be reviewed in detail.

It is necessary to turn from the British to the American scene in order to review the beginnings of an indigenous theology in the New World. Essential Wesleyan theology was introduced in America and sustained by the writings of Wesley and Fletcher as well as those of second-generation British theologians. When American editions of the works of Wesley, Fletcher, and Watson appeared around 1830, they received appreciative notices in the *Methodist Quarterly Review*.[7] The Course of Study for Methodist preachers invariably included the books of these early English Methodist writers. The *Methodist Quarterly Review* (1818) and the *Christian Advocate* (1826) were instituted out of the same concern for Methodism's integrity; their editorials and articles regularly refer to Wesleyan sources for authoritative guidance.

Though largely confined to the basic elements of experiential appeal, the theology of the early Methodist preachers, such as Francis Asbury and Freeborn Garrettson, was consciously Wesleyan. Since theirs was essentially a theology of salvation, Methodists found the American revival tradition a congenial force, supporting and being supported by it. They concurred in its stress

[6] Clarke, with Watson and Pope, is studied in detail by Dunlap, "Methodist Theology in Great Britain," chap. II. For a brief general survey of Clarke's thought see *Christian Theology*, selections from his writings edited by Samuel Dunn, and Maldwyn Edwards, *Adam Clarke*.

[7] See the *Methodist Quarterly Review* (hereafter MQR, variations in title ignored), 14 (1832), 49-71, 129-49; 11 (1828), 413-20; 12 (1830), 272-307, 361-93. See also Scott, "Methodist Theology," pp. 12 ff., on Wesley's relation to early American evangelicalism, and Appendix 3, "Wesleyan Doctrinal Standards in America," pp. 546-52; and Frederick A. Norwood, "Continuity and Change in Methodism," *Religion in Life*, 29 (1960), 521.

on a plain, simple theology of fundamentals. But also, as a result of their evangelical commitment they resisted scholastic disputation, the substitution of romantic feelings for evangelical conversion, and the temptation to accommodate themselves to the world.[8]

Methodism's evangelical pragmatism ideally suited it to life on the frontier and in rural America. Its stress on equality, responsibility, and practical results was heartily endorsed by the free American spirit, which found Methodism more comfortable than austere and rigorous Calvinism. It is likely, however, that these environmental forces did not so much add new dimensions to Methodist theology as sustain and underscore its characteristic tendencies.[9]

Thus experiential and pragmatic allegiance to Wesleyan theology resulted in a significant continuity of doctrinal and scriptural interpretation. It tended, however, to exaggerate the subjective experience of grace and to accent its emotional accompaniments. Further, it helped confirm Methodism in an uncritical theological attitude which it seldom escaped for long. After 1810, however, the native American leaders, who largely replaced those sent from England, became increasingly dissatisfied with the oversimplifications of revivalism and the frontier. Reluctant merely to quote the primary Wesleyan authorities, these men display more independent theological judgment.[10]

Of greatest importance for the development of an indigenous

[8] Leland Scott provides a comprehensive and well-documented summary of the evangelistic concern for the conviction, conversion, and sanctification of the sinner, in chap. 7, "The Message of Early American Methodism," of *The History of American Methodism*, I, 291-307. For more general discussions see *They Gathered at the River*, a fascinating study by Bernard A. Weisberger, and H. Shelton Smith, Robert T. Handy, and Lefferts A. Loetscher, *American Christianity*, II, 10-64.

[9] Theodore L. Agnew includes a wealth of interesting material on the frontier, camp meetings, revivalism, and the early preachers in his "Methodism on the Frontier," chap. 10 of *The History of American Methodism*, I, 488-545. See also Jerald C. Brauer, *Protestantism in America*, pp. 89 ff., 101; and Sidney E. Mead's modification of the "Turner thesis"—that the frontier was the determinative factor shaping American life and thought in *Church History*, 22 (1953), 42-45. For a simple elaboration of the Turner thesis see P. G. Mode, *The Frontier Spirit in American Christianity*.

[10] Sanders, "An Appraisal of John Wesley's Sacramentalism," pp. 489, 198 ff.; Scott, "Methodist Theology," pp. 21 f., 84 f.; and Brauer, *Protestantism in America*, pp. 112 ff.

Methodist theology in this period was the theological challenge of Calvinism. Though it debated with Socinians, Unitarians, and Universalists, Methodism had its chief doctrinal encounter with Calvinists. One of the first Americans to give independent treatment to the Wesleyan inheritance was Nathan Bangs (1778-1862). He served early Methodism in many ways, as a writer, church historian, founder and editor of several publications, and as an editor of the Book Concern. He was a primary leader of the movement for an educated ministry and successfully encouraged the development of American Methodist theological literature. Both of these activities were important in Methodism's effort to establish itself in the public mind alongside an older and more entrenched Calvinism. Bangs was the first notable leader in the Methodist polemic against revisionist Calvinism as typified by Hopkinsianism.

His volume *The Errors of Hopkinsianism Detected and Exposed* shows Bangs to have been a formidable opponent, thoroughly familiar with the points at issue between Methodism and Calvinism. Bangs chides Williston, a defender of Hopkinsianism, asserting that his version of Calvinism has largely come over to Methodism on "the moral agency of man, the universality of the atonement, and justification by faith." Its distinction between natural ability and moral ability represents a basic denial of human depravity. The Methodist understanding of prevenient grace whereby "light, grace and ability is given to every man" sufficient "to enable him to repent and believe in Christ" saves Methodism from the impossible dilemma from which Hopkins struggled to escape. Thus Bangs rests the basic issue with Calvinism on the gracious origin of man's responsible participation in salvation.[11]

[11] Nathan Bangs, *The Errors of Hopkinsianism Detected and Exposed*, pp. 93, 14. See the account of this debate in Scott, "Methodist Theology," pp. 48 ff., and Appendix 8, "The Bangs-Williston Controversy," pp. 576 f.; and see David C. Shipley, "The Development of Theology in American Methodism in the Nineteenth Century," *London Quarterly and Holborn Review*, 28 (1959), 251 f., hereafter referred to as "Theology in American Methodism." Abel Stevens, *The Life and Times of Nathan Bangs*, is also pertinent. The story of the Calvinist controversy and the roles in it played by Bangs and Fish is unfolded by Scott in his section on "Methodism and New England Calvinism," in *The History of American Methodism*, I, 346-57.

Wilbur Fisk (1792-1839) was a second influential leader in this period. As one of the first college-trained Methodists, as a persuasive writer, and as president of Wesleyan Academy and Wesleyan University (a leader among the theological schools and activity of the time), he occupied a respected place in the forefront of Methodist leaders. He was particularly important for his part in the growing Calvinist-Arminian debate, which continued through most of the century. In his *Calvinist Controversy*, against the determinism of Old School Calvinists, Fisk stresses the universality of gracious ability as the ground of man's morally responsible voice in salvation. Against the freedomism of New School Calvinists, he contends that grace is indispensably required to restore freedom and responsibility to fallen men. Thus Fisk argues that Methodism stands between the irreconcilable extremes of Calvinist theology, free from the distortions of both sides.[12]

Francis Hodgson, Asa Shinn, and Stephen Olin also contributed to the development of Methodist theological literature toward the end of this period. Hodgson was especially committed to a refutation of the New Haven views of Barnes, Beecher, and Finney. Shinn presaged many of the emphases in the moralistic revision of Wesleyan theology which came to dominate the second period of Methodist theology. With one voice all Methodists of the period invoked the Wesleyan strictures on predestination wherever they met it. The controversy between Calvinism and Methodism continued through most of the nineteenth century, shifting generally from soteriological to anthropological grounds, with modifications in their original positions bringing them closer and closer together. At the same time Methodism and revisionist Calvinism were never identical, and their rivalries persisted until newly emerging the-

---

[12] Wilbur Fisk, *Calvinist Controversy*, pp. 8, 48-54, 94; this volume, first published in 1835, was composed of a lengthy sermon and several later articles originally appearing in the *Christian Advocate*. The controversy between Old and New School Calvinists is helpfully discussed by H. Shelton Smith in *Changing Conceptions of Original Sin*, chaps. V and VI; and Scott, "Methodist Theology," pp. 43-77, "Methodism's Warfare for the Public Mind," and Appendix 13, "Wilbur Fisk: *Calvinist Controversy* and Its Issues," pp. 597 ff. The best biography of Fisk is by Joseph Holdich, *Life of Wilbur Fisk, D.D.*

ologies crowded their convictions aside toward the end of the century.[13]

Wesleyan Orthodoxy in Richard Watson

Richard Watson was born in Lincolnshire in 1781. His father Thomas Watson, a saddler, wanted the best for his only son, who with three sisters survived from among eighteen children. Richard early showed unusual ability, beginning the study of Latin at six, reading widely in voluminous histories before he was ten, preaching his first sermon at sixteen, publishing his first pamphlet at nineteen, and becoming a full member of the Wesleyan connection during his twentieth year. He was largely self-educated and was continuously and widely employed throughout his active ministry as traveling preacher, executive of the Missionary Society, secretary of the Conference, occasional teacher, and prolific writer on a number of subjects. He was well known and respected throughout England, and his work greatly enriched early Methodism until his untimely death at fifty-two.[14]

Watson's major theological contribution, the *Theological Institutes: Or a View of the Evidences, Doctrines, Morals and Institutions of Christianity*, appeared between 1823 and 1829. In 1831 his *Biblical and Theological Dictionary* made available to the English-speaking world one of the most careful and comprehensive resources of its kind. Sermons, letters, reviews, and miscellaneous pieces flowed from his productive pen throughout his busy life. Shortly after Watson's death, Thomas Jackson collected and published his works in thirteen volumes, 1834-1837. In his remarkable activity and varied interests, Watson was a true son of Wesley. His most lasting contribution to the Methodist Church, however, was made through his *Theological Institutes*.[15]

[13] Scott, "Methodist Theology," pp. 78-81.

[14] Thomas Jackson, *Memoirs of the Life and Writings of the Rev. Richard Watson*, supplies a good account of Watson's life and work; see also Dunlap's review of Watson, "Methodist Theology in Great Britain," chap. II.

[15] The generations have been lavish in their praise of Watson and his *Institutes*. They have been regarded as "the scientific and moral standard" of Methodist belief by W. B. Duncan, *Studies in Methodist Literature* (Nashville: Publishing House MECS,

Before Watson finished writing his *Institutes*, its first part began to issue from presses in America. It went through numerous editions, at least one of them running to more than thirty printings. Various editors added indexes, and in 1850 John McClintock prepared a ninety-page outline of its contents as a guide to its use in the Course of Study, where it continued until 1876. Its influence in America was immense. In 1877 Daniel Curry wrote, "To no other single agency is the continued doctrinal unity of Methodism so much indebted as to the extensive use of Watson's *Theological Institutes.* . . . This great work has been the standard of Methodist theology for a full half century." It was said that T. O. Summers, an important theologian in the southern church, "measured all things in heaven and earth by Watson's *Institutes.*" [16] Recent studies of Methodist theological history are just as emphatic in their recognition of Watson's place. "Richard Watson, directly or indirectly, was the determinative theological force in the mind of the Methodists. It was Watson's systematic treatment of the theological motifs of Wesley and Fletcher . . . which proved to be the *standard* theological source in American Methodism for at least three decades following the early 1840's." [17]

1914), p. 100. Watson is said to have left "the stamp of his character and the work of his genius" on Methodist theology by Edward J. Brailsford, *Richard Watson, Theologian and Missionary Advocate,* p. 128. He is called the "greatest theological thinker of his day" by John Fletcher Hurst, *The History of Methodism,* III, 1318. In him "was given to the Methodist Church its first great theologian," according to J. R. Gregory, *A History of Methodism* (London: Charles H. Kelley, 1911), I, 245. He is characterized as "a Prince in theology and the *Institutes* as the noblest work in Methodism and truly valuable" by Dr. John Brown, quoted by Thomas Neely, *Doctrinal Standards of Methodism,* p. 64.

[16] Curry's words are in the Introduction to Miner Raymond's *Systematic Theology,* I, 3; A. T. Bledsoe's judgment of Summers is quoted by Edwin Mims, *History of Vanderbilt University,* p. 61. Henry C. Sheldon wrote that the *Institutes* "for a considerable period ranked as the unrivaled textbook of American Methodism," in "Changes in Theology Among American Methodists," *American Journal of Theology,* 10 (1906), 32.

[17] Scott, "Methodist Theology," p. 143; see pp. 143-49 for an appraisal of Watson's American influence. Dunlap, "Methodist Theology in Great Britain," p. 266, notes that "Watson was equipped with a sharp mind and keen native ability, but . . . did not live long enough to reflect the maturity of age and experience in his work." Further, the heavy demands of connectional duties prevented him from "familiarity with historical and comparative theology."

Later American theologians who transparently imitated the *Institutes* in their own systematic presentations further extended Watson's influence. Thomas Ralston's *Elements of Divinity* (1847), Luther Lee's *Elements of Theology* (1853), Samuel Wakefield's *Complete System of Christian Theology* (1858), and Amos Binney's *Theological Compend* (1858), each in its way, hoped to be a "judicious abridgement of the *Institutes*," more helpfully addressed to the needs of a later day.

Watson takes up his pen as the orthodox chronicler of Wesleyan theology seeking to provide aid for those Methodists, particularly younger ministers, who wished instruction in their theological heritage. According to Thomas Jackson, his biographer, Watson "expressed a wish to write something that would assist them in obtaining an accurate and comprehensive acquaintance with the entire system of evangelical truth, and with the evidence upon which every vital doctrine is grounded." [18] Though significant polemical interests are evident in the *Institutes* as Watson engages Calvinists at considerable length and takes note also of Socinians, Pelagians, and Romanists, his dominant purpose is to present Wesleyan evangelical truth and to sustain it with appropriate evidence.

Watson had the highest regard for Wesley and his theology. In a theological review he writes that the wider his acquaintance with other theologies becomes, "the more do we admire the unity, clearness, and consistency with the Scriptures, which characterize the experimental discourses of the venerable Wesley, who, as the theologian of the heart, stands unrivaled in modern times." [19] His work is filled with references to and quotations from Wesley. Almost never does he deign to correct or criticize his master.

Watson's extended and varied efforts to establish the divine authority of Scripture clearly hint that his ultimate allegiance was to evidence external to Scripture itself. In this he is supported by only meager and occasional passages in Wesley, for whom the Bible assumes living authority in evangelical experience, not in rational

[18] Jackson, *Memoirs of . . . Watson*, p. 253.
[19] *The Works of the Rev. Richard Watson*, VII, 506.

verification. Though he preserves the substance of Wesleyan theology, Watson compromises its spirit. Tending to be more preoccupied with the evidences for faith than with faith itself, he typifies the scholastic inclinations of second-generation Methodist theology.[20]

FROM WATSON TO MILEY, 1840-1890

In 1844, as civil tensions in America mounted, the Methodist Episcopal Church divided north and south. Theological conversations and exchanges between the two branches continued, however, and no marked theological differences are to be traced to the separation. Much more significant for theology was its encounter with the surrounding American culture. Methodist theology faced important philosophical influences and the disturbing challenges of evolutionary science and discussed them in its periodical literature. Through theological training for its ministers it sought a more informed and articulate theological expression. Specifically, Methodism's theological response in the period from 1840 to 1890 had two foci: a tendency to revise theological categories in the light of a philosophical doctrine of free personal agency, and an effort to integrate these categories in a comprehensive and representative statement. Around 1890 both tendencies reached their culmination in John Miley, who through them hoped to clarify and sustain the Wesleyan-Arminian heritage.

Moralistic Revision and Systematic Integration

The broader intellectual and cultural developments of the second period of Methodist theological history were noted by Methodists. Reference is found to American transcendentalism, the romantic emphases of Coleridge and Schleiermacher, and the writings of Bushnell and Maurice. Butler continued to be read, and the writings of William Paley on Christian evidences and natural theology

[20] Dunlap, "Methodist Theology in Great Britain," pp. 477, 217.

gained considerable vogue. Methodism's most portentous encounter with philosophy, however, was with the common-sense philosophy of Reid, Stewart, and Cousin. Stressing the ultimacy of moral and religious intuitions, it seemed to provide an unassailable place for morality and religion even as it granted a place to modern science. For Methodism and for American Protestantism generally, intuitional realism (common-sense or Scottish philosophy) played a decisive role in theological reinterpretation.[21]

An impressive periodical literature served as an important medium of exchange between Methodism and its religious and cultural context. After 1840, under the editorship of George Peck and John McClintock, the *Methodist Quarterly Review* reflects an awareness of German biblical criticism and philosophical developments. Under Daniel Whedon's editorship from 1856 to 1884, it exhibits the impact of Darwinianism, the development of biblical criticism, and a growing tide of philosophical influence from abroad. Daniel Curry, Whedon's successor, was more traditionally oriented but no less committed to the policy of informing Methodism about world developments with theological bearing. From 1847 on, the southern church had its own *Review,* somewhat more conservative, aiming to preserve Wesleyan motifs. Yet it did introduce new trends and men to its readers. The *Reviews,* together with the more popular *Christian Advocate,* gave Methodism

[21] Sydney E. Ahlstrom shrewdly probes the meaning of the conquest of the Scottish philosophy at Princeton, Harvard, Yale, and Andover, not to mention its sway over nineteenth-century Methodists. He attributes its appeal to the need for an apologetic philosophy to counter the current fears of French infidelity, Hume's skepticism, and various metaphysical heresies. The cost to theology of surrendering to this philosophy he specifies in terms of the displacement of biblical revelation by human consciousness and needs; the surrender of a vitiated human nature for a benign anthropology; and the acceleration of trends toward rational theology, giving new life to Locke, Butler, and Paley; see Ahlstrom, "Theology in America: A Historical Survey," in James Ward Smith and A. Leland Jamison, eds., *Religion in American Life,* Vol. I, *The Shaping of American Religion,* pp. 259-69; see also Ahlstrom's "The Scottish Philosophy and American Theology," *Church History,* 24 (1955), 257-72, and Scott's review of the impact of this philosophy on Methodism, *The History of American Methodism,* I, 352-56. Compare parallel developments in Britain in Dunlap, "Methodist Theology in Great Britain," chap. V.

the most widely circulated periodical literature of the time.[22]

Advances in the training of its ministers contributed to the development of Methodist theology. The Course of Study became even more determinative after 1844 when the General Conference listed specific theological texts for examination. Widespread suspicion of college education among Methodists declined. More settled pastorates, the rising educational level of the laity, the debate with Calvinism, and reluctance to have Methodists trained in non-Methodist seminaries encouraged the establishment of advanced theological institutions, whose influence increased throughout the century.[23]

After the Civil War, Methodism gave more and more attention to the challenge of science, particularly as expressed by Darwin and the evolutionists. Methodism's response varied from outraged rejection to cautious acceptance. Biblical interpretation was affected, not only by the evolutionary threat to Genesis, but also by the critical historical studies of Strauss, Wellhausen, and other German scholars, whose conclusions were brought back to America and pressed by Hurst, Warren, and others.[24]

[22] John A. Faulkner, "The Methodist Review: The First Century," MQR, 99 (1917), 850-65; Wade Crawford Barclay, History of Methodist Missions, Vol. III, Widening Horizons, 1845-95, pp. 110-12. Scott gives an excellent review of the character and influence of the Methodist Quarterly Review in the period 1840-1870 in The History of American Methodism, II, 383-86.

[23] Barclay, History of Methodist Missions, Vol. II, To Reform the Nation, pp. 439-41 on the Course of Study and 410-14 on education and schools. See also Sweet, Methodism in American History, pp. 207-28; S. M. Duvall, The Methodist Episcopal Church and Education up to 1869, pp. 17-25; Scott, "Methodist Theology," p. 134, listing factors encouraging and deterring theological education; and Hurst, History of Methodism, II, 746-52. The History of American Methodism gives extended consideration to the development of theological education; for the more important discussions see I, 565-71, II, 193-96, 303-9, 322-24, 649-59.

[24] Brauer, Protestantism in America, pp. 218-24; H. S. Smith et al., American Christianity, II, 215-19; John Dillenberger and Claude Welch, Protestant Christianity, pp. 189-206; H. S. Smith, Changing Conceptions of Original Sin, pp. 164-97. An excellent review of "Evolutionary Science and the Theistic Adaptation" is found in Scott, "Methodist Theology," pp. 334-47. Compare parallel developments in British Methodism in Dunlap, "Methodist Theology in Great Britain," pp. 434-38. By 1877 a gradual change began in the Methodist view toward science, moving from opposition, to skepticism, to support. By the end of the century "Methodism came to accept without serious question the contribution of Biblical scholarship."

The Methodist theological response to these environmental forces generally confirmed its own developmental tendencies. Together, external demands and internal necessities converged to produce both a moralistic revision and a systematic integration of Methodist theology. For a comprehensive study it is important that more extended consideration be given to each one of these developments.

First the tendencies toward moralistic revision should be noted. The stress in common-sense philosophy on the intuitions of freedom and responsibility found a cordial reception among Methodists, whose tradition had always supported a lively debate about free grace and free will. The struggle with Calvinist New Divinity heightened interest in the doctrine of freedom. Thus it comes as no surprise to discover that in 1853 when A. T. Bledsoe, a Baptist from the south, issued his *Theodicy*, forcefully arguing that moral character can be predicated only of the specific acts of an individual moral agent, Methodists greeted it with enthusiasm and quoted it profusely for fifty years. Contemporary books by R. S. Foster and H. P. Tappan contained supporting arguments.[25] All these forces met in Daniel D. Whedon (1808-1885), whose *Freedom of the Will* (1864) exerted enormous influence on the moralistic revision of theology.

College educated and persistently inquiring, Whedon was well prepared for his most strategic position as editor of the *Methodist Quarterly Review*. Articles, editorials, and reviews flowed from his pen. With these, and the contributions he encouraged and the selections he chose for publication, almost single-handedly he guided the theological education of a generation. T. O. Summers esteemed

[25] See Albert Taylor Bledsoe, *A Theodicy*, H. P. Tappan, *The Doctrine of the Will*, and R. S. Foster, *Objections to Calvinism*, and Scott's discussion, "Methodist Theology," pp. 165-69. In the same vein a bit later Gilbert Haven argued that "Wesley saw that this one principle [freedom of the will] was the key to his system," in "Wesley and Modern Philosophy," *MQR*, 61 (1879), 210. The contemporary discussion also included D. D. Whedon, "Doctrines of Methodism," *Bibliotheca Sacra*, 19 (1862), 241-73; John F. McClintock, "The Conflict of the Ages," *MQR*, 36 (1854), 169-90; D. D. Whedon, "Wesleyanism and Taylorism—Reply to *The New Englander*," *MQR*, 42 (1860), 656-69.

him "the foremost theologian in America," a judgment which Methodists generally upheld.[26]

Against Edwards and later revisionist Calvinism as represented by Taylor, Finney, and Beecher, Whedon maintains the essential freedom of the will as a binding requirement of the "Maxim of Responsibility." True responsibility, he argues, demands essential and intrinsic freedom, including the power of contrary choice. Such freedom must derive from man himself; "every free agent is thus an original creator even out of nothing." Motives to the good, Whedon contends, have their source in God's prevenient grace, not man's sinful nature. Once given, however, they may be elected or rejected by man as an intrinsically free agent.[27]

Whedon's work was widely heralded within and received considerable notice beyond Methodist circles. It was roundly criticized from Calvinist quarters, the most important arraignment being that of H. P. Smith, who challenged its thesis and correctly indicated its contradictions with Wesleyan tradition.[28]

The philosophical doctrine of moral responsibility had far-reaching implications for doctrinal revision. It required the subjection of biblical revelation to philosophical intuition and the analysis of human consciousness; the rejection of original guilt and the reinterpretation of the meaning and mode of original depravity; the elimination of substitutionary themes and the encourage-

[26] Quoted in Scott, "Methodist Theology," p. 187; see the whole of chap. IV, "Daniel Whedon on the Freedom of the Will."

[27] Daniel D. Whedon, *The Freedom of the Will as a Basis of Human Responsibility and a Divine Government*, pp. 396, 42. See Scott, "Methodist Theology," Appendix 16, "Whedon's Definition of the Will and Freedom," pp. 611 f., and Appendix 17, "Whedon's Critique of Necessitarian Arguments," pp. 614 ff. About revisionist Calvinists, Whedon writes elsewhere that "they are in a doubtful transition state; standing on unmaintainable ground and liable to wake up, next generation, Pelagian"—*MQR*, 40 (1858), 138. Whedon remembers the Wesleyan heritage of grace, but more generally grounds freedom in nature; compare pp. 15, 22, 249, 365, 397, in *The Freedom of the Will*. Note also his preference on this point for Raymond's *Systematic Theology* over that of Pope in his review of the latter's systematics in *MQR*, 64 (1882), p. 362.

[28] Henry B. Smith, *Faith and Philosophy*, chap. X, "Whedon on the Will." Scott, "Methodist Theology," pp. 221-25, traces to Whedon the generally unified tradition on the freedom of the will which emerged in American Methodism supported by Tigert, Raymond, Summers, Foster, Hurst, Merrill, and Miley. Daniel Curry was one of the few significant objectors, in "A New Orthodoxy," *MQR*, 68 (1886), 445-54.

ment of the governmental theory of the atonement; and finally, the devaluation of the role of prevenient grace and the magnification of man's inherent freedom.[29]

The second outstanding feature of Methodism in the period 1840-1890 was its effort to systematize these revised theological motifs. Interest appeared at mid-century with the publication of the first catechism for church members, and of *Wesleyana*, a compendium of Wesley's theological statements. Silas Comfort's *Exposition of the Articles of Religion* (1847) and A. A. Jimeson's *Notes on the Twenty-five Articles* (1853) proposed to interpret the Methodist tradition for the common reader. Watson's American influence was at its height, and his *Institutes* was issued, as it were, in American translations by Ralston, Wakefield, Lee, and Binney. At the same time, both for the instruction of the church and for the argument with Calvinism, there was evident a desire for a fresh statement of Wesleyanism, freed from the dictation of Watson's outline and categories.[30] Whedon was a major force moving Methodism away from Watson, as W. F. Warren was also. But neither man produced a systematic theology.

Not until 1877 was the first American text in systematic theology written—by Miner Raymond (1811-1897) of Garrett. Raymond's work combines careful exegesis of Scripture and analysis of the history of doctrine with elements from Watson's thought. It also supports the growing Methodist effort to reinterpret the-

---

[29] It is important to note that these developments were not peculiar to Methodism in the nineteenth century. Discussing Calvinist theology in this period, Sydney Ahlstrom, in Smith and Jamison, *Religion in American Life*, I, 255, observes "a distinct tendency . . . to formulate a 'governmental' rather than a 'satisfaction' theory of the atonement, to inveigh against the ideas of a limited atonement with the insistence that Christ died for all men, to deny the imputation of Adam's sin, to conceive of original sin as privative or dispositional rather than forensic, and to insist that God's permission of sin in the world was essential to a moral (as against a purely mechanical) order."

[30] Shipley, "Theology in American Methodism," p. 252; Scott, "Methodist Theology," pp. 137-48; James Roy, *Catholicity and Methodism*, pp. 92-94. Daniel Curry pleaded for the "Present Necessity for a Restatement of Christian Beliefs," *MQR*, 68 (1886), 750-60. For a more detailed discussion of these and related matters see "Early Attempts at a More Systematic Theology," which Scott contributed to *The History of American Methodism*, II, 380-83.

ology in the categories of free personal agency. Raymond's theology was intended as a statement of Methodist Arminian principles for the general church, not simply for its scholars. By Whedon and many others it was received as a standard exposition of the thinking of American Methodism.[31] Raymond's work was on the Course of Study from 1880 until 1908.

William F. Warren (1833-1929) was one of the most creative of the Methodist thinkers of this period and the first Methodist to achieve international recognition in theological circles. He did advanced study in Berlin and Halle, taught at the Methodist mission seminary in Germany, served as foreign correspondent to the *Methodist Quarterly Review*, and made several important literary contributions. He became president of Boston University and on his retirement was named dean of the School of Theology. His *Einleitung*, published in Germany, was received as a creative statement of the need for a new methodology, remaining evangelical yet relevant to the new world of thought. Methodism's loss was great when the systematic theology projected in the *Einleitung* failed to appear—Warren's interest turned to comparative religion and other fields. Warren stands as a landmark in nineteenth-century Methodism's effort to make evangelical Christianity relevant to its new intellectual context.[32]

Thomas O. Summers (1812-1882) was the outstanding theologian of the Methodist Church, South. He served as Book Editor for the denomination, as editor of its *Quarterly Review*, and as dean and professor of theology at the School of Theology at Vanderbilt. Summers was aware of the newer developments of his

---

[31] In reviewing Raymond's theology, in *MQR*, 59 (1877), 734, Whedon found the "clearest, most modern and most American aspects" of Wesleyan Arminianism. Consult Scott, "Methodist Theology," chap. VI, "Miner Raymond: American Methodism's Representative Theologian"; Shipley, "Theology in American Methodism," pp. 255-57; and Raymond's major work, *Systematic Theology*.

[32] Scott, "Methodist Theology," p. 244, writes that "no other man within the period of our study was at once so fully cognizant of Methodism's specific doctrinal orientation and so genuinely sensitive to the emergent demands of a revolutionary intellectual epoch"; and see chap. V, "William F. Warren and Advanced Theological Scholarship." See also Shipley, "Theology in American Methodism," pp. 253-55.

day and felt that they should be honestly discussed and not summarily dismissed. He was loyal to the Wesleyan tradition, however, as interpreted by Watson and by his own English contemporary, W. B. Pope. He was reluctant to dismiss original guilt, yet made a place for Whedon on the will; he endorsed substitutionary elements, yet also asserted a governmental theory of the atonement; he investigated biblical criticism, yet remained prevailingly conservative. His two-volume *Systematic Theology, A Complete Body of Wesleyan Arminian Divinity* (1888) was based on lectures on the Twenty-Five Articles. After his death it was edited by his student and successor at Vanderbilt, John Tigert.[33]

Other influential men of the period contributed to the development of its theological literature. John McClintock, Daniel Curry, and John Tigert were editors of Methodism's noted *Reviews*. John Fletcher Hurst wrote extensively as a historian and advocate of Methodism and did as much as any other single man to widen its intellectual horizons. Several of the many books by Bishops R. S. Foster and S. M. Merrill appear on the study lists. James Strong and John McClintock assumed the editorship of an imposing *Cyclopedia of Biblical, Theological and Ecclesiastical Literature* (1867-1887). George Crooks and J. F. Hurst projected an important *Biblical and Theological Library*, of which seven volumes finally appeared (1877-1900), Miley's *Systematic Theology* being among them.[34]

Methodism's theological unfolding in this second period was not unanimously approved. A conservative opposition made a continuing protest against what it took to be unwarranted innovations. The decline of the class meeting became a matter of concern after 1850 and was often thought to stem from a loosening of ties to tradition-

---

[33] In Scott's judgment ("Methodist Theology," p. 487), both Summers and Warren supported the transitional development, that was to be clearest in Miley, "through their severe criticism (i) of the Lockean epistemology, (ii) of Calvinism's 'theistic fatalism,' and (iii) of the Calvinistic doctrine of original guilt." Refer to Scott's chap. VIII, "T. O. Summers and Evangelical Orthodoxy"; Shipley, "Theology in American Methodism," pp. 257-60; and O. P. Fitzgerald, *Dr. Summers, a Life Study*.

[34] Shipley, "Theology in American Methodism," p. 260; Scott, "Methodist Theology," pp. 344-47, and Appendix 14, "McClintock and Strong's Cyclopedia, 1867-87," p. 605.

al theology. In 1864, over vocal opposition, the General Conference passed a doctrinal test for members, requiring them to subscribe to the doctrines of Scripture "as set forth in the Articles of Religion." In 1880 the General Conference noted with displeasure the decline of evangelical and experiential elements once central to the Methodist heritage. Bishop E. M. Marvin and Daniel Steele voiced their distress over the neglect of man's depravity by Methodist theology, which, they said, tended to weaken every other evangelical doctrine.[35]

Men apprehensive over the loss of the Wesleyan heritage increased the pressure for enforceable doctrinal standards for the ministry. The *Methodist Quarterly Review,* in several contributions, proposed the reinstatement and, again, restatement of the Articles of Religion. In their later constitutional histories of Methodism Thomas Neely and John Tigert reflect the fear of this period that the traditional standards of Methodism were being disregarded. This conservative protest, however, was destined to fall before newer theological developments.[36]

Throughout this middle period of Methodist theological history,

[35] Scott, "Methodist Theology," pp. 348-57. Refer also to Frederick A. Norwood, *Church Membership in the Methodist Tradition,* pp. 50-52, 70-87; E. M. Marvin, *The Doctrinal Integrity of Methodism;* Daniel Steele, *The Holy Spirit, the Conservator of Orthodoxy;* Barclay, *History of Methodist Missions,* Vol. III, *Widening Horizons, 1845-95,* pp. 72-76, 90-92; Peters, *Christian Perfection and American Methodism,* pp. 163-65; Henry Wheeler, *History and Exposition of the Twenty-five Articles,* pp. 9 f.

[36] Neely, *Doctrinal Standards of Methodism;* Tigert, *A Constitutional History of American Episcopal Methodism.* The debate in the pages of the *Methodist Quarterly Review* includes the following sampling: J. Pullman, "Methodism and Heresy," 61 (1879), 334-57; A. Brunson, "Proposed New Articles of Religion," 54 (1872), 229-46; R. Wheatly, "Methodist Doctrinal Standards," 65 (1883), 26-50; H. Liebhart, "Present State of Protestant Theology," 65 (1883), 120-36; R. Crook, "The Doctrine of the Atonement," 67 (1885), 329-52; D. Curry, "A New Orthodoxy," 68 (1886), 445-56; "Present Necessity for a Restatement of Christian Beliefs," 68 (1886), 750-60; "The New Theology," 70 (1888), 284-86; and "Revolution in Theology," 74 (1892), 281-88. The General Conference of 1880 added these questions to the requirements for ministers' admission into full connection: "Have you studied the doctrines of the Methodist Episcopal Church? After full examination, do you believe that our doctrines are in harmony with the Holy Scriptures, and will you preach and maintain them?" See *General Conference Journal,* 1880, pp. 365 f. Barclay, *History of Methodist Missions,* Vol. III, *Widening Horizons, 1845-95,* pp. 72-74, surveys the controversy about the Articles in the General Conferences from 1868 to 1880.

despite opposition, a steady change took place. While the advocates of the newer developments intended to maintain or enhance the integrity of Methodism's theological heritage, they were also firmly resolved to retain relevance to movements of the day. Characteristically, both the leaders of revisionist and systematic tendencies and their conservative opponents were devoted to the Wesleyan heritage. Whatever the practical consequences of their work, the innovators of the period professed loyalty to this heritage. The concern that pervades their efforts is almost as conspicuous by its absence after 1890 in Methodism's major systematic theologians.

Ethical Arminianism in John Miley

For the middle period, John Miley is the representative theologian par excellence for he logically explicates and systematically integrates its emergent characteristics. In his efforts to free anthropological and soteriological doctrines of "unethical" elements and join them in an integrated statement of Arminian-Wesleyan theology, he catches up both characteristic motifs of the period.

John Miley was born in 1813 in Butler County, Ohio. In 1832 he entered Augusta College, Kentucky, where he received both B.A. and M.A. degrees. Entering the Methodist ministry through the Ohio Conference (1838), he served Ohio pastorates until 1852, when he transferred to the New York East Conference. In the pastorate, Miley became known for his able, deliberate preaching and his continuing theological study. His understanding of and concern for the Methodist community was disclosed in his first publication, a treatise on *Class Meetings* (1851). Upon the election of Randolph S. Foster to the episcopacy, Miley succeeded to the chair of systematic theology at Drew Theological Seminary in 1873. His first significant publication as professor of theology was *The Atonement in Christ* (1879), which was well received and widely discussed and was placed on the Course of Study the next year. The two volumes of his major *Systematic Theology* were published in

1892 and 1894 and immediately placed on the Course of Study. They gave way in 1908 to Sheldon's *System of Christian Doctrine*.[37]

High value was placed on Miley's work by his contemporaries. In the *Methodist Quarterly Review*, J. H. Mendenhall wrote, "It has not been surpassed by any work from the pens of scholars during the century," and predicted, "It will make its way into the living thought of the Church as the standard authority on all questions of theology." W. V. Kelley also extolled Miley's "exposition of the victorious Wesleyan-Arminian belief." "His work is good, great, true, and contains that which will enable us to wage war and win victories." In the *New York Christian Advocate* J. M. Buckley gave it his enthusiastic endorsement. Though much more critical, John Tigert in the southern *Review* found Miley's work "more profound and critical than Raymond's," and "as a whole, a most creditable and satisfactory exhibition of the theology of our common Methodism." [38]

Miley reflects a prevailing disposition among Methodists to relate themselves to James Arminius and his sixteenth-century Dutch movement. The basic affinity in Miley, as in most of them, however, is not with Dutch sources but with Americans such as Whedon and Bledsoe. The literature of historic Arminianism serves to confirm rather than direct American doctrinal development. Indeed, Miley veers away from both Dutch and Wesleyan sources as he consummates the nineteenth-century American Methodist

---

[37] See the sketch of Miley's life as well as the excellent interpretation of his thought in Scott, "Methodist Theology," chap. IX, "John Miley on the Logic of Methodist Arminianism." Additional details are found in Barclay, *History of Methodist Missions*, Vol. III, *Widening Horizons, 1845-95*, p. 69, and in Ezra S. Tipple, ed., *Drew Theological Seminary, 1867-1917*, pp. 153 ff.; and see James R. Joy, *The Teachers of Drew, 1867-1942*, pp. 85-90.

[38] These appraisals of the *Systematic Theology* are taken in turn from: Mendenhall, *MQR*, 74 (1892), 497; Kelley, *MQR*, 76 (1894), 835, 838; Barclay, *Christian Advocate*, 70 (1895), 258; and Tigert, *Quarterly Review of the Methodist Episcopal Church, South* (hereafter *MQRS*, variations in title ignored), 40 (1894), 259. Compare also J. F. Chaplain's more reserved review of Miley's *Atonement in Christ*, *MQR*, 62 (1880), 698-709.

movement toward the abstraction of anthropological emphases from their evangelical context.[39]

Free personal agency is the critical and constructive principle of Miley's ethical Arminianism. His efforts to eliminate all remnants of Augustinian realism by his critique of native guilt, his insistence on governmental justice as the key to the atonement, and his tendency to compromise the gracious basis of man's freedom in his philosophical doctrine of responsibility—all are expressions of this principle. More clearly and consistently than any other Methodist he explicates and relates these tendencies. Yet he retains an emphasis on man's helplessness and moral ruin in his "native" condition, and dependence on grace for every movement toward good.

Desiring to serve his Wesleyan heritage, Miley feels he can best do so by purging it of unethical and illogical elements. Hence he continuously corrects British Methodist sources, including Wesley. It is in his work that Richard Watson disappears as a determining force on the form and content of Methodist doctrine. His theology is characterized by its thoroughness, its systematic and orderly arrangements, its close and logical definitions and arguments, and its appeal to and continuous concern for Arminian-Wesleyan doctrine. His finished work represents the denouement of nineteenth-century trends in Methodist theology. There is every reason to approve Scott's judgment that Miley should be interpreted "as something of a culmination of a transitional tendency emergent in mid-nineteenth century American Methodist theology." [40]

[39] Scott, "Methodist Theology," pp. 447, 483, 455, questions that Miley's theology is a return to original Arminianism since characteristically Wesleyan elements remain, e.g., depravity, prevenient grace and free will; also, Miley often criticizes Arminius; finally, he depends more on American than on Remonstrance literature. Compare also Shipley, "Methodist Arminianism, in the Theology of John Fletcher," unpublished Ph.D. dissertation, Yale, 1942, p. 202, and Tigert's review, MQRS, 40 (1894), 260, in which he remarks that "if St. Paul had omitted Romans v 12-21 from his writings, Dr. Miley's easy solution might have been accepted and the Arminian 'system' might have been less complex." By ignoring facts for the sake of our system it is "easy to frame simple explanations."

[40] Scott, "Methodist Theology," pp. 471, 483, 498, and the fine summary statement on pp. 469 f., which merits quotation at length: "Nineteenth-century American Methodism, in its most peculiarly indigenous theological thought, moved increasingly in the

Coming as it did at the end of an era, Miley's work was to endure only briefly. Doctrinally, as well as chronologically, it stood at the dividing line between two centuries. The theologies of Curtis, Sheldon, and others, written only five or ten years later than his, reflect a different world. Regularly they draw conclusions to the premises which Miley admitted, but which his loyalty to the Wesleyan heritage would not permit him to draw. His successors were not thus bound.

FROM MILEY TO KNUDSON, 1890-1935

By the turn of the century, the references to John Wesley in Methodist theological literature were infrequent. When they did appear, more often than not their purpose was to correct rather than to find corroboration in Wesley. Also infrequent visitors in these pages were Methodist theological figures from the nineteenth century. Drawn chiefly from the surrounding culture, a new set of determinative and widely acknowledged forces appeared: science and its evolutionary world view, the critical study of the Bible, and philosophy as set forth by Ritschl, Lotze, and Schleiermacher. The theological responses to these cultural forces varied. Some radically rejected traditional theology to embrace the new world view. Others sought to mediate between the new views and historic faith. Still others clung to orthodoxy and stubbornly resisted all

direction of a quite specific philosophical anthropology. Indeed, the dialectic with Calvinism—which occasioned Methodism's most extended theological efforts—was shifted almost entirely from a soteriological to an anthropological orientation. The uniqueness of Methodist theology was formulated increasingly in terms abstract from the universal objectivities of redemptive grace—the stress rather being on that free personal agency considered necessary to responsibility. John Miley represents the logical integration of this transitional tendency emergent in nineteenth century American Methodism—a tendency initially evident in the writings of Bangs, Shinn and Fisk, a tendency definitively shaped in Bledsoe and Whedon, and a tendency systematically incorporated and sustained in Miner Raymond. Not only did Miley indicate the direction of such a transitional development through his own historical recapitulations; he further specified what he took to be its necessary implications, including a radical critique of the tradition of British Wesleyanism. Indeed, it is in John Miley that one clearly discerns the disappearance of Richard Watson as a determinative theological influence, either on the content or structure of systematic theology in American Methodism."

theological modifications.[41] Methodism generally fell within the second group, seeking to mediate between Christ and culture, though in it the third response also was represented by fundamentalist orthodoxy. Its reconstruction of theology was carried on by men of liberal spirit who held theology to be a "progressive science" and who felt under obligation to make it relevant to the cultural forces of the day.

Cultural Impact and Liberal Reconstruction

Following the Civil War an amazing transformation swept American life as the technological application of science hastened industrialization, expanded and complicated urban life, and drastically modified rural society. Darwinism could not be ignored or rejected indefinitely and gradually was accepted by making God the dynamic power immanent in man and the universe. Assimilation of the scientific attitude and method by most religious disciplines gave rise to empirical methodologies, the historical study of religious development, and the descriptive comparison of religious traditions.

The critical historical investigation of the Bible by European scholars was reported by Americans studying abroad, encouraged by American interpreters, and discussed in the religious journals of the day. In time, it led to fierce intradenominational warfare. It confirmed the tendency of science to treat the Bible as a historically conditioned book and to deprive it of its status as infallible arbiter in historical and scientific matters.[42]

[41] H. S. Smith *et al.*, *American Christianity*, Vol. II, chaps. XVI-XVIII, elaborates and illustrates in some detail this threefold response to the challenges of the new age. One of Methodism's transitional theologians, Milton Terry, contended that Christian theology was "a progressive and improvable science" and opined that among earlier Methodists only Watson and Pope had given careful attention to "scientific method" in their dogmatics; see "Scope and Methods of Christian Dogmatics," *MQR*, 77 (1895). 190, 194-96.

[42] Smith, *et al.*, *American Christianity*, Vol. II, pp. 215-21; See also Henry Steele Commager, *The American Mind*, chap. IV, "John Fiske and Evolutionary Philosophy," and chap. IX, "Religious Thought and Practice." Compare Dunlap's judgment, "Methodist Theology in Great Britain," pp. 426-32, that in Britain the Methodists were about a

Study abroad brought back not only German biblical research but also the philosophies of Schleiermacher, Lotze, and Ritschl. Ritschlianism in particular penetrated the English-speaking world. Commenting on the time, a Methodist wrote, "theological seminaries in America are filled with professors who have either sat in the Ritschlian lecture rooms in Berlin, Marburg, Gottingen, etc., and have come back devotees of the faith, or have imbibed at Ritschlian springs nearer home." [43] It encouraged the further moralization of theological categories and also gave support to the emphasis on the Kingdom of God in the Social Gospel movement which helped polarize growing liberal conviction, inherited from revival and perfectionist traditions, that the whole of life must be brought under God's rule. [44]

The emphasis on religious experience, enhanced by Schleiermacher, helped pave the way for empirical method in theology and confirmed romantic philosophical tendencies. The emphasis on personal theism articulated by Lotze, and rooted back in Hegel, developed into personal idealism. Though not as influential as Ritschlianism in American Protestantism, within Methodism and particularly through its seminary at Boston, personal idealism became a decisive force. In the impact of these three philosophers is il-

------

quarter-century behind in the general controversy over higher criticism. See also Scott, "Methodist Theology," pp. 489-95, and Barclay, *History of Methodist Missions*, Vol. III, *Widening Horizons, 1845-95*, pp. 76-81.

[43] John A. Faulkner, *Modernism and the Christian Faith*, pp. 218, 28; Dillenberger and Welch, *Protestant Christianity*, chap. IX. C. W. Rishell, "The Ritschlian Theology," *MQR*, 73 (1891), 194-211, gives a critique of this philosophical emphasis, charging that it "added another element of confusion" even while acknowledging that work such as Ritschl's was "sadly needed." In breaking a new path, "the wonder is that he did not make more mistakes." See the summaries of the emphases and importance of Schleiermacher, Hegel, and Ritschl by Henry P. Van Dusen, "The Farther Background: Theology in the Nineteenth Century," in *The Vindication of Liberal Theology*, pp. 176-86.

[44] Methodism strongly championed the Social Gospel and very early adopted a Social Creed (1908). For representative discussions see Harry F. Ward, "Which Way Will Methodism Go?" *MQR*, 104 (1921), 685-95; Herbert Welch, "The Church and Social Service," *MQR*, 90 (1908), 707-15; William M. Balch, "Social Salvation," *MQR*, 91 (1909), 742-50. Consult also the entire four-volume study *Methodism and Society*, edited by the Board of Social and Economic Relations of the Methodist Church, in which Schilling's *Methodism and Society in Theological Perspective* is Vol. III.

lustrated one of the distinctive traits of this period—the displacement of theology by philosophy of religion.[45]

Among those who led the movement in American Methodism toward a liberal theology, Borden Parker Bowne (1847-1910) stands out as one whose "thinking has probably reached the minds of more professing Christians than [that of] any other philosopher of religion in the United States."[46] A brilliant student, Bowne studied abroad and was deeply influenced by the German philosophers particularly Leibnitz, Kant, Hegel, and Lotze. He taught at Boston University from 1876 until his death, serving variously as dean of the graduate school and head of the department of philosophy. Many of his students have since become important teachers and writers: McConnell, Brightman, Knudson, and Flewelling, and a second generation among whom Bertocci, DeWolf, Muelder, and Johnson may be mentioned.

Bowne based his philosophy on the ultimate significance of

[45] H. S. Smith *et al.*, *American Christianity*, II, 223, 308, and chap. XVII, "The Christo-centric Liberal Tradition." See the account of the development of personal idealism in James Edward Will, "Implications for Philosophical Theology in the Confrontation of American Personalism with Depth Psychology," unpublished Ph.D. dissertation, Columbia, 1962, chaps. II and III. The pervasive importance of personalism and the decisive role of Boston University School of Theology is underscored by the following. Its seminary catalogue typically proclaims "personal theism undergirding Christian theology" to be its special trust, enabling it to offer "the church and the world a confident Christian faith" (1954-1956), p. 12. "A Survey of Ten Theological Schools" (Nashville: Board of Education, mimeo, ca. 1947), p. 41, notes that at the time, eight of the eleven doctorates held by Boston faculty members had been earned at Boston, and comments, "It is undoubtedly an unwise policy to build a faculty in this way." Finally, a survey for the Commission of College Teachers of Religion of the Methodist Conference on Christian Education (mimeo, 1949), p. 5, discovered that of 144 graduate degrees reported among teachers at Methodist colleges, 48 were from Boston. Drew and Garrett, the next largest contributors, together had only 24.

[46] H. N. Wieman and B. E. Meland, *American Philosophies of Religion*, p. 134. Sydney Ahlstrom, in Smith and Jamison, *Religion in American Life*, I, 288, judges Bowne to be "probably the most influential of the late nineteenth-century philosophers as far as the churches were concerned." See H. N. Schneider, *A History of American Philosophy*, pp. 249 ff.; Francis J. McConnell, *Borden Parker Bowne*; Peter A. Bertocci, "Bowne: Philosophical Theologian and Personalist," *Religion in Life*, 29 (1960), 587-97; Albert C. Knudson, "Bowne in American Theological Education," *The Personalist*, 28 (1947), 247 ff. Finally, see Scott, "Methodist Theology," pp. 492-95, and Appendix 34, p. 667.

personality (the self) for both epistemology and metaphysics. In epistemology, the self is essential as that which unites subject and object and abides through successive states, building knowledge of the experienced world by its structural categories. In metaphysics, only the continuous causal activity of the divine personality provides a satisfying explanation for the world of things.

Bowne's philosophy attempted to mediate between science and religion, between pure idealism and empiricism. It employed an analytic, synoptic method aimed not at absolute proof but at coherent probability—"warranted belief." It appealed to the practical reason for the right to believe what life requires, in the absence of positive disproof. The inclusive nature of personal idealism promised a place to the most diverse realities. Taken together, these features won for this philosophy a most sympathetic hearing among American Methodists.[47]

The last fifteen years of the nineteenth century saw the theological leadership of American Methodism change hands almost completely. The shift signaled the end of one theological era and the beginning of another. "Liberal evangelicalism" had prevailed in Whedon, Warren, Curry, Foster, and Miley. The new generation of Terry, Tillett, Curtis, Sheldon, Rall, and Knudson was dedicated to something different—"evangelical liberalism." In this substantive transition Methodism was one participant in the general reorientation of American Protestantism. A scholar of the New England theology noted thus its abrupt disappearance: "It had endured more than 150 years; it had become dominant in a great ecclesiastical denomination; it had founded every Congregational seminary; and, as it were, in a night, it perished from off the face of the earth."[48] Another observer comments, "From the perspective of more than half a century the nineties emerge as the years

---

[47] For typical statements of Bowne's views on epistemology, see *Metaphysics*, pp. 100-137, 483; on metaphysics, *Theism*, pp. 32-56; and on the practical reason, *ibid.*, pp. 9-18, and Bertocci, "Bowne: Philosophical Theologian and Personalist," *Religion in Life*, 29 (1960), 590-93.

[48] Frank H. Foster, *A Genetic History of New England Theology*, p. 543.

when religious leaders pleasantly bid good-by to their predecessors." [49]

The new leaders come recently to chairs of theology in Methodist seminaries included Milton Terry at Garrett, 1895; Wilbur F. Tillett at Vanderbilt, 1882; Olin A. Curtis at Drew, 1896; and Henry C. Sheldon at Boston, 1895. As Methodist theologians of transition each one deserves notice.

Milton Terry (1840-1914) studied at Yale but was largely self-educated, acquiring nine languages along the way. He was a fine scholar of recognized competence. He began teaching at Garrett in 1884 as head of the department of Hebrew and Old Testament. An active supporter of higher criticism, he became its able champion in its early formative years. He wrote widely in the biblical field and made important contributions through several lesser books in theology. His collected correspondence with Warren, Bowne, and Tillett shows him to have occupied an important place in the transitional period at the turn of the century. Evidence of Ritschlian influence may be found in his doctrinal works.[50]

Wilbur F. Tillett (1854-1936) represents the theology of the southern church. Tillett was a man of broad sympathies with a loyalty to the Methodist tradition inculcated by his teacher T. O. Summers. He was one of the early Methodist leaders in the ecumenical movement. He wrote several books in theology, contributed to various periodicals, and was widely influential throughout the southern church. He rendered an important service by

[49] Winthrop Hudson, *The Great Tradition of the American Churches*, p. 158. Dunlap, "Methodist Theology in Great Britain," pp. 467-69, records the transition which was beginning in British Methodism. For contemporary documents on this transition see W. F. Tillett, "Some Currents of Contemporaneous Theological Thought," *MQRS*, 50 (1901), 483-95, H. C. Sheldon, "Changes in Theology Among American Methodists," *American Journal of Theology*, 10 (1906), 32-50; R. G. Hobbs, "Progress in Theology," *MQR*, 77 (1895), 913-20.

[50] Consult his "Scope and Methods of Christian Dogmatics," *MQR*, 77 (1895), 190-206, and Scott, "Methodist Theology," pp. 364, 491, 532. Terry's theological stance is suggested in a representative volume, *The New and Living Way*, p. 5, where he writes deploring the fact that many studies of doctrine, unfortunately even some now current, "pay little or no attention to the exegesis and learning of the scriptural teachings and nearly all of them devote a large amount of argument to the issues of old Calvinist and Arminian controversies, which ought to be now considered obsolete."

introducing many to the considered findings of biblical research.[51]

Olin A. Curtis (1850-1918) studied at Boston, Leipzig, Erlangen, Marburg, and Edinburgh. He taught several years at Boston, but the period of his major productivity was spent as professor of systematic theology at Drew. He acknowledges his debt to Whedon, Bowne, and Carlyle. To Bowne's personalism he joins a strong emphasis on racial solidarity to form an important theological work, *The Christian Faith* (1905), which was on the Course of Study in 1908 and 1912. This volume gained a considerable circulation and won for Curtis a deserved reputation as a leading Methodist theologian.[52]

Henry C. Sheldon (1845-1928) attended Yale and Boston. He was professor of historical theology at Boston from 1875 to 1895, moving thence to systematic theology, where he worked until 1921. He wrote copiously in several fields and gained the respect of the scholarly circles of his day. He was strongly influenced by Bowne, under whom he studied and with whom he taught for many years. His major theological work, *A System of Christian Doctrine*, first appeared in 1903 (revised in 1912) and was listed on the Course of Study through 1928. Though he purports to write without reference to any particular point of view, his *System* is indebted to Warren, shows marks of Ritschlian influence, and exhibits some of the categories of personalism.[53]

[51] For Tillett's general position see *A Statement of Faith of World-Wide Methodism*. He was far less inclined toward traditionalism than Summers, his predecessor, yet he had a Wesleyan interest. "The theology of Wesley and his followers is the Arminianism of Holland baptised with the Holy Spirit and infused with spiritual life" (p. 127). See also Peters, *Christian Perfection and American Methodism*, pp. 167 f.; and Mims, *History of Vanderbilt University*, pp. 157-68.

[52] For Curtis' acknowledgments and emphases see *The Christian Faith*, p. 5 and chaps. IV and X, and for his relationships to the theological forces of his time, "The Best Recent Books Bearing on Systematic Theology," *MQRS*, 48 (1899), 434. Also Joy, *The Teachers of Drew*, pp. 108-12.

[53] See *A System of Christian Doctrine*, pp. 30-39, 294-302, 434-41. It bears mention also that though Sheldon frequently refers to Bowne in this work, he does not mention John Wesley. Knudson asserts that Sheldon "marks an epoch" as he "made the transition from the older to the newer type of Methodist theology," in "Memoir," *Journal, Main Conference*, 1927, pp. 131-33, quoted in Barclay, *History of Methodist*

Before this third period of Methodism theological history ended, yet another generation of theological leaders appeared. In their work evangelical notes are less evident, while distinctively liberal notes are sounded even more clearly. They are occasionally concerned to criticize and clarify the Methodist theological heritage but in the main devote themselves to the reconstruction of theology by appeal to liberal principles.[54] Among this later generation three names may be mentioned.

Harris Franklin Rall (1870-1964) studied at Yale, the University of Berlin, and Halle-Wittenberg. He was strongly influenced by Harnack and the Ritschlian school and became one of the important Methodist interpreters of modern biblical studies. He was president of Iliff School of Theology from 1910 to 1915 and replaced Terry at Garrett in 1915 as professor of Christian doctrine. Rall wrote widely in both biblical and theological fields. Various of his works appeared on the study lists from 1916 to 1956. He served for years as the theological mentor of Methodist laymen through his column in the *Christian Advocate*. He helped lead the church through the fundamentalist-modernist, millennialist, and Course of Study controversies in the early decades of the century.[55]

Edwin Lewis (1881-1959) came to the United States from England at an early age. His training at Drew was under Miley and

Missions, Vol. III, *Widening Horizons, 1845-95*, p. 74 n. Compare Knudson's appraisal in "Henry Clay Sheldon—Theologian," *MQR*, 108 (1925), 175-92. Interesting judgments by Sheldon are found in his "Changes in Theology Among American Methodists," *American Journal of Theology*, 10 (1906), 38.

[54] Though basically liberal, the continuing evangelical disposition of this generation is evident in these articles: Ernest F. Tittle, "The Use and Abuse of Creeds," *MQR*, 99 (1917), 866-74; Harris Franklin Rall, "Methodism Today," *American Journal of Theology*, 24 (1920), 481-501; Edwin Lewis, "The Social Theology," *MQR*, 102 (1919), 226-38; George Croft Cell, "The Decay of Religion: I & II," *MQR*, 107 (1924), 64-78, 207-19.

[55] For Rall's reflections on his own thought see "Theology, Empirical and Christian," in *Contemporary American Theology*, ed. Vergilius Ferm, II, 245-76; compare a representative volume, *A Faith for Today*, and *Theology and Modern Life: Essays in Honor of Harris Franklin Rall*, ed. Paul A. Schilpp, especially the first essay by Irl G. Whitchurch. McCutcheon presents an appreciative review of Rall's thought, including a summary of his response to the impact of European crisis theology, in *The History of American Methodism*, III, 280-84, 301-3.

Curtis, and after teaching in the Bible department he became professor of systematic theology in 1916 succeeding Curtis. In his earlier career, Lewis' thought was strongly influenced by British idealism and exhibited the characteristic marks of evangelical liberalism. Lewis was a productive writer, his books appearing on the study lists from 1932 to 1952. His publication in 1934 of *A Christian Manifesto* marked his theological conversion. Informed by rising currents of neo-Protestant theology both in this country and abroad, along with G. C. Cell's *The Rediscovery of John Wesley* (1935), this book points the way to a critical reappraisal of Methodist theology.[56]

Albert C. Knudson (1873-1953), the third main figure in this period, is the outstanding Methodist representative of theology fashioned on the basis of personal idealism. His theology is given detailed consideration in the chapters which follow. That Knudson has been more influential than Rall would be difficult to establish; that he is more representative of the dominant stress in Methodism, however, can be argued with some cogency.

It should not be supposed that Methodists were of one mind in accepting all these changes. A sizable and potent group opposed both the dynamic forces of the New World and the attempts of the liberals to reconstruct a theology relevant to them. The opposition existed in the holiness movement, which expanded in the last half of the nineteenth century. It drew most of its strength from Methodism, in which the stress on a "second blessing" had become increasingly unpalatable. The 1896 General Confer-

[56] David W. Soper, *Major Voices in American Theology*, pp. 17-36, gives a brief analysis of Lewis' thought. In H. S. Smith *et al.*, *American Christianity*, II, 438-43, see the comments on Lewis and the lengthy reproduction of his prophetic article "The Fatal Apostasy of the Modern Church," *Religion in Life*, 2 (1933), 483 ff. The significance of the works by Lewis and Cell was immediately apparent. Wieman and Meland, *American Philosophies of Religion*, p. 92, termed Lewis' volume "a very stirring exposition of the supernaturalist gospel" and Cell's "another notable expression of this view." Sweet, *Methodism in American History*, p. 409, was unenthusiastic about the books and their impact, dismissing Cell's as an attempt "to make John Wesley a Calvinist without much success." For an illuminating account of Lewis' "theological conversion" see McCutcheon, *The History of American Methodism*, III, 304-15.

ence repudiated this theme and thereby hastened the proliferation of separate holiness sects, each claiming superiority to Methodism in doctrinal integrity.[57] The early part of the twentieth century also displayed a renewed concern for the preservation of the Methodist theological heritage. Between 1894 and 1918, volumes by G. L. Curtis, E. R. Hendrix, H. M. Du Bose, H. Wheeler, and T. B. Neely strove to direct Methodism to its historic and still legally binding standards.[58]

Resistance to the newer critical studies of the Bible became increasingly vocal, as illustrated in half a dozen articles controverting "higher criticism" published in the nineties by J. W. Mendenhall, editor of the *Methodist Quarterly Review*. Somewhat protected by its practical and experiential emphases, however, Methodism was not as violently disrupted as were many denominations by the fundamentalist-modernist controversy.[59]

The determination to resist the accommodation of Methodist theology to currents of the new age may be noted in frequent protests published in the *Methodist Quarterly Review*. It is seen also in books in which Bowne and his kind are the chief foils—G. Wilson, *Methodist Theology vs. Methodist Theologians* (1904), and G. A. Cooke, *Present and Future of Methodism* (ca. 1900). Wilson was very critical because the Methodist greats, Wesley, Clarke, Watson, Fletcher, Pope, and Miley, were ignored by Bowne, Tillett, and Huntington, who "hurl from them the testimonies, doctrines and teachings concerning every vital truth which

[57] See Peters, *Christian Perfection and American Methodism*, pp. 147-50, 175-80; and Elmer T. Clark, *The Small Sects in America*, p. 92.

[58] For example, H. M. Du Bose, in *A History of Methodism*, p. v, is convinced "of the transcendent historical importance of Methodism as the successor and heir of the great intellectual and doctrinal movements of England and German Protestantism." He contends for the "historical fitness, confessional sufficiency, and prophetic destiny of the Twenty-Five Articles."

[59] The Mendenhall articles appear through the years 1890 to 1900. See also Sweet, *History of American Methodism*, pp. 389-94. H. S. Smith *et al.*, *American Christianity*, II, 315, 324-32, 340-56, has illuminating documents and interpretation, and William F. Warren, in "Current Biblical Discussion: The Proper Attitude of Theological Faculties with Reference to Them," *MQR*, 81 (1899), 368-81, defends his colleagues Mitchell and Bowne.

has made us a distinctive people." Through the first quarter of the twentieth century, John A. Faulkner, church historian at Drew, maintained an informed critique of liberalism as he addressed himself to the arresting contrasts between *Modernism and the Christian Faith*. He indicated a clear preference for John Wesley as a supporter of the latter.[60]

The growing estrangement between progressive theology and traditional conservatism could not be excluded from General Conference consideration. The test for membership which had been instituted in 1864, requiring subscription to the Articles of Religion, had come under heavy fire. Despite conservative resistance it was removed in 1916. The Course of Study drawn up by the commission of the 1916 General Conference departed radically from previous lists and brought a storm of protest. But the defenders of orthodoxy, led by Harold Paul Sloan, fought a losing battle and after the Conference of 1928 were unable again to muster a decisive body of dissenting opinion.[61]

Thus conservative apologetics brought all religious, philosophical, and scientific developments under attack. However, the liberal reconstruction of Methodist theology successfully pursued its course. The surveys of modern Methodist theology by Schilling and McCutcheon impressively document the extent to which Methodism was dominated by liberalism in the first third of the twentieth century.[62] In general character and spirit, this theology had

---

[60] George Wilson *Methodist Theology vs. Methodist Theologians*, pp. 5, 128, 347. See also John A. Faulkner, "Methodism and Andover Theology," *Andover Review*, 18 (1892), 487-509, and H. F. Rall, "Do We Need a Methodist Creed?" *MQR*, 89 (1907), 221-30. For a discussion of Faulkner see *The History of American Methodism*, III, 267-70.

[61] Cole, *History of Fundamentalism*, pp. 165-74. Thomas Neely, *Present Perils of Methodism*, p. 81, warned that in the 1916 Course of Study "Methodism was largely eliminated," and that the course "contained books that positively taught doctrines contrary to Methodist teaching." A like criticism was made by Harold P. Sloan in "The New Course of Study," *MQR*, 104 (1921), 792-99. See also McCutcheon's section on "Conservative Reaction," devoted primarily to the polemics of John A. Faulkner and Harold Paul Sloan, *The History of American Methodism*, III, 267-73.

[62] Schilling, *Methodism and Society in Theological Perspective*, chaps. III and IV, summarizes the thinking of representative Methodist scholars and church leaders about "Wesleyan Emphases" and "Basic Christian Beliefs in Methodist Social Thought."

much more in common with the theology current in other denominations than it did with its own heritage. In some respects, lacking a sense of theological identity, Methodism was even more susceptible than other denominations to reconstruction under the criteria of liberalism.

Personal Idealism in Albert Knudson

Albert Cornelius Knudson was born of Norwegian parents in Grandmeadow, Minnesota, in 1873 and died at the age of eighty in 1953. His father was a preacher in the Norwegian Danish Methodist Church, where he was loved and respected for his devotion and service. The fourth of nine children, Albert was a studious youth who completed the reading of Adam Clarke's *Commentary* at the age of fifteen and entered the University of Minnesota at sixteen. He was graduated in 1893 as salutatorian of his class, having studied Greek and Latin and taken all the philosophy offered. He went to Boston to study under Mitchell, Sheldon, and Curtis and received his theology degree in 1896. He devoted the following year to the study of philosophy under Bowne, which proved to be "a veritable *Aufklärung*. It brought me a mental relief and an intellectual illumination that may be described as akin to a redemptive experience." [63]

Knudson went abroad to study at Jena and the University of Berlin under Wendt, Weiss, Harnack, and Kaftan. He began his teaching career at Iliff School of Theology and in 1906 was called back to Boston to replace Mitchell as professor of Old Testament. In 1921 he became professor of systematic theology and in 1926 dean of the School of Theology.

Knudson's major work in systematic theology appeared in two companion volumes *The Doctrine of God* (1930) and *The Doc-*

Chap. V is a 1959 report of a survey of responses from 5020 laymen from 267 Methodist churches selected from the entire country. McCutcheon's review of Methodist theology in the period 1919-1960 gives conclusive support of this judgment; the argument is further buttressed by additional evidence in his doctoral dissertation.

[63] In his theological autobiography, "A Personalist Approach to Theology," in *Contemporary American Theology*, ed. Vergilius Ferm, I, 217-41, see pp. 222 f.

trine of Redemption (1933). His last book, *Basic Issues in Christian Thought* (1950), also contains helpful material. In it he addresses himself more directly to the "theological irrationalism" or neo-orthodoxy which had made such inroads in American theology during the intervening twenty years.

Knudson is the pre-eminent theologian of the second generation of Boston personalists. He was deeply committed to the philosophy of personalism, which had rescued him from uncertainty and confusion about intellectual forces in the New World and given him an intellectually satisfying rationale for his own religious life and experience. In his essay in *Contemporary American Theology* Knudson asserts, "The great theological task of the present is to reinterpret Christian doctrine in the light of the personalistic type of thought." [64] In his final book, commenting on an unreserved endorsement of personalism which he had written more than twenty-five years earlier, he affirms, "I share its confidence and enthusiasm as fully today as I did then." [65]

Perhaps the most critical issue in the evaluation of personalist theology is to determine whether in it personalism or Christian faith is the controlling element. In careful doctoral studies Jones and Will both maintain that Knudson's theology is controlled by his personalism; they see his work as a clear illustration of the subordination of theology to philosophy of religion. Cauthen, in his helpful interpretation of Knudson's thought, effectively demonstrates its basic identity with the evangelical liberalism of the period. Though particular emphases are directly attributable to it, his personalist philosophy more widely serves to confirm and en-

[64] *Ibid.*, p. 234; see also *Personalism in Theology*, ed. E. S. Brightman, pp. 16, 234.
[65] *Basic Issues in Christian Thought*, pp. 45, 69. It is instructive to note as well Knudson's understanding of the major outlines of Methodist history and the central emphases of Methodist theology in his article on "Methodism" in *An Encyclopedia of Religion*, ed. Vergilius Ferm (New York: The Philosophical Library, 1945), pp. 487-89. McCutcheon provides a satisfactory summary of Knudson's theology in the context of the general development of Methodist theology in the twentieth century in *The History of American Methodism*, III, 276-80, 299-301.

hance the fundamental principles of continuity, autonomy, and dynamism characteristic of religious liberalism.[66]

Coming at the end of this period, Knudson's theological impact was limited as the energies of increasing numbers of students and teachers were given over to the claims of neo-Protestantism, including neo-Wesleyanism. The significance of his work was further restricted by being intertwined with a special philosophy which gained only a limited hearing, chiefly within his own denomination.[67] This philosophy was also effectively challenged in its own right by Dewey, Whitehead, and others. Knudson's reconstruction of theology in the liberal mold was comprehensive, consistent, and

[66] Curtis K. Jones, "Personalism as Christian Philosophy," unpublished Ph.D. dissertation, Union, 1944, pp. 213, 196, argues that "personalism neither begins nor really ends with Christianity. It begins with some speculations about the self and the world and ends with an hypothesis about God." As a consequence, "there seems to be a raveling out of the distinctively Christian theological concepts when the attempt is made to recast them in personalist categories." It is Will's contention ("Implications for Philosophical Theology in the Confrontation of American Personalism with Depth Psychology," pp. 2, 65) that in the "attempt to base Christianity upon reason, personalism sought to discover ultimate truth and value not so much through, as in the person's self conscious apprehension of himself." It fails "sufficiently to recognize the distortions of man's personality under the conditions of sin and evil in existence," and therefore is too sanguine about the possibilities of unaided human knowledge and too cavalier in its dismissal of the non-rational reaches of the human ego. McCutcheon ("Theology of the Methodist Episcopal Church during the Interwar Period, 1919-1939," unpublished Ph.D. dissertation, Yale, 1960, pp. vi, vii) levels this summary criticism at Knudson (and Brightman): They "subordinated the Scriptures as a source of ultimate religious authority to the standards of reason and coherence. They seemed, moreover, to have lost the Wesleyan note of evangelicalism while focusing their sole attention upon individual personality and its inherent metaphysical and theological freedom." McCutcheon draws suggestive comparisons among the liberal views of Knudson, Rall, and Lewis in *ibid.*, 188-91. In *The Impact of American Religious Liberalism* by Kenneth Cauthen see pp. 35, 108-110, 209-27. Consult also the appreciative and critical response to Cauthen's theses in Van Dusen, *The Vindication of Liberal Theology*, "The Indictment of Liberal Theology," pp. 55-90, and *passim*.

[67] Walter Marshall Horton says that Knudson's major theological work came too late and failed to achieve wide currency. See "Systematic Theology," in *Protestant Thought in the Twentieth Century*, ed. Arnold S. Nash, p. 109. But note McCutcheon's more positive estimate of Knudson's influence. He feels that Knudson's contact with students and the widespread distribution of his writings have made him "one of the most influential theologians in the Methodist Episcopal Church. In addition to colleges and universities of the church which were staffed with Boston-trained men, professors in the church's seminaries offered courses in theology using his texts as basic readings." *The History of American Methodism*, III, 277.

clear. But the days of its life were numbered. The creative expression of Methodist theology fell into new hands, which have yet to produce a representative, systematic statement.

The preceding survey provides a background for the following detailed elaboration of the elements of continuity and change in "fundamental doctrines" in American Methodism. The discussion includes basic transitions from revelation to reason, from sinful man to moral man, and from free grace to free will. In the next three chapters these changes, which have been adumbrated in the historical survey, receive additional documentation. The concluding chapter offers some generalizations about the anatomy, dynamics, and implications of theological transition, together with a brief summary of the whole.

CHAPTER III
FROM REVELATION
TO REASON

More than 2600 entries in eight sizable volumes compose John
Telford's edition of Wesley's *Letters*. In this vast correspondence,
brief passages are often most illuminating. To one of many accusations of heresy, Wesley retorts, "If I am a heretic, I became such
by reading the Bible." Lamenting the Quaker tendency to make
Scripture "a secondary rule, subordinate to the Spirit," Wesley insists rather that "the Scriptures are the touchstone whereby Christians examine all real or supposed revelations." Another correspondent charged that all who come into Methodism "must
renounce their reason." Wesley bluntly replies, "Sir, are you awake
... ? It is a fundamental principle with us that to renounce reason
is to renounce religion." Finally, in debate with Dr. Middleton,
Wesley prophesies that, unless the Christian apologists among his
contemporaries lay more stress on "internal evidence" or personal
experience, they will eventually "give up the external and . . . go
over to those whom they are now contending with; so that in a

century or two, the people of England will be fairly divided into real Deists and real Christians." [1]

This sampling reflects Wesley's staunch convictions about first principles and suggests some of the problems with which he wrestled. A significant chapter in the history of Methodism chronicles the struggle of Wesley's heirs with similar problems concerning theological sources, authority, and method.

WESLEYAN "SCRIPTURAL, EXPERIMENTAL RELIGION"

Revelation Through Scripture

In the Preface to his *Sermons*, Wesley announces his intention to describe "the true, the Scriptural, experimental religion," neither adding to nor omitting in them "what I find in the Bible." Amazingly well read in ancient and contemporary literature, he never wavers in his insistence that in final allegiance he is "a man of one Book." [2] Nor is this an idle claim. His sermons are biblical from end to end. Together with his *Notes*, they furnish the standards for doctrinal judgment in Methodism, the only Christian communion to rest its doctrinal standards on expositions of Scripture. The Scripture is also the rule of faith and practice and the test of all the workings of the Holy Spirit. Again and again Wesley "opened his Bible" confident that his need would be supplied from the "Oracles of God." [3]

There is more than a little evidence for the belief that Wesley was a literalist who believed the Bible to be "infallibly true." "Given by the inspiration of God," it is free from any "material error." [4] God employed virtuous and upright men wholly open to

---

[1] These citations are taken in turn from Wesley's *Letters*, IV, 216; II, 117; V, 364; II, 385.

[2] *Sermons*, Preface, I, 31 f.

[3] *Letters*, II, 44; *Sermons*, I, 245; *Notes*, Ro. 12:6; *Works*, VII, 294; VIII, 449. Franz Hildebrandt comments on the scriptural character of Methodism's doctrinal standards in *Christianity According to the Wesleys*, pp. 9-26.

[4] *Sermons*, I, 205, 225; *Natural Philosophy*, II, 447; *Letters*, IV, 369.

his direction whose work is eminently trustworthy. Wesley often refers to their words as "Spirit dictated." [5] Such citations, supporting the verbal inspiration of the Bible, can be multiplied. However, the logic Wesley uses in "A Clear and Concise Demonstration of the Divine Inspiration of the Holy Scriptures" is no more convincing than the evidence he offers for its "Divine authority" in his *Natural Philosophy*.[6] The significance of these essays is to be found, not in their logic or evidence, but in the serious purpose they represent. For Wesley, the divine authority of the Scriptures is essential to Christianity.

Yet his "literalism" has important qualifications which save it from being merely a wooden scholasticism. In his *Notes upon the New Testament* he does not hesitate to make substantially a new translation of the New Testament, and to add to it a critical and often most helpful exposition. He voices skepticism regarding some of the passages in Romans which imply predestination. He chooses among the Psalms when fashioning a Prayer Book for the American Methodists, omitting some as "highly improper for the mouth of a Christian Congregation." [7] He recognizes that the Apostles used fallible memories and often quoted Scripture inexactly.

His literalism has further restrictions. Though the words of the Bible are divinely inspired, they often require interpretation. Here Wesley offers several guides. The literal sense of the text is to be taken if possible. Where there is obscurity, parallel passages are to be considered and interpretations made "according to the grand truths which run through the whole." [8] Moreover, passages can be given a faithful reading only when they are set in context. Having considered a text in all these ways, one should seek to con-

---

[5] *Notes*, Preface, p. 9, and John 19:24.

[6] See *Works*, XI, 478 f., and *Natural Philosophy*, II, 447-49.

[7] Cited in S. N. Duvall, *The Methodist Episcopal Church and Education up to 1869*, p. 10; *Notes*, Ro. 8 and 9, Heb. 2:7, Matt. 2:6; see John Deschner, *Wesley's Christology*, pp. 7-12, for a review of the background and significance of the *Notes*.

[8] *Letters*, III, 129; *Works*, VI, 395; *Notes*, Ro. 12:6; *Sermons*, I, 32. For specific accounts of Wesley's understanding and use of the Bible see also Colin Williams, *John Wesley's Theology Today*, pp. 23-29; and Lycurgus M. Starkey, Jr., *The Work of the Holy Spirit*, pp. 85-90.

firm its meaning in reason, experience, and Christian tradition.[9]

But most important for its understanding, the Bible is to be approached in "serious and earnest prayer," and its meaning sought in meditation and self-examination. Wesley insists that the Spirit which gave the Bible is needed to "continually inspire" and "supernaturally assist" those who read it.[10] The "letter of Scripture" is of little avail apart from the Spirit, for the unregenerate mind has no access to the Word.[11] The function of the accompanying Spirit is not to convince man of the authenticity of what he reads. Rather, it is "to apply and enable man to receive with faith the illuminating and saving meaning of God's revelation." [12] That is, significant knowledge of God is saving knowledge. It follows, then, that the essence of revelation is the Word spoken in Christ, not ideas or ideals. In Scripture man confronts not a dead record but a living presence. For Wesley, reading the Bible is expectant listening to the Word, as evidently present in it as in the sacrament. In his perceptive study of the *Notes* John Deschner defines and defends this Christological emphasis in revelation as true to Wesley's view.[13] Surely it is misleading to dismiss as a mere literalist one who describes in these terms the Bible's mediating function between God and man.

Experience and Reason

Commentators have discussed at considerable length Wesley's emphasis on experience. For some it is an impressive anticipation of Schleiermacher's religion based on feeling; for others it is an image of more recent empirical method. When liberal theology made common appeal to experience, Methodists seized eagerly on this aspect

---

[9] *Works*, VI, 354 f.; *Journal*, I, 471 f.; *Letters*, III, 172. Williams, *John Wesley's Theology Today*, pp. 28-38, writes judiciously on the manner in which Wesley sees Scripture confirmed in tradition, reason, and experience.

[10] *Works*, XIV, 267; *Notes*, II Tim. 3:16.

[11] *Sermons*, I, 242 f.; *Notes*, Acts 7:38, John 3:21.

[12] Starkey, *The Work of the Holy Spirit*, p. 89.

[13] *Wesley's Christology*, p. 110; see also Hildebrandt, *From Luther to Wesley*, pp. 26-29.

of their tradition to show the compatibility between *John Wesley and Modern Religion*.[14] However, the effort to make an empirical theologian of Wesley misconceives the meaning of experience for him. Experience generally, and "religious experience" broadly defined, is of passing interest to him, no more. His persistent preoccupation is with the encounter between man's need and God's grace. In Wesley, clarity is served by regularly reading "experience" as "evangelical experience." Invariably his concrete interest is with the truth that saves.

Further, the Wesleyan concern for evangelical experience is antithetical to a stress on subjective states and emotions which has often followed in its wake. Wesley advises an anxious seeker not to be overly preoccupied with moods and feelings, but devoted rather to the sure promises of God.[15] The God who makes himself known

[14] The title of Umphrey Lee's book on Wesley. Lee is concerned to qualify interpretations overly enthusiastic about the importance of experience for Wesley, though he too retains an empirical emphasis. "Certainly, before the work of Schleiermacher had much influence in England and America, the Methodist Revival had prepared millions to minimize orthodoxy and to rely on inner experience rather than upon syllogisms. On the whole Schleiermacher influenced the theologians, John Wesley the preachers. . . . The contribution of the Methodists to the break-down of the older orthodoxy and rationalism was in their emphasis upon a milder conception of God, upon Christian experience as taking precedence over dogma, and in their stress on feeling" (pp. 302, 136-43). Piette notes that religious experience is dear to twentieth-century Methodists, some of whom find it in a return to the Revival while still more "have been won over to the acceptance of religious experience as understood by theorists such as Schleiermacher—the father of liberal Protestantism—and William James, the prophet of religious pragmatism." See Maximin Piette, *John Wesley in the Evolution of Protestantism*, trans. J. B. Howard, p. 477. One of the most thoroughgoing portrayals of Wesley in terms of religious empiricism may be found in Henry Bett's *The Spirit of Methodism*, pp. 93-105. See also Shipley's discussion of John Fletcher and Schleiermacher in "Methodist Arminianism," pp. 148 ff.

[15] *Letters*, VIII, 190; VII, 120. Williams, *John Wesley's Theology Today*, pp. 107-12, argues cogently against a subjective "psychologism" in the description of the work of the Spirit in human life. George C. Cell, *The Rediscovery of John Wesley*, p. 97, records this general contention: "A religion of ideas and feeling, whose primary trust is in considerations of natural reason or floats on the changeful tides of emotion or limits its confidences to a round of good works, is not the Wesleyan type, but its antithesis. Considerations of natural reason and systems of opinion, codes of conduct and work-righteousness, the wind and weather of subjective states and feelings, are radically subordinated therein to the objectivity of Christian experience and the Christian faith, to that of revelation and the atonement. The reference in Christian faith to a living and saving God is what really counts." In Fletcher's account of his own

in the depths of human experience is transcendent and objectively real. In no sense is he produced by man's feelings, desires, or reason. Thus Wesley gives primacy to the revelatory act of God in Christ, applied to the heart of the believer by the Spirit. In his theology of revelation the Word of God must become a living Word *pro mea*, for me.[16] The encounter carries its own testimony and requires no external confirmation. Held fast, this truth frees Wesley from the necessity of trying to "authenticate," "certify," or "justify" faith, dominant enterprises of his successors.

On the one hand, Wesley's assertion of the reality of God's work in the life of man was considered "a very horrid thing" by his rationalistic contemporaries, who called him a ranting enthusiast. On the other hand, the devout charged that he set experience and his own private notions above Scripture. To the latter group he writes, "I have declared again and again that I make the Word of God the rule of all my actions, and that I no more follow any secret impulse instead thereof than I follow Mahomet or Confucius."[17] Experience is not the primary source of faith standing in judgment on Scripture; its function rather is to confirm scriptural truth. "Whereas it is objected that experience is not sufficient to prove a doctrine unsupported by Scripture; . . . we answer, Experience is sufficient to *confirm* a doctrine which is grounded on Scripture."[18]

---

conversion, he acknowledges distress over his poverty of feeling and adds, "But I found relief in Mr. Wesley's *Journal,* where I learned, that we should not build on what we feel, but go to Christ with all our sins, and all our hardness of heart." Quoted by Wesley, *Works,* XI, 284.

[16] Paul W. Hoon, "The Soteriology of John Wesley," unpublished Ph.D. dissertation, Edinburgh, 1936, p. vii, commenting on the experiential character of Wesley's theology, observes, "Religion is real when God is experienced in a saving way." For Wesley, however, this experience "was specifically one of the Christian religion as it saves people and restores them to life with God. It was not, for example, merely mystical; it was primarily redemptive."

[17] *Letters,* II, 205; *Sermons,* I, 202 f.

[18] *Sermons,* II, 357 f. Cell, *The Rediscovery of John Wesley,* p. 72, rightly contends that Wesley's "theology of experience" rests on two pillars—Scripture and experience—which are not "alien and antagonistic, but cognate and congenial principles," Succinctly, Robert E. Cushman, "Theological Landmarks in the Revival Under Wesley," *Religion in Life,* 27 (1957-58), p. 108, makes the same point: "The Word was

The reality of scriptural Christianity is also confirmed by the witness and the fruits of the Spirit. A privilege of those born of God is the Spirit's testimony to the fact, an experience which Wesley did not require, however, of all his converts in his later ministry. To this witness or assurance Wesley joins the fruits of the Spirit's work. These marks of regeneration indirectly attest to God's love. Thus both inner and outer testimonies are important to Wesley as he turns to "living witnesses." [19] Such appeal was critical to his own conversion and continues to occupy an important place in his work. In the face of contrary Christian experience, he is willing to reconsider and, occasionally, to modify some point of faith or practice. Without question, then, experience receives distinctive treatment in Wesley's theology. It roots in his passion for religious reality and underlies his approval of the testimony of early Christians: "What the Scripture promises, I enjoy. Come and see what Christianity has done here, and acknowledge it is of God." [20]

As Wesley regularly appeals to reason, in addition to Scripture and experience, he reflects the influence of the Age of Reason. It is

---

life. It came to life under the power of the Holy Spirit. Doctrines of the New Testament—justification, new birth, sanctification—took on flesh and blood in the lives of individuals. Here was visible and ample proof of the truth of Scripture."

[19] Wesley's understanding of the work of the Spirit is perhaps best approached through his three sermons on the subject, "The Witness of the Spirit: I," "The Witness of the Spirit: II," and "The Witness of Our Own Spirit," found in *Sermons*, I, 202-18; II, 343-59; I, 219-36. In *Works*, X, 295, Wesley writes, "My comfort stands not on any opinion, either that a believer can or cannot fall away; not on the remembrance of anything wrought in me yesterday; but to what is today; on my present knowledge of God in Christ, reconciling me to Himself." For a careful review of Wesley's position see Starkey, *The Work of the Holy Spirit*, pp. 63-78; see also R. Benjamin Garrison, "Vital Interaction: Scripture and Experience: John Wesley's Doctrine of Authority," *Religion in Life*, 25 (1956), 567 ff., who contends that the witness and fruits of the Spirit and the appeal to the community of believers are also aspects of Wesley's total doctrine of experience.

[20] *Letters*, II, 387. John Fletcher shared Wesley's feeling for the immediacy of Christian reality. See Fletcher's *Works*, VII, 361, quoted in Shipley, "Methodist Arminianism," p. 112: "If, because we have the letter of the Scriptures, we must be deprived of all immediate manifestations of Christ, we are great losers by that blessed book. . . . If we can have no discovery of the glorious original, have compassion on us, take back Thy book and impart Thyself to us as Thou didst to Thine Ancient People."

important to understand his conception of reason. Reason enables man to know much about the world and the Creator behind it. Man's desire for knowledge far exceeds these discoveries, however, and tends to draw him toward fuller knowledge of God. Reason is to be employed "as far as it will go," and no one is justified in remaining in ignorance or in shirking opportunities to learn. But "The Imperfection of Human Knowledge" is an abiding fact. An inescapable residue of ignorance is designed by God to "hide pride from man" and prevent him from coming to rest in his own achievements. Reason is good and helpful but "it is utterly incapable of giving either faith, or hope, or love; and, consequently, of producing either real virtue, or substantial happiness." [21] A necessary task for the man of faith is "the overturning of all the prejudices of corrupt reason . . . that blind leader of the blind, so idolized by the world." [22]

For Wesley, reason means logic, careful, consistent deduction from premises, and induction by inference based on experience. It does not mean discursive or metaphysical construction. Quite often reason simply means "common sense," including that which is right, fair, and impartial. It is this to which Wesley appeals when he speaks to "men of reason." [23] Though reason aids in the interpretation and understanding of the Scriptures, it does not set itself above them. Neither is it a final authority in the interpretation of evangelical experience. Wesley employs reason carefully and thoroughly throughout his life and writings. But he knows its weaknesses and limitations. It is for him a useful instrument, never a final authority. Wesley is more trusting of reason than are the

---

[21] Works, VI, 360, 337; VIII, 197 f.

[22] Sermons, I, 149; II, 216; Works, XII, 137, 402, Cushman in "Theological Landmarks in the Revival Under Wesley," Religion in Life, 27 (1957-58), 106 f., argues that the Wesleyan Revival rooted in a rediscovery of the Bible which implied "a most emphatic protest, from within the church, against the substitution of philosophy and ethics for the faith and doctrine of the Bible."

[23] In such essays as "An Earnest Appeal to Men of Reason and Religion" and "A Farther Appeal to Men of Reason and Religion," Works, VIII, 266 and 466; many additional essays in Vols. X and XI in the Works bear this out. In the Preface to the Works, I, iv, Wesley addressed his "maturest thoughts" to "serious and candid men" proposing to speak agreeably to "Scripture, Reason and Christian Antiquity."

Reformers, but he is a world removed from the "reasonable" men of his day who grieved at his "irrational excesses."

A final note should be added about Wesley's valuation of Christian tradition. It is abundantly clear that he had no desire to sever himself from his catholic heritage. Methodism claims no innovations, he declares; "It is the one old religion; as old as the Reformation; as old as Christianity; as old as Moses; as old as Adam." [24] The Christian tradition which he valued so highly included the writings of the early church fathers, the ecumenical creeds and the Homilies and the *Book of Common Prayer*. Though this traditional evidence is not as authoritative as other evidence for Christianity, and though it is "clogged and encumbered," it is not to be despised. It gives us knowledge of true Christians and genuine Christianity; its writings are blessed by the Spirit and merit greater respect than any others except those of the Bible.[25] As his *Journal* shows impressively, Wesley read voluminously; his theology is enriched by his acquaintance with much of the great writing of the past.

Wesley's Theological Method

There is of course no discussion by Wesley on theological method. Yet, in the light of his understanding of scriptural, experimental Christianity, it is possible to describe how he worked as a theologian. He edited *A Survey of the Wisdom of God in the Creation: or, A Compendium of Natural Philosophy*, which, along with scattered other references, contains some elements of a natural theology.[26] God is a good and powerful Creator who has marvelously ordered the world, giving due cause for wonder and thanksgiving. But Wesley places little confidence in arguments for the existence of God. Natural theology receives but scant space in his writings, and, when it does appear, the knowledge derived from it is shown to be

[24] *Letters*, IV, 131; III, 291.
[25] *Ibid.*, II, 384 ff.
[26] *Natural Philosophy*, I, 313; II, 184, 447-49; *Letters*, II, 71, 379; IV, 90 f.; *Works*, VI, 325-27; VII, 271; VIII, 197.

entirely wanting in power to bring man to salvation. Wesley is sensitive to the "dangers of philosophical speculation" and convinced that it is impossible to "pass from things natural to things spiritual" because there is "no proportion between the finite and the infinite." [27]

Wesley knows that theology must look to another foundation—God's revelation through the Scripture. Thus the Evangelical Revival began as scriptural Christianity; although Wesley never claimed it to be more than this, neither did he ever desire it to be less. His appeal to Scripture is characteristically orthodox; his distinctiveness lies in his insistence that Scripture be confirmed in evangelical experience. At times Wesley refers to this confirmation as the "internal evidence" for Christianity, which he opposes favorably to "external evidence." He argues that such experience is self-authenticating, depending on nothing for its validity except the immediate conviction of the Holy Spirit. But as the enthusiasts taught him all too well, supposed encounters with the Spirit require verification by Scripture as well as by reason and the fruits of the Spirit. Thus guarded against distortion by the historical revelation, the divine disclosure in empirical experience plays a preeminent role in his theology.[28]

[27] *Works*, VIII, 14, 197. Williams, *John Wesley's Theology Today*, pp. 30-32, examines Wesley's use of the rudiments of natural theology and concludes that he "makes no use of arguments for the existence of God and draws his ethics entirely from revelation"; for him "reason has no pre-established principles which would enable it to develop a 'natural theology'"; finally he emphasizes "the existential irrelevance" of such natural knowledge as is possible. The possibility of basing a "natural theology" on the universal manifestations of the Spirit's work (prevenient grace) is examined by Starkey, *The Work of the Holy Spirit*, pp. 41-45. He finds much more ground for such a theology in Wesley than in Luther or in Calvin. Harald Lindström, *Wesley and Sanctification*, pp. 47-49, denies, while E. D. Dunlap, "Methodist Theology in Great Britain," pp. 31-33, affirms, that a natural theology is possible on this basis. Cell, *The Rediscovery of John Wesley*, p. 158, observes that Wesley "agreed with Calvin and Luther alike in banishing philosophy and speculation and in reserving the interpretation of the Gospel to historical and experiential reasoning."

[28] Garrison, "Vital Interaction," *Religion in Life*, 25 (1956), 564, proposes this summary: "Thus the basis of the Scripture's authority is 'other foundation can no man lay, than that which is laid, even Jesus Christ.' By experience we build upon that foundation; judging tradition (the record of other men's experiences and of the New Testament experience) in the light of reason." See also Shipley, "Methodist

The doctrines derived from scriptural revelation and attested by experience are to be ordered and set forth clearly and logically by reason. In this undertaking, reason functions as servant, never as master. It does not add to the content of revelation but only states it. It makes appeal to Christian tradition, but never as though to a higher authority. "Granted then, the interaction of Scripture and experience, [Wesley] sought corroboration of these in the experience and Scriptural interpretation of the Church's history (particularly of the Patristic writings) and then he searched the whole in the light of reason." [29] Or as summarized by Paul Hoon, "The procedure by which Wesley arrives at a doctrine consists, first, in deriving it from and formulating it on the basis of Scripture; second, in testing and modifying it in accord with experience; third, in testing it by reason; fourth, in testing it by tradition. . . . This might be said to be the *ordo auctoritatis* for Wesley. The distinctive feature of this method lies in the high place given to experience and in the manner in which Wesley systematically appeals to experience." [30]

There is little reason to doubt that Wesley's "intuitive apprehension of truth" and his "theological pragmatism" occasionally lead him into theological difficulty. He prefers to obey "his instinct at the expense of logical consistency." [31] Yet both his theological creativity and his inadequacy may root in this preference. Wesley theologizes as one intensely involved in experimental Christianity. The experience out of which he works is not only personal but also corporate, growing out of an intimate knowledge of his people. Though his sensitivity to experience did not guarantee him against

---

Arminianism," p. 142: "The final religious authority in the intrinsic sense is empirical revelation, but this requires in varying degrees the concomitant verification of the extrinsic authorities—the Scriptures, the Church, reason, and experience."

[29] Garrison, "Vital Interaction," p. 571. Sugden contends that Wesley "first worked out his theology by strict logical deduction from the Scriptures; and then he corrected his conclusions by the test of actual experience." He concludes, in *Sermons*, I, 196 n., that "his class-meetings were a laboratory in which he verified or modified his hypothesis."

[30] Hoon, "The Soteriology of John Wesley," p. 343 n.

[31] *Ibid.*, p. 336.

theological error, it did save him from a circumspect but impotent orthodoxy. In the final analysis, transcending "peculiarities," he maintains views consonant with the classical Christian heritage.

WATSON ON "THE DIVINE AUTHORITY OF SCRIPTURE"

For more than fifty years Wesley carried on a creative and productive evangelical ministry surrounded by the dispassionate adherents of the Age of Reason. Yet it is possible to read dozens of his pages on end without confronting logical proofs and disputations. He addressed problems prior in importance and more deeply rooted than the misuse of reason. A different atmosphere pervades the pages of Richard Watson. With the possible exception of sermons, exhorting sinners to repentance, his writings are a continuous reminder that his Christianity sought to maintain a place in a world enamored of reason. His discussion of the foundation, character, and value of Christianity was aimed at the reasonable mind. True, he wrote as a Wesleyan, and the distinctive Wesleyan marks remain. But the mood and voice have changed. The Scriptures continue as the ultimate source and norm for faith and practice. The rational demonstration of their credibility, however, has become a central concern. For Watson, they seem to serve as much to confirm the probability as to convey the actuality of new life in Christ. Watson is Wesleyan and he is not. The evidence of his departure from his heritage is most extensive and unequivocal in his discussion of revelation and reason.

Scripture as Revelation

Men ought to be able to recognize, understand, and find revelation credible, says Watson. It should be thought of as "the communication of Divine truth," on "all subjects connected with our moral state and relations." [32] He quotes with approval an earlier

[32] *Sermons and Sketches of Sermons*, II, 474; I, 138; see also II, 107, 279, and 369. Quotations from Watson's sermons will be taken from this American edition, which is more readily available than his complete *Works*.

authority, Doddridge, who defines revelation as "a discovery of some proposition to the mind, which came not in by the usual exercise of its faculties, but by some miraculous Divine interposition and attestation, either mediate or immediate" (I, 71).[33] In these passages and throughout his writings, Watson interprets revelation almost exclusively as the communication of divine truths or "propositions to the mind." He finds little warrant in Wesley, however, for his interpretation. For Wesley, revelation is relational, not propositional, and it intends not credible ideas but salvation itself.

Revelation is confined to the Bible, which therefore must be used as the source and authority for all thought about the Christian religion. Just this Watson seeks to do, states his publisher in the advertisement to the *Institutes*. The author endeavors "to exhibit what he believes to be the sense of the Holy Scriptures, to whose authority, he trusts, he has unreservedly subjected all his own opinions" (I, i). The first part of the *Institutes* Watson devotes to the "Evidences of the Divine Authority of the Holy Scriptures." In it he seeks to demonstrate for others what he knows to be true: the Scriptures are the source of and authority for the whole of theology. In them "we have the confirmation of a *Divine* and therefore an *infallible authority* for everything in RELIGION: so that this is no longer left to the conflicting and doubtful opinions of men." [34]

Watson has no discussion of the inspiration of the Scriptures in

---

[33] *Theological Institutes: Or a View of the Evidences, Doctrines, Morals, and Institutes of Christianity,* ed. John M'Clintock, I, 71. The Institutes is by far the most important source for the study of Watson's theology and will be quoted repeatedly. Therefore, references to it in the interpretative sections on his thought, in the chapters on revelation, sin, and grace, will be given in the text, by volume and page. In these chapters in comparable sections, references to the systematic theologies of Miley and Knudson will be made in the same manner.

[34] *Conversations for the Young,* p. 17; see also Sermons, II, pp. 192 ff., 278. Dunlap, "Methodist Theology in Great Britain," p. 155, accurately describes Watson's intention in these words: "'The Holy Scripture was the basic foundation upon which Methodist theology rested. Throughout the whole of Richard Watson's writings, particularly the *Institutes,* it is apparent that the final appeal is always made to Scripture and in the face of the testimony of Scripture all rational conclusions must give way." Dunlap notes also that there is little evidence that biblical criticism had much direct or positive influence on Watson's work (p. 157).

the *Institutes*. In his infrequent remarks elsewhere, he defends their plenary inspiration, regarding them as unerring reproductions of the Divine mind: "*The whole* was authenticated or dictated by the Holy Spirit with so full an influence, that it became truth without mixture or error." Consequently, the Scriptures are infallible and secure from "all error, both as to the subjects spoken and the manner of expressing them." [35] Close study of their claim to antiquity, their careful preservation, and the reliability of their writers amply establishes that they were "early and faithfully made" and have come to us "uncorruptly kept." They are authentic, reliable records of the divine revelation (I, 105–46).

Watson's reserve in discussing the inspiration of the Scriptures reflects an assumption which underlies all his treatment of evidence: to be decisive, evidence must be external to that which it establishes. Thus objective and impartial, it can be logically conclusive. If it is to claim truth, religion must possess a rational ground outside the religious experience itself. This assumption, common to Christian writers in the Age of Reason, appears again and again in Watson's writings.

Evidence of Divine Authority

It might be supposed that having contended for a divinely inspired, authentically transmitted record Watson would rest his case. Not so. In his mind these considerations have little to do with the "evidence" for the divine authority of the Bible. To establish this evidence he devotes more than two hundred pages to a review of "presumptive," "external," "internal," and "collateral" proofs. Though he says that external evidence is the best by far, yet he labors the others at length. Perhaps he is aware that external evidence, founded on miracle and prophecy, is not as compelling as he would like to have it.

1. As a moral agent, man requires a rule whereby he can judge

[35] *Conversations for the Young*, p. 16; see also *The Works of the Rev. Richard Watson*, XII, 332-50.

his actions. It is reasonable to assume that such a rule has come from God in a disclosure regarding his divine government. This presumption is sustained by the notorious inability of man to devise his own rule and the necessity that God "restore, enlarge and promulgate" religious knowledge among men. Thus we can presume that God will make a revelation "by which we are instructed ... both as to what we are to believe and to do." [36]

2. "The principal and most appropriate evidence of a revelation from God, must be *external* to the revelation itself." If a man claims to have received a revelation, under what circumstances are we to believe him? "His belief has no authority to command *ours*. He may have actually received it; but we have not the means of knowing it without proof." Such a man "would be asked for some external authentication of his mission" (I, 71). Quite in keeping with the Christian apologists of the eighteenth and nineteenth centuries, and despite the doubt cast by Hume, Watson regards miracle and prophecy as the two great external proofs of the mission of Jewish and Christian authors. External to that which they are employed to establish, miracle and prophecy give indisputable evidence for the divine authority of the Scriptures.[37] His discussion is extensive and studied. Yet this argument became increasingly sterile as the years passed. That his apologetics was largely ineffectual was not its chief fault. But rather, engrossed by it, he was tempted to neglect some fundamental accents in the Wesleyan heritage.

3. Evidence internal to the Scriptures, though really not needed, confirms external proof. It arises from the "apparent excellence and beneficial tendency" of the doctrines of the Scriptures. Some doctrines are "undiscoverable by the unassisted faculties of man" (I, 204). When revealed, however, they impress man with their

[36] *Works*, XII, 303.

[37] *Ibid.*, XII, 318-34; see also *Sermons*, I, 9, 146, 176; II, 21, 474. In an article on "Henry Clay Sheldon—Theologian," MQR, 108 (1925), 180, Knudson observes, "The Methodist theologians from Watson to Miley and Foster were authoritarian rationalists. They based the Christian faith on the divine authority of Scripture, and this authority they believed could be established by purely rational considerations."

excellence and carry the same demonstration as all other truth. In its essence Scripture exhibits a moral tendency also. It has improved "immense numbers of individuals" and is therefore "worthy of God" (I, 204–32; cf. 88–94).

4. Collateral evidence consists in the agreement of revealed doctrines through the ages; the suitableness of the Christian revelation to the state of the world; the consistency of its historical record and monuments with those of the time; its "marvelous diffusion" and its "beneficial effect" on mankind. A multitude of facts support these empirical proofs (I, 232).

Now Watson can rest his case. To the strong presumption that God would make a revelation is added the direct evidence of miracle and prophecy (external to the revelation itself), the goodness of the revelation (internal to it), and the empirical benefits (which follow from it).

In this disputation about evidence, where is the confirmation of Scripture in evangelical experience so central and distinctive in John Wesley? It has little place. "Experience" fails to appear in either the index or the extensive study outline provided by McClintock in the 1850 edition of the *Institutes*. When Watson discusses faith, a familiar insistence on trust is heard, and in his sermons he regularly solicits a personal surrender to the gospel. But even in these instances trust is generally commended on the basis of evidence.[38] Watson does not directly deny the importance of experience; he neglects it. While Wesley strives in behalf of the experiential appropriation of Scripture, Watson strives to establish the evidences for Scripture. Their concern for Scripture provides both men with common materials and produces many similarities in their writings. Their divergent convictions about Scripture, however, lead them to identifiably different theologies. If the differences are

---

[38] In one sermon, *Sermons*, I, 343, Watson writes, "By prophecy, miracles and the unanimous testimony of experienced Christians the Gospel is confirmed to us as the sure word of God." 343. In another, *ibid.*, I, 337, he sounds his more general theme, "The conversion of St. Paul proves the truth of the religion which he embraced, by showing how satisfactory, how irresistible, are its evidences when suffered to present themselves fairly to the mind." See also *ibid.*, II, 376, 387, and 409.

not apparent, and if they are not recognized by Watson, none the less they lie close to the surface, available for such use as other hands might make of them.[39]

Authority and Method in Theology

"Systematic" theology is simply ordered and informed exegesis and exposition of the Scriptures. Having established them as the infallible truth of God, Watson regards it as his further duty "to examine their contents, and to collect from them that ample information on religious and moral subjects which they profess to contain, and in which it has become necessary that the world should be supernaturally instructed" (I, 263). Theological method is concerned first to adduce the evidence for the divine authority of the Scriptures and second to explicate systematically the *"leading DOCTRINES of the Scriptures as they are found in that perfected system of revealed religion"* (I, 468, 2, 87, 573).

What is the place of reason in these methodological responsibilities of theology? We have considered at length the evidence for the authority of Scripture, which is addressed to reason, "the only faculty which is capable of receiving it." The examination of evidence, then, is the first use of reason. After this evidence is approved, the second use of reason is to interpret scriptural revelation by the same "common-sense rules which are adopted by all mankind" to determine the meaning of writing (I, 96 f.).

A common principle in biblical interpretation at the time held that nothing contrary to reason was to be deduced from revelation. Watson regards this principle as potentially dangerous. In addition to his discussion in the *Institutes,* one of his earliest writings, *Remarks upon the Eternal Sonship of Christ and the Use of Reason*

[39] Scott, "Methodist Theology," pp. 159 f., concludes that American Methodists generally failed to integrate and develop the emphasis on "experiential" evidence in their heritage. They followed Richard Watson so closely that they rarely got back to the vital experience of Wesley; thus their "apologetics were limited almost completely to the methodology of 'natural theology.' "

in Matters of Revelation, addresses this problem.[40] It was prompted by the public views of a fellow Methodist, Adam Clarke, which were far too rationalistic for Watson. Watson insists that divine reason must be normative. Man's limited and erring reason cannot be elevated to a supreme position. If man's reason could receive and understand all rational demonstrations as they appear to the mind of God, it would find no contradiction between itself and divine reason. But, in fact, the most important doctrines of revelation do contradict human reason and expectation. Consequently, reason is morally obligated to proceed humbly in areas which, by their nature, are incapable of investigation.[41] As he strives to define the limits within which reason may be used, Watson's biblical orthodoxy again comes to the fore. Having won a place for the Bible itself, he bids reason affect a becoming modesty when subsequently the doctrines of the Bible are under examination.

Limited to its previous knowledge and experience, reason is unable to anticipate or evaluate new revelation. Therefore, initially the idea of God must be given to man. In this matter Watson is clearly aligned with the sensationalism of John Locke, which held that the mind knows only what comes to it from without by way of the senses. There are no intuitive first principles to which God is a rational necessity, nor can any segment or combination of experiences of the empirical world produce the idea of God. Once revealed, however, the idea is capable of rational demonstration. In his theory of knowledge Watson is clearer than Wesley though not basically different.[42] Wesley too followed Locke, though he talked also about "spiritual senses" which, except as they are clouded by sin, enable men to apprehend the things of God. Though this

---

[40] The original English edition is used (London: T. Cordeux, 1818). In the *Institutes* see chap. IX, "The Uses and Limitations of Reason in Religion," I, 95-104.

[41] *Conversations for the Young,* p. 11. See also *Remarks upon the Eternal Sonship of Christ,* p. 49: "What is said by the God of truth must be true; what appears reasonable to me, may or may not be true; and the position which best becomes our humility, as fallible creatures, is not that Scripture cannot be true if it be contrary to my reason; but that my reason cannot be true if it contradict Scripture."

[42] Watson quotes Locke with favor in a number of places in his *Remarks upon the Eternal Sonship of Christ,* p. 62 and *passim;* see also *Sermons,* I, 273 ff.

idea finds little space in Watson, for both men knowledge in general is built up from sense experience. But for John Wesley, the saving experience in which God encounters man is self-authenticating. A more certain reality neither is required nor exists by reference to which the experience of God can be validated.

Watson's epistemology is the point most frequently attacked by his American successors who fell under the influence of intuitional realism and the common-sense philosophy of Reid, Stewart, Cousin, etc. The restriction of knowledge to the world of sensation greatly distresses them. It unnecessarily limits knowledge, it casts doubt on universal intuitions of reason, and it gives encouragement to atheism. Demands for a new theology to replace Watson's listed the revision of his theory of knowledge as a first concern.[48]

While revelation announces the *idea*, it cannot "prove" the *existence* of God. His existence is demonstrated by a natural philosophy fashioned by reason. Watson's epistemology makes impossible a priori proofs for the existence of God. However, no such disqualification attaches to a posteriori proofs. Man's investigation of God rightly proceeds from existence, intelligence, motion, design, and personality. The logical implications of these aspects of experience provide the revealed idea of God with "irresistible corroborative evidence." [44] In the *Institutes* nearly half the material on natural theology is quoted from other authors, in particular William Paley and his disciple John Howe (I, 227–325), Their

---

[48] This sentiment is expressed in the *Methodist Quarterly Review* in articles by W. M. Bangs, 19 (1837), 332 ff.; and 20 (1838), 80 f.; and by B. F. Cocker, 44 (1862), 181 ff.; and 46 (1864), 5 ff. Daniel Whedon, 46 (1864), 155, says that Watson's views on the inability of reason to discover God (his Lockean epistemology and psychology) are "now somewhat obsolete." See also Scott, "Methodist Theology," pp. 145-47, for a discussion of the growing contention about the necessity of replacing Watson's *Institutes*.

[44] *Sermons*, I, 281, 335; *Works*, VII, 312; *Conversations for the Young*, pp. 9-11. Dunlap, "Methodist Theology in Great Britain," p. 144, concludes that "this shift toward philosophical discussion represents something basically new in Methodist theological circles. It is illustrative of Clarke's more rationalistic interest and methodology. In his *Institutes*, Watson also dwells on the attributes [of God] but insists that the knowledge of such matters comes strictly by revelation which, when received, is subject to 'copious and irresistible' rational evidence." See also *Works*, IX, 378-460.

statements of the arguments from design Watson found most convincing. But the extent of his dependence on them and the general tone of his discussion suggest that he is not at home in philosophical theology.

The idea of God is given by revelation; the existence of God is established by reason. Into which domain then does the consideration of God's character and attributes properly fall? Remembering the limitations and distortions of reason, Watson again turns to revelation and, in the investigation of God's being and government, requires reason to serve the dictates of revelation (I, 335, 447).

These final issues epitomize the scholastic tendencies widely evident in Watson. To resolve the conflict between his competing loyalties to Scripture and reason, he assigns to scriptural revelation the idea and attributes of God, and to reason the demonstration of his existence. But this gratuitous division of labor only superficially veiled his basic rationalism. And it proved ineffectual. In this area Watson was limited in his ability to speak with conviction to the questioning mind of the world, and perhaps, in some degree, to the seeking hearts of needy men.

MILEY ON "THEOLOGICAL SCIENCE"

To move from Watson to Miley, it is necessary to span an ocean and three-quarters of a century, to exchange the rationalism of England for new science in America, to replace an atmosphere of more traditionally orthodox Christianity with one independently pragmatic. On the face of it, these two men are a world apart and their writings reflect the fact. Yet, despite their differences, their views possess basic similarities. That there should be differences between them is not surprising. They are easily pointed out. That there should be identities is naturally supposed, since they share a common tradition. It is more exacting and important, however, to discern the identities, which reside not in their fidelity to but in their common modifications of that tradition. Miley reflects the epistemological and methodological problems and interests of the latter nineteenth century. Many of his terms and concepts are taken from it and addressed to it. But the assumptions which guide his use of these materials are, several of them, remarkably akin to those which governed Richard Watson in his service to his age.

Sources of Theology

Miley, beginning his *Systematic Theology* with a consideration of the sources of theology, indicates that theologians often limit themselves either to revelation or to nature. By confining theology to revelation, they hope to protect it from dilution, but actually they weaken its appeal; by confining theology to nature, they unwittingly promote infidelity such as deism. They can avoid these errors by using both sources even though "they are very far from any equality; in fullness, clearness, and authority comparable only by contrast" (I, 8). Each has a separate function, though, compared to revelation, nature suffers distinct limitations.

The "light of nature" should be taken to mean "all things and events" which manifest God or give theological truth. Such truth may be an intuition of moral reason, a conclusion of logical reason, or a product of religious consciousness. The truth of nature is distinguished by the mode of its acquisition, coming always by "the use of human faculties." Universal ideas regarding God, providence, moral obligation, and future existence "are traceable to the light of nature, and rationally traceable to no other source" (I, 9). The Bible itself assumes that nature is an adequate source for these conceptions. Yet it recognizes also "a profound moral need of higher forms of religious truth which the light of nature cannot discern" (I, 11).

Revelation is "religious truth communicated through a supernatural agency of God" (I, 11). As a source of theology it is clearly set apart by the supernatural agency which bestows it. Revelation is not restricted to the Bible. When given outside the Bible, however, it lacks "the seal of a divine original" and therefore is far from equal to the biblical revelation. In a strict sense, "revelation and the

Scriptures are one"; they are "by all pre-eminence *the* source of theology," containing the "highest religious truths ever attained by mankind" (I, 12). They give the doctrines of salvation, which cannot be derived from reason or any other source. They complete and give a final seal of authority to the truth of nature.

Thus with characteristic clarity Miley defines the issues at hand. His understanding of revelation as "religious truths" is not at variance with Watson's "propositions to the mind." But, as they interpret revelation as the communication of truthful propositions, both men depart from Wesley's much more existential view. Further, Miley makes a far-reaching decision affecting theology when he insists on the essential compatibility of nature and revelation, though he has assigned distinct priorities to each. In effect, he carries one step farther the strictures on revelation made by Watson.[45]

Scientific Certitude

A double motivation is evident in Miley's theological work. In ways rarely hinted at by his Methodist predecessors and contemporaries, he seeks with notable success to make theology both "scientific" and "systematic."

A sense of certainty is the essence of science, according to Miley. He distinguishes experimental science, which is inductive and grounded in fact, from abstract science, which is deductive and constructed on axiomatic principles. Both achieve scientific status by virtue of the certitude which they possess. "If theology is to receive a scientific construction, it [too] must possess the requisite grounds of certitude" (I, 23).

[45] In *The Atonement in Christ*, p. 20, Miley argues that truth must accord with truth. Therefore no systematic contradiction is possible in theology, and further, a proper theological system cannot contradict Scripture. It is instuctive to compare the essays in this area by Watson, *Remarks upon the Eternal Sonship of Christ and the Use of Reason in Matters of Revelation,* and by Miley, "The Idea of God as a Law of Religious Development." Threatened by the rationalistic speculation of Clarke, Watson is eager to fix limits on the place and uses of reason. Distressed by the reluctance of the orthodox to give critical appraisal to religious doctrines, Miley magnifies the importance of reason by showing the ultimate dependence of religious life on relgious ideas. In their appeal to external evidence to validate revelation, however, both men stand on common ground.

Science cannot be restricted to empirical facts on the belief that they alone possess certainty. The scientist uses discursive reason in classification and deduction and is continuously dependent on mathematics. He cannot deny to others the same rights he enjoys. Nor is theology disqualified as a science because it deals with faith. Faith does not rest on blind authority, but rather on rational grounds. It has "respect to evidence" and in its proper sense is a "thoroughly rational state or act of mind" (I, 37). Further, science itself requires too much faith (in the uniformity of nature, in generalizations, and in its practitioners) for it to "dispute the scientific claim of theology" (I, 39).

Miley elaborates four grounds for certainty in theology: the proofs of God's existence in natural theology; the demonstration of the "divine verity" of the Scriptures; the fact of man's religious nature; and the experimental confirmation of religion. For their certainty, the first two depend primarily on exact deductive science, the third and fourth largely on scientific induction from empirical fact.

1. In "Theism," Part One of his *Systematic Theology*, Miley develops a natural theology. The first question of all religion, the existence of God, he addresses initially to nature. He rejects the contention found in Watson that the idea of God can be accounted for only by revelation. Rather, the idea is universally and necessarily produced by the moral intuition—"the faculty of immediate insight into truth" (I, 62). "The idea of God does not wait for our reasoning processes. It springs into life before the logical faculty gets to work" (I, 70). However, moral intuition and logical reason are not mutually exclusive. Moral intuitions in religion depend on "mental development" and are closely tied up with the sensibilities or feelings. Consequently they are often weak and distorted. Logical reason, therefore, is indispensable in proving the existence of God. It gives incontrovertible certainty to this "first truth of theology" by the elaboration of the theistic proofs. These make the existence of God "more certain than the existence of a physical universe as studied in the light of sensationalism" (I, 26).

2. The Scriptures are another ground of scientific certitude. Their doctrinal value "hinges upon the question of their divine original," which Miley attempts to establish. In the Introduction to his *Systematic Theology* he argues for the possibility and probability of God's revelation, in the Scriptures, attested by miracles (I, 28–34). His demonstration does not vary in any important respect from Watson's earlier, more extensive exposition.

Through the nineteenth century the argument for the authenticity of the Scripture gradually shifted. As external evidence was threatened by the newer science and philosophy, increasingly, Christian apologists found refuge in contentions for the inspiration of the Scripture. Later, fundamentalism was to base Christianity squarely on a doctrine of the verbal inspiration of the Bible.[46] Miley seems caught between allegiance to external evidence and to verbal inspiration. At the same time, he is aware of the new literary, historical study of the Bible.

Significantly, he relegates his discussion of inspiration to an appendix in his second volume, which was published two years later than the first one (II, 479–89). He defends a "dynamical" view of inspiration, which he distinguishes from "mechanical" or "verbal" views. It implies a threefold operation of the Spirit in the illumination, communication, and publication of revealed truth, not uniformly throughout the Scriptures, but only "with respect to their higher truths" (II, 482). A reviewer noted in disappointment that Miley's treatment of inspiration "gives the conventional theories, and is sufficiently reasonable in its remarks upon them. But it does not touch with any living connection the questions that are seething and burning" in inquiring minds.[47] If his remarks on inspiration are not challenging, neither are his arguments from ex-

[46] W. F. Warren, "The Impending Revolution in Anglo-Saxon Theology," *MQR*, 45 (1863), 455 ff., warned that many traditional beliefs were involved in a now antiquated physical theory. He urged serious attention to the scientific revolution confident that eternal truth would not be undermined. Those who feared such prompting took refuge in a Bible directly and infallibly inspired by God. See also Stewart G. Cole, *The History of Fundamentalism*, chap. IV, "The Rise of Fundamentalism."

[47] William Kelley, "Review of Miley's 'Systematic Theology,'" *MQR*, 76 (1894), 838.

ternal evidence nor his interpretation of currently disputed biblical passages. On the understanding and use of the Bible, Miley failed to provide creative leadership for his disturbed generation.

3. Man's inherent religious nature is an empirical fact giving further certitude to theology. It is witnessed to by human history and consciousness—more certain facts "than the facts of physics or the properties of matter" (I, 27). They are open to "scientific treatment" in the "light of philosophy" (though they cannot be completely tested in the physical realm). In his third division, "Anthropology," Miley examines man's nature apart from salvation and explicates the significance for theology of its natively religious bent (I, 355–533). Largely inductive, this study has suggestive anticipations of later empirical theology. Earlier, Watson had found little of doctrinal interest in such "moral and religious facts." Wesley, however, placed great stress on them, though he and Miley "find" somewhat different "facts," to which they often give variant interpretations. It is unfortunate that other assumptions did not allow Miley to make more of this essentially Wesleyan theme.

4. A final ground of certitude is found in the evidence of religious experimentation. "By applying experimental tests and by realizing promised results" the validity of Christianity can be demonstrated (I, 35). The offer of salvation is certified, in those making the venture, by a consciousness of sonship wrought by the Holy Spirit. The witness to such experience comes from all ages with surprising unity. But on this issue Miley does not write with his accustomed clarity. His basic appeal seemingly is to verification by results, loosely related to Wesley's fruits of the Spirit. There is some hint, too, that he also recognizes the intrinsic authority of direct encounter with God. That this encounter is not decisive, however, is evident from his comments on the nature of Christian consciousness. He argues that Christian consciousness is *formed* by right doctrine, which cannot "find its proof, much less its source in such a consciousness" (I, 19). Equivocally, he adds, "The internal consciousness only attests and confirms the truth [of doc-

trine] after having learned it from Scripture" (I, 22). Miley comes much closer to Wesley's confirmation of Christianity in evangelical experience than does Watson. But, consistent with his view of the wider role of deductive reason, he hedges his position. Thus a distinctive note, basic to Wesley, is allowed to languish in uncertainty.

Systematization of Theology

Miley's interest in the "scientific" basis of theology is directly related to his interest in its "systematic" character. The requisite certitude having been adduced, the "facts" of Christianity are opened to "scientific construction" (I, 47). The definitive "facts" of systematic theology are the doctrines of Christianity. "Doctrine" is not to be regarded as esoteric or peculiar to Christianity. It is "any principle or law reached and verified through a proper induction" (I, 5).

Working with these "facts," systematic theology has a double function. First, after studying the elements of doctrinal truth, "whether furnished in the book of nature or the book of revelation," it must construct a doctrine in scientific form, consistent within itself and with the ruling principle of the system. Second, the separate doctrines thus constructed must be combined in a system. The elements in the system, as within each doctrine, must be in "scientific accord," else theology is denied "systematic" character (I, 51). Since "there is no one principle or doctrine from which the others may be deduced," systematic theology is first constructive, then synthetic (I, 53).

Not only does systematic theology satisfy the mind's need for order; it also shows the wider meaning and application of particular truths, which give the "highest knowledge" when joined together. Doctrines should be arranged in "the order in which they arise for thought, and for most intelligible treatment," each truth so related to preceding truth "as shall set it in the clearest light" (I, 51, 53).

Admiration is due Miley's pursuit of scientific, systematic theology. He displays a comprehensiveness and consistency unsurpassed by any other Methodist theologian of the century, paralleled only by Pope in England, and approached only by Summers and Raymond in America. Surely Scott's judgment is well taken: "In his independence of theological insight, in his comprehension of doctrinal issues, and in the consistency with which he wrought out a complete 'system' of theology, John Miley stands somewhat uniquely among theologians of American Methodism. . . . His treatment of . . . theological method ('scientific,' 'systematic') gave to his work a proper significance outside the Methodist community of thought." [48]

Obviously, reason is essential in the pursuit of systematic theological science. It has even wider bearing. Miley opens his discussion of the place of reason in religion thus: "There is no question of either natural or revealed religion that is not open to rational consideration" (I, 40). Reason has several uses. It demonstrates that theism is a rational faith. It receives and approves revelation. It is the necessary tool of apologetics, for the Scriptures and for theology generally. It is indispensable for the systematization of theology.

Miley denies that rationalism inevitably results from the use of reason. Basically rationalism errs in rejecting revelation on the ground that it is irrational; the truth is that revelation *is* reasonable. Even those revealed truths which surpass or transcend rational comprehension are not irrational (I, 46). Thus Miley carries one step farther Watson's view that though revelation may contradict human reason, it does not contradict divine reason. It contradicts neither!

And so Miley's underlying rationalism is again evident. He is unable to relax his hold on rational certitude as the basis for theology, even though several elements in his theology offer opportunity for him to do so: his stress on the "facts" of religion and human nature, his appeal to experimental results, and his willingness to consider contrary evidence. Therefore, his certification of the facts of theology is at bottom the same as Watson's authentication of the

[48] Scott, "Methodist Theology," pp. 467 f.

Scripture. Ultimately, both men ground the authority of the Christian faith in its relation to a rationally verified reality external to itself; methodologically they are more concerned with the evidences for revelation than they are with revelation itself. Miley struggles with the contradiction implicit in his position, but he is unable to free himself from it.

A remaining issue first appears in one of Miley's earliest theological writings, "The Idea of God as a Law of Religious Development" (1865). In it he argues that man's religious development depends on the particular ideas about God which he holds. Right doctrine is indispensable for right faith and practice. Conversely, "Most of the perversions of the religious life result from perverted views of the divine goodness and justice." [49] And, consistently, religious reformation entails "first a reformation of doctrine, and then, through faith in the better doctrine, a new and better religious experience and life. . . . Such is the chronological order because it is the logical order." [50]

Unswervingly, Miley maintains the priority of the intellect over the affections or "sensibilities." This view is found in his discussion of the moral intuition of God, his estimate of the significance of

[49] "The Idea of God as a Law of Religious Development," MQR, 47 (1865), 21. See also Scott, "Methodist Theology," Appendix 39, "Miley: 'The Idea of God . . . ,'" pp. 684 ff. One of Miley's critics, A. H. Strong, in his Systematic Theology (New York; A. C. Armstrong, 1902), p. 452, charged that Miley's emphasis on the primacy of "moral and religious intellection" in moral and religious experience sounded dangerously like the doctrine that one may convert his own character by the apprehension of and commitment to religious truth. Miley regards the charge as wide of the mark, since he holds that choice and achievement are separate realities, the latter possible only under the power of the Holy Spirit.

[50] "Pope's Christian Theology," MQR, 59 (1877), 390. See also "The Idea of God" for these further comments: "We assimilate to the character that we attribute to [God]. Our idea of his character determines the type of our religious development" (p. 20). "Where this idea is partial, erroneous, or perverted, so must be the religious life formed under its influence. But as this idea is truthful and complete, so will the religious life be the more perfect, symmetrical and complete" (p. 21). In Miner Raymond, Systematic Theology, I, 38-44, 247-62, may be found traces of this tendency to regard ideas as preceding and having determinative influence on acts. Daniel Whedon's thinking, in Freedom of the Will, p. 368, also stresses the influential character of ideas. Man's moral sense assumes responsibility, he says, because the intellect affirms it. "Here as in all cases, the moral sense pronounces its decisions upon this case as it is made up and presented by the intellect."

Christian consciousness, his assignment of reason to a "high place" in theology, his assumptions regarding the nature of human freedom, and his insistence on the decisiveness of right doctrine. Assertion of the priority of the intellect, however, is incompatible with Richard Watson's theory of knowledge and expression of rationalism. And it flatly contradicts Wesley's insistence on the centrality of the existential encounter between God and man. Yet it is one of the consistent principles running throughout Miley's theology. However strenuously he might try to remain faithful to the heart of his Wesleyan tradition, with this underlying assumption Miley is able to achieve only indifferent success.

KNUDSON'S "RATIONAL JUSTIFICATION OF FAITH"

Occasionally Miley refers to the work of a newly emerging figure in American philosophy of religion, Borden Parker Bowne. His citations are few and generally confined to the doctrine of God. But forty years later a "school" of numerous and often distinguished men were exponents of Bowne's personal idealism. One of them, Albert Knudson, gave American Methodism a systematic theology fully informed by this philosophy. What was a peripheral interest in Miley and Watson becomes a dominant concern in Knudson. As Watson and Miley elaborate the Wesleyan heritage, they reflect their basic philosophical loyalties, the former to Locke and Paley, the latter to the common-sense philosophy or intuitional realism. But these philosophies make only hurried appearances, ostensibly cast in minor roles. In Knudson, however, philosophy is neither preliminary nor incidental to some special problems. It dictates the setting and tools as well as the method of justification and mode of expression for Christian theology. Although philosophical influence on theological formulation before Knudson was not new to American Methodism, never before had it been so extensive and comprehensive, and rarely had its modifications of the tradition been so drastic.

Religion and Theology

Knudson's empirical interests are considerable, and evident at the very beginning. Religion, he says, is a native manifestation of man's existence. It springs up spontaneously in human life as a feeling of trustful dependence, a longing for salvation, and a sense of obligation to man as well as God (I, 48).[51] As a given reality, religion is prior to conceptual knowledge about it. It is a "profound personal attitude, a vital experience," deeper than doctrine. In a sense, religious experience is self-justifying. However, religion is prone to be imperfectly self-conscious and self-directive. It tends to pick up mythology and superstition and go astray both in thought and in practice. Therefore, while theology cannot create religion, it can perform for it an important regulative function. This then is theology's first service to religion: to clarify, to eliminate accretions, and to provide for its systematic exposition (I, 63 f.).

Religion is not merely subjective experience, however. By its "very nature it refers to a Divine Object" (I, 65). If a super-world is affirmed by religion, then the question concerning the validity and implications of this affirmation, "the crucial question of our day," lays upon theology a second most pressing task. It must provide rational justification for religion. In brief, "Theology may be defined as the systematic exposition and rational justification of the intellectual content of religion" (I, 19).

Knudson is more concerned for the justification than for the exposition of faith. Is reason capable of this undertaking? Though religious faith stands in its own right, it is not opposed to or irreconcilable with reason, or incapable of support by its use. Only

[51] *The Doctrine of God*, p. 48. For convenience in this and subsequent interpretative sections on Knudson's thought, this book will be identified in the text as Volume I and *The Doctrine of Redemption* as Volume II of Knudson's major discussion of systematic theology. Cauthen, *The Impact of American Religious Liberalism*, p. 110, shows that for Knudson Christianity is but one version of a universal religious phenomenon (the principle of continuity) and theology is more an elaboration of man's experience of God than it is a description of God's redemptive activity (the principle of autonomy). Thus Knudson begins theology with a discussion of religion generally and throughout gives priority to man's rationally interpreted religious experience.

when improperly conceived, by being restricted to logical, mathematical thinking or limited to the phenomenal world, does reason seem to be inadequate to its task.[52] Reason is required to ward off heresy, to make faith articulate, to systematize it, and to commend it to the unbelieving world. Faith and reason belong together; one involves the other and, without both, theology is incomplete (I, 67–84).

In demonstrating the truth of religion, theology and philosophy stand on the same ground. As Christian theology lives within a particular tradition and is a servant to the church, it is distinct. But, with philosophy, it is concerned for the "rational justification of faith." "Both base their case on a rational interpretation of our total human experience, both subjective and objective. This rational interpretation has expressed itself in two fundamental disciplines. One is metaphysics or the theory of reality, and the other is epistemology, or the theory of knowledge." Thus Knudson sets the problem in his last book, *Basic Issues in Christian Thought* (p. 44). His text in systematics does not state the issue in quite this way—the epistemological concern is not so explicitly defined (I, 147-70). But the general tenor of his writings upholds epistemology and metaphysics as the double focus of his rational justification of faith.

Epistemology and the Right to Believe

In Knudson the marks of Kantian epistemology are discernible. Knowledge is inescapably subjective owing to the dualism of thought and thing and the impossibility of grasping the thing-in-itself. The sources of knowledge are external to man and cannot be transported into his mind to produce certain and unerring knowledge. The mind, however, is not merely a passive recipient of external stimuli but is itself active in the process of thought and

[52] Knudson deplores the mistaken conception of reason which restricts it to the "narrow field of purely logical thinking, where conclusions are deduced from premises and truth is demonstrated with mathematical certainty," and which "limits its range to the world of phenomena"; see *Basic Issues in Christian Thought*, p. 42.

knowledge. To produce meaningful experience, the concepts of the mind must be added to the percepts of the senses. Consequently, all experience, including the religious, is interpreted experience.[53]

Experience is interpreted by the a priori categories of the mind. Here Knudson extends the Kantian notion of the a priori to include categories for moral, aesthetic, and religious experience. Added to the theoretical reason, they represent four distinct, autonomous, native capacities of the human mind. Together they are constituent and permanent factors in that deeper reason which underlies and expresses itself through them. If each of these capacities stands in its own right, it follows that religious experience and knowledge are independent.[54] Thus Knudson secures religion against those who flatly deny it as well as against those who oppose it to, or place it beyond the reach of, reason.[55]

The religious a priori seems to promise an immediate, intrinsically authoritative encounter with God. But the promise is withdrawn forthwith. The immediacy of religious experience makes it forceful and appealing and often encourages impressive claims to knowledge. Such claims, however, are misleading. For religious experience also must be interpreted by reason, with error as a prevalent possibility. Religious knowledge is produced by the same rational processes that produce knowledge in science, morality, and art. The probability in each is the same.[56]

At best, knowledge possesses no more than the probability of truth and validity, because reason cannot establish, but must as-

[53] Knudson elaborates this thesis at some length in *The Validity of Religious Experience*, pp. 28-30, 58-71.

[54] *Ibid.*, pp. 175, 232. See also *Present Tendencies in Religious Thought*, pp. 184 ff., 246. In *Basic Issues in Christian Thought*, p. 48, Knudson writes, "There is no extra mental standard of truth in religion or science or morality or art. Each of these fields of mental activity has its own a priori, and these a prioris are all normative. They carry within themselves their own standards."

[55] *Present Tendencies in Religious Thought*, p. 247. The religious a priori shows that "religion is permanently grounded in the deeps of the human reason, that it has its own autonomous validity, and that it can never be displaced." See also *The Philosophy of Personalism*, p. 257.

[56] *Present Tendencies in Religious Thought*, pp. 143-45; *Basic Issues in Christian Thought*, p. 47.

sume, its own trustworthiness. And this assumption is an original act of faith; it underlies every act of knowing; it is immediate and instinctive; it embraces theoretical, moral, aesthetic, and religious experience. Ultimately, trust in reason and in the parallelism of thought and thing must rest in a monism which transcends both. This unifying principle is found in theistic personalism. Reason can be trusted because thought and thing are both expressions of the same God.[57]

While Watson and Miley had struggled to maintain a place for revelation, Knudson consistently denies it independent status. He frequently voices distress over the growth of "theological irrationalism." He writes at length about faith (the knower and his knowing), but his words on revelation (the givenness of God in evangelical experience) are scattered and generally historical or critical.[58] Further, the faith which Knudson requires in order to cross the "epistemological gulf" is qualitatively different from that faith which receives saving revelation. The former is based on the best possible evidence (and it may be only the absence of contrary evidence) and has no necessary relation to sin and grace.

The final item in Knudson's epistemology constitutes a bridge to his metaphysics. He affirms, with Kant, the primacy of the practical reason. Faith in the intelligibility of the world springs out of the vital needs and interests of the mind. The *need* to believe is essential to man's nature and justifies his *right* to believe. Knudson often quotes Bowne's formulation of the law of the practical rea-

---

[57] *The Philosophy of Personalism*, pp. 147-54; *The Validity of Religious Experience*, pp. 98 f.

[58] These issues are most pronounced in Knudson's last book (1950) *Basic Issues in Christian Thought*; see the section on theological irrationalism, pp. 29-44. Cauthen's observations on Knudson's procedure, in *The Impact of American Religious Liberalism*, p. 113, are illuminating: "The distinction between revelation and reason is reduced by a combination of the principles of continuity and autonomy. The highest insights of the mind, he urges, are themselves to be regarded as divine revelations. Moreover, nothing that purports to be revelation is to be accepted that is not in harmony with what is reasonable. . . . All faith involves reasoning, and all reasoning involves an element of belief beyond absolute certainty. . . . All truth is part of one continuous whole, so that no radical gap can exist between reason and revelation." For a careful summary of Knudson's reaction to the wave of European crisis theology see McCutcheon, *The History of American Methodism*, III, 299-301.

son: "Whatever the mind demands for the satisfaction of its subjective interests and tendencies may be assumed as real in default of positive disproof." [59] If the scientist and the philosopher have the right to believe, so also does the man of religion. And his concerns with purpose and values are even more essential to human personality than are the concerns of the theoretical reason.[60]

The right to believe includes the right to make affirmations about reality which constitute a sort of "faith" metaphysics. Thus Kant had postulated God, freedom, and immortality on the basis of the practical reason. Knudson asserts that the objective validity and cognitive significance of such metaphysical affirmations are greater than Kant supposed and that it is quite legitimate to base the "philosophy of reality upon the moral and spiritual nature of man." Perhaps one should ask no more. Yet metaphysics "ethically grounded" is liable to the charge of subjectivism. And the charge can be largely discounted by the more objective metaphysics of theoretical reason (I, 160 f.).

Metaphysics and Personalism

Ethically grounded metaphysics based on the right to believe does not deny the need for or the value of supplementary considerations drawn from inductive and speculative arguments. What man feels and does religiously should find some justification or explanation in the activity of thought. The most compelling theory of reality for this purpose and the preeminent philosophy for Christian faith is personalism.

Personalism . . . is voluntaristic rather than rationalistic. It lays more stress on the will than the intellect and inclines to the view that life is deeper than logic. To formal argumentation it allows a place, its abstract

[59] Bowne's formulation appears in *Theism*, p. 18. Some of Knudson's references to it appear in *The Validity of Religious Experience*, p. 176; *The Philosophy of Personalism*, p. 162; *Present Tendencies in Religious Thought*, p. 185; and *Basic Issues in Christian Thought*, p. 46.

[60] *The Philosophy of Personalism*, pp. 308, 164 ff.; *Basic Issues in Christian Thought*, p. 47.

validity it does not question, but mere reason, it holds, cannot bridge the gulf between thought and reality. At this point faith alone will suffice. So in the last analysis all knowledge rests on faith. Faith is the ultimate ground of every philosophical system. Demonstration is, then, impossible when it comes to belief in God. But we can, nevertheless, go a long way toward establishing it by showing that it is the line of least resistance, and that in it human nature finds its completest satisfaction.[61]

Obviously Knudson's epistemology is integral to and decisive for his metaphysics. Both begin with the reality that puts man closest to the inwardness of being—the experience of the self.

For the personalist, even more than the existence of God, the reality of the self, or soul, or "I" is *the* fundamental presupposition. Personality is an ultimate in experience and thought which "cannot be explained." It is the limiting concept reached by the analysis of experience. It is therefore the key by means of which reality can be explained.[62] The antinomies of human thought, of identity and change, of unity and plurality, of freedom and necessity, find their most satisfying resolution in a philosophy which makes the uniqueness of personality central. It also provides the most plausible explanation for religious perplexities about the world, creation and providence, and miracles and revelation (I, 139–45).

The theoretical "arguments" drawn from personality furnish the "least line of resistance" for belief in the existence of God (I, 241). To the religious argument, based on the religious a priori, and the moral argument, based on the practical reason, Knudson adds theoretical or "rationalistic" proofs: the causal, including the cosmological and teleological; the conceptual or ontological; and the

---

[61] *The Philosophy of Personalism*, pp. 67, 337.

[62] *Present Tendencies in Religious Thought*, p. 75. Consistently Knudson argues for the "unique epistemological and metaphysical significance of personality. Around this one insight the whole system [of personalism] revolves, and that it is able to take up into itself without contradiction so many factors that have previously been regarded as mutually discordant is proof of the fruitfulness of the fundamental principle by which it is animated." See *The Philosophy of Personalism*, p. 421; see pp. 171, 237 f.; and *Basic Issues in Christian Thought*, pp. 71-75.

epistemological (God as the source of the parallelism of thought and thing, and as the Author of intelligibility). While these arguments fall short of certain demonstration, they add weight to the spiritual interpretation of the universe.[63]

Finally, God's character is most helpfully illuminated by theistic personalism. Personalism affirms the intelligence and freedom of a God who seeks communion with others, and whose trustworthy goodness is manifested in righteous love. Personalism "seeks to provide religion with a philosophical underpinning, to give it a cosmic framework in which it will fit, to create for it an intellectual atmosphere in which it will thrive." Though it has "manifest limitations and difficulties," personalism gains strength when compared with other philosophies, which have "still more serious difficulties." [64] Knudson calls others to the task at which he worked—the reinterpretation of doctrine in the light of personalist thought, that "powerful bulwark of the Christian faith." [65]

Method and Authority

According to Knudson, then, philosophy not only shapes theology but also determines theological method (I, 189 f.). The method dictated by his philosophy he describes as follows. It is *critical,* beginning with an inquiry into the subjective conditions of knowledge and denying external authoritative standards. It is *anthropological,* affirming that theology must begin with man, and not miraculous divine revelation. It is *empirical,* not speculative, though wary of preferring concepts of immediate experience to metaphysically interpreted experience. Finally, it is *historical,* re-

---

[63] *The Philosophy of Personalism,* chap. IV, pp. 247 ff., and *The Doctrine of God,* chap. VI, pp. 202 ff.

[64] *The Philosophy of Personalism,* pp. 328, 427; see also p. 80: "That the personality of God and the sacredness of human personality express the true genius of the Christian religion, whatever may be said of its theology, is hardly open to question; and that these beliefs have received their completest philosophical justification in modern personalistic metaphysics, would seem equally clear. Personalism is *par excellence* the Christian philosophy of our day."

[65] *Basic Issues in Christian Thought,* p. 45.

nouncing the "cult of contemporaneity" and finding guidance in the history of thought.[66]

Theology has three duties, the first two of which we have examined. First, as a normative science, theology determines and expounds "the essential nature and content of the Christian faith," as indicated in the section on "Religion and Theology." Second, functioning philosophically, theology establishes "the validity of the Christian faith," as outlined in the sections on epistemology and metaphysics. In both of these theological duties, reason plays a dominant and decisive role. The third duty of theology is to render service to the practical needs of the Christian tradition and the church within which it lives (I, 196–98).

The Christian theologian has sources suited to his task, of which the Bible is chief. The history of the church "supplements Scripture" and helps regulate its interpretation. But neither is immune to rational criticism. Whatever its source, religious truth becomes real to us to the degree that it is able to commend itself to our conscience and intelligence. The judge of the Bible, as of theology and philosophy, is the illuminated mind.[67] The mind has distinctive norms for religious experience in the religious a priori. But they do not insure the attainment of truth. The mind must constantly engage in self-criticism, in which both the Bible and Christian tradition are allies.[68]

Christianity is absolute in two senses, writes Knudson. It is a revelation of the Absolute; and it is the highest revelation known to man (I, 117). But to guarantee this absoluteness, Christianity has no objective standard in the creeds or in the Bible. Only in its "es-

[66] "A Personalist Approach to Theology," in *Contemporary American Theology*, ed. Vergilius Ferm, p. 232. Compare the discussion of these characteristics in *The Doctrine of God*, pp. 189-96.

[67] Knudson's position is crystal clear; see *Present Tendencies in Religious Thought*, p. 113. Reason "acknowledges no foreign master; it cannot be coerced. The only condition on which it can recognize the authority of Scripture is on the proof or conviction that scriptural teaching is itself rational. The Bible to win the modern mind must itself become modern."

[68] *Basic Issues in Christian Thought*, pp. 48-50.

sence" can Christianity be said to be absolute (I, 174 f.). One of the great strengths of modern thought is its effort to determine the essence of faith. "It is not so clearly defined as the older standards, but it is derived from them and retains what was really authoritative in them. We learn from Scripture and the history of the church what the Christian faith in its essence is; and the task of Christian theology is to expound its intellectual content and justify it so far as possible from the standpoint of the common reason and the common religious experience." Knudson's conclusion echoes again his initial assertion about the religious life: "Its ultimate justification, it must find in itself" (I, 124).

What are we to make of Knudson's discussion of religion, philosophy, and theology? Since his principles of construction and validation are often derived from the newer cultural forces of his day, it is not always apparent whether the results of his work are essentially compatible with the Wesleyan tradition. Several elements in his work seem to propose important qualifications of its generally rationalistic aspect: his view of the probability of knowledge, his affirmation of the right to believe founded on man's vital needs, and his empirical emphasis. How significant are these qualifications?

Knudson's strictures on reason rest on the epistemological assumption that knowledge requires an initial act of faith, quite a different ground from that in Wesley! His assertion that knowledge is equally probabilistic in all areas is a denial of the distinctive and self-authenticating nature of revelation. His declarations about the necessity of adequate conceptions to prevent distorted religious belief and practice are frequent reminders of Miley's stress on the determinative character of religious ideas.[69] His discussion of authority, sources, and norms clearly makes reason the decisive factor in securing theological truth. The metaphysics of personalism, which he also uses to rationally justify faith, is predicated, he says, upon the immediate intuition of the self. But the manner of knowing the self is direct and orderly, and the self thus known is

[69] Ibid., p. 14; and The Doctrine of God, pp. 52, 205.

readily intelligible and strangely lacking in subconscious and compulsive dimensions.[70]

Though Knudson vigorously contends for the primacy of the practical reason, it is a question whether his total theology is shaped by his contention. For him, the right to believe has epistemological warrant, room for which has been cleared by philosophical speculation. In fact, he depends on speculation and not on the practical reason and surely not on the revelatory encounter, which determines Wesley's thinking, and which Watson and Miley endeavor to retain in forms more compatible with their own systems.

Knudson stresses experience and, by appealing to the religious a priori, defends distinct and valid knowledge derived from it. But in the derivation, religious experience (revelation) is so subjected to the categories and canons of reason that it becomes its handmaiden.

In all this Knudson does not try to deceive himself or others. He acknowledges that epistemology is of first importance, and that it determines the limits of philosophy and thus the method and shape of theology. He makes honest and extended efforts to come to terms with the forces of the new world and not to ignore any problem or challenge. In the end, however, reason, somewhat chastened by empirical observation and philosophical agnosticism, generally constricts the divine realities, imposes its own standards, and has its autonomous way.

[70] In his discerning study, Will explicates this judgment; see "Implications for Philosophical Theology in the Confrontation of American Personalism with Depth Psychology," unpublished Ph.D. dissertation, Columbia, 1962, especially chap. V.

CHAPTER IV
FROM SINFUL MAN
TO MORAL MAN

In 1738, eighteen days after his conversion experience, John Wesley delivered the sermon "Salvation by Faith" at St. Mary's, Oxford. This sermon has often and appropriately been referred to as the manifesto of the Wesleyan Revival. Six years later, after he had preached on "Scriptural Christianity," officials of the university decided to end his appearances in their pulpit. In 1757 the longest of more than 350 pieces of Wesley's collected works issued from the press in reply to an earlier volume by John Taylor of Norwich. Elsewhere, Wesley had termed Taylor's writings "poison" and his disciples "sweet-tongued Anti-Christs." "No single person since Mahomet has given such a blow to Christianity as Dr. Taylor," he charged.[1] The persistent controversy illustrated by each of these events involves the same basic issue—man's status as a fallen creature. Its central importance for Wesley's theology can be am-

[1] The two University Sermons are found in *Sermons*, I, 35-62 and 87-111; the "Doctrine of Original Sin," in reply to Taylor's book, in *Works*, IX, 191-464; and Wesley's appraisal of Taylor in *Journal*, IV, 200; III, 374; see also *Letters*, IV, 48.

plified from dozens of additional sources, which together indisputably document his espousal of the inescapable fact of the sinfulness of man.

MAN AS SINNER IN WESLEY

Adam and Original Sin

Wesley's understanding of the sinfulness of man is derived from scriptural sources, among which the Genesis story of Adam and his fall is most important. He argues for a literal interpretation of this account against the rationalistic modifications made by Taylor and others in order to fit it into their views of Christianity. Its portrayal of man's fallen condition Wesley sees amply confirmed in experience—his own, that of his people, and that of the race.

In his primitive state Adam was without sin. He was created in the image of God and enjoyed God's favor. The image of God in man was threefold. It included the *natural* image—immortality, understanding, and freedom of the will; the *political* image—the power of ruling over other, lower creatures; and the *moral* image—love, justice, mercy, truth, purity; man was "filled with righteousness and true holiness." [2] It was in their moral likeness that man and God had their most distinctive resemblance. Man was "capable of God . . . of knowing, loving or obeying" him.[3] This capacity for God set man apart from the inferior creatures and made him the chief end of creation.

However, Adam did not continue in the state of perfection. Through unbelief, pride, and the desires of the flesh, he succumbed to temptation and transgressed the law of God. His sin was not due to some sinful propensity stronger than his inclination to holiness. Rather, it presupposed his freedom and liability to temptation at the hands of Satan. In consequence of his rebellion, Adam's punishment was swift and sure. God's favor was lost and the image of

---

[2] *Sermons*, II, 227 f.
[3] *Works*, VI, 244.

God defaced—the moral image completely, the natural image in part: Adam "commenced unholy, foolish and unhappy." [4]

Without exception Adam's posterity have been afflicted by the ravages of inbred or original sin. Wesley acknowledges that he cannot with certainty account for the manner in which sin is propagated from father to son, though of the fact he is absolutely sure. He suggests two modes of its transmission. First, Adam was the federal head or representative of mankind, just as Christ—the second Adam—was a type or figure of the race. Both represent and act in behalf of all men. But as "representative" and "federal head" are not scriptural words, Wesley refuses to contend for them, being satisfied to insist on the reality to which they point. When Adam sinned, he did so on behalf of the entire race. The guilt of his sin is "imputed" to each of his descendants, who as a consequence suffers the punishment of spiritual, temporal, and eternal death.[5]

The second means whereby Adam's sin blights his children is through physical generation. As Adam is the primogenitor of mankind, all who descend from him must be of "his kind"—depraved in nature and corrupt in all their faculties. "The loathsome leprosy of sin, which he brought with him from his mother's womb, . . . overspreads his whole soul, and totally corrupts every power and faculty thereof." [6] The communication of depravity through physical generation does not presuppose that the body itself is sinful. Sin is not located in man's physical nature but is better thought of as an infection of the soul, transmitted from parent to child.[7]

God's justice is at stake in the imputation of Adam's sin to "in-

[4] *Ibid.*, VI, 223; see also IX, 345, where Wesley traces sin to the "power of yielding to temptation," not to any sort of innate sinful propensity, and *Notes*, Matt. 13:27, 8.

[5] *Works*, IX, 332, 379 f., 418, 458; see also *Notes*, Ro. 5:12, 14; I Cor. 15:45, 47; and *Sermons*, I, 117.

[6] *Sermons*, I, 323; see also *Works*, XI, 384; and IX, 262, 275-82, 378, and 428 f.

[7] Shipley establishes this as a viable reading of the Wesleyan tradition, in "Methodist Arminianism," p. 182. On one occasion Wesley replied to a correspondent who had asserted that "there are but three opinions" concerning the transmission of original sin: "I care not if there were none. The fact I know, both by Scripture and by experience. I know it is transmitted; but how it is transmitted I neither know nor desire to know"; see *Letters*, III, 107.

nocent" men. It is therefore necessary to note that the sin was Adam's, not God's. Maintaining the conditions under which the consequences of Adam's sin inevitably afflict his descendants does not make God the author of sin any more than supplying power to the murderer's arm makes God a murderer.[8] Wesley knew, however, that such logic merely drives the problem back a step. With disarming candor he affirms both God's unlimited love toward, and his universal condemnation of, sinful man. Ultimately he sees no incongruity in doing so because of his doctrine of prevenient grace. If "all may recover through the Second Adam, whatever they lost through the first," then God may not be charged with injustice in punishing man for Adam's sin.[9] But this is a delicate issue in Wesleyan anthropology. Though in reality sin and grace are rarely divorced, the failure to keep them distinct leads to drastic modifications in the doctrine of man. More extended consideration must be given to this issue in the next chapter.

Original Guilt and Depravity

There is widespread agreement among interpreters of Wesley's theology that he is one with Paul and Augustine in his understanding of original sin.[10] All men are totally corrupt; they are "children of wrath" and subjects of divine displeasure. Prior to any act of his own, each man shares in the depravity and guilt of Adam's sin. In general, Wesley suggests that man inherits depravity through physical generation and that he is the subject of guilt through representative participation in Adam's transgression.

---

[8] *Works*, IX, 335. Wesley is aware of the logical incompatibility between God's omnipotence and human freedom but insists on man's freedom despite the mystery (*ibid.*, p. 337): "I am as sure of this as I am that there is a God; and yet, impenetrable darkness rests on the subject."

[9] *Ibid.*, p. 332.

[10] Lycurgus M. Starkey, Jr., *The Work of the Holy Spirit*, pp. 124 ff.; George C. Cell, *The Rediscovery of John Wesley*, pp. 25, 272; William R. Cannon, *The Theology of John Wesley*, p. 200; Robert E. Cushman, "Salvation for All," in *Methodism*, ed. William K. Anderson, pp. 106-8. Harald Lindström, *Wesley and Sanctification*, p. 12, lists continental interpreters of Wesley who concur: von Eichen, Scott, Schmidt, Lerch, and Lang; this is also the chief principle that informs Hildebrandt's *From Luther to Wesley*.

The *depravity* or corruption flowing from inbred sin totally envelops human existence. In *The Doctrine of Original Sin* Wesley catalogues at length evidence for this fact taken from the history of mankind and various societies around the world. Even so-called "Christian countries," he says, exhibit ample proof of the havoc wrought by sin. The Scriptures bear overwhelming witness to the utter corruption of man. Finally, personal experience shows no one to be exempt from its ravages. Together this wealth of evidence constitutes incontrovertible proof of man's total corruption. It is expressed variously as atheism, idolatry, pride, self-will, and love of the world. Man is "deeply corrupted, inclined to evil and disinclined to all that is spiritually good." [11] His will is in bondage, unable to choose the things of God. "Leave the unrenewed will to itself, it will choose sin and reject holiness; and that as certainly as water poured on the side of a hill will run downward and not upward." [12] Man's ability to comprehend the things of God has been lost. "He has no more intercourse with, or knowledge of, the spiritual world" than he had with the external world when shut up in his mother's womb.[13] So complete is his affirmation of the depravity of man that Wesley is subject to the same charge that was leveled at Calvin: he conceives man to be utterly determined toward good and evil.[14]

Original *guilt* is also affirmed by Wesley, though on this point some of his interpreters strongly demur.[15] The mere fact that man shares in the universal corruption justly brings him under condemnation; the possession of a corrupt nature occasions guilt. Condemnation is grounded also in man's representative participa-

[11] *Works*, IX, 273; see also 208 ff., 221, 238-40, 263, 320, 356 ff., 439 ff. Further samplings of Wesley's judgments are in his treatise on original sin. Sermon references illustrating the theme include *Works*, VI, 23, 277, 344; VII, 282, 340, 400.

[12] *Ibid.*, IX, 450; or again, "I am inclined and was ever since I can remember, antecedently to any choice of my own, to pride, revenge, idolatry" (p. 294).

[13] *Ibid.*, VI, 70; also VII, 351.

[14] *Ibid.*, IX, 273 f., 286.

[15] See Lindström, *Wesley and Sanctification*, pp. 34-37; Cannon, *The Theology of John Wesley*, pp. 104 ff.; and John L. Peters, *Christian Perfection and American Methodism*, p. 42.

tion in the Adamic sin and illustrated in the universality of suffer-ing—for Wesley an infallible sign of punishment. Before he acts in any way, the individual incurs the displeasure or wrath of God. Newborn children are condemned for Adam's sin and would per-ish eternally but for the gracious provision made by God through Christ.[16]

In a detailed and generally adequate interpretation of Wesley's doctrine of sin, Harald Lindström argues that Wesley limits the imputation of guilt so that man is not eternally condemned because of it. Only "personal guilt, deriving from the actual sins of the individual," leads to eternal death. Because man is an heir of Christ, as well as of Adam, he is not condemned apart from his own transgression.[17] It is possible, however, that Lindström's desire to interpret Wesley in terms of sanctification leads him to shade this point. Shipley seems closer to the truth when he affirms that, in spite of the universality of prevenient grace, both Wesley and Fletcher insist on the reality of original guilt. Further, the appeal to Wesleyan sources in the debate over original guilt in nineteenth-century Methodism is inconceivable apart from serious affirmations about it by Wesley himself.[18]

In the interpretation of Wesley's theology of salvation, the point at which prevenient grace is introduced and the sort of qualifica-tions which are drawn from it are of critical import. Compromising and ambiguous judgments about guilt and freedom inevitably re-

[16] See David C. Shipley for an excellent discussion of guilt in the Arminian and Wesleyan traditions, "Methodist Arminianism," pp. 176-95; also Paul W. Hoon, "The Soteriology of John Wesley," pp. 13-14, and Wesley's own words, "God does not look upon infants as innocent, but as involved in the guilt of Adam's sin," in *Works*, XIV, 143.

[17] Lindström, *Wesley and Sanctification*, pp. 34 f.

[18] Shipley argues, "Methodist Arminianism," pp. 169-76, that though the logic of prevenient grace implies the cancellation of original guilt, inconsistently, Fletcher and Wesley hold that all men are guilty now despite prevenient grace. Henry Sheldon ob-serves that "in its first stratum Methodism was undoubtedly committed to the conclusion that guilt, as well as corruption of nature, is inherited by the whole posterity of Adam." At the close of the nineteenth century, however, original guilt was rejected by Raymond, Miley, Foster, and Tillett, while Summers and Curry upheld it. See "Changes in Theology Among American Methodists," *American Journal of Theology*, 10 (1906), 38, 39.

sult if the irreconcilable tension between sin and grace which forms the bedrock of Wesley's theology is neglected. It is true that some of his statements in this area are unguarded and inconsistent. But to restrict the implications of guilt in Wesley is to weaken his doctrines of sin and grace and eventually to erode the dynamic of his theologizing.

The depraved descendant of Adam is corrupt in every power and faculty—understanding, affections, passions, and will. All are "out of frame," so that there is "no soundness" in his soul. The righteous judgment of God is visited upon him and he is given over to the reign of temporal, spiritual, and eternal death. His body is corruptible and mortal; his soul, separated from God, dies; and, being dead in body and in spirit, "he hastens on to death everlasting." [19] Such is the end of the race of man.

Sinful Man

Wesley often suggests that the doctrine of original sin is the fundamental distinguishing point between Christianity and paganism.[20] It keeps to the truth that man has turned away from God and turned in upon himself. No matter how man may strive to do so, he "cannot move beyond the circle of self"; he acts for himself, preferring his own interest to that of others.[21] This universal propensity finds expression in actual sin; from the evil root, evil fruit is born. From the carnal mind, which is enmity against God, come the sins of pride, self-will, and love of the world. Man continues to "heap sin upon sin," making himself worthy of eternal death. Inward sin gives rise to outward sins, which mark the final disruption of man's relationship to God.

What then is the essence of sin for Wesley? This is a question of

---

[19] *Sermons*, I, 156, 117; see also *Works*, IX, 291.

[20] *Works*, IX, 194; VI, 54, 63.

[21] Colin Williams, *John Wesley's Theology Today*, p. 50; note also Wesley's words, in *Works*, IX, 456: "Yea, self is the highest end of unregenerate men, even in their religious actions. They perform duties for a name; for some worldly interest; or, at best, in order to escape hell. They seek not God at all, but their own interest. So that God is only the means, and self their end."

some importance because his writing is equivocal, depending on whether justification or sanctification is under consideration. As reviewed above, his doctrine of sin generally deals with fallen man prior to and as a subject of justification. As Wesley examines the life of the believer more directly, his stress in the doctrine of sin changes. A common assertion has it that he regards sin as a thing, a quantum, hypostasis or substance. And it is true that he sometimes refers to sin as a "root of bitterness," "thing," or "old man." He talks variously of "erasing," "extinguishing," "extracting," or "rooting it out." [22] But as Lindström is at pains to show, he also regards it as a disease, virus, or leprosy which must be cured.[23] Peters agrees that it is unfair to charge that Wesley regards sin as a substance which can be eradicated. Such an interpretation is not "congruous with a teaching which calls for such a sense of momentary reliance" in salvation, nor does it give sufficient weight to "the possibility of backsliding and restoration" which Wesley maintains.[24] Sin is not so much ontological degradation or demolition of human reality as it is illness or contagion; not so much biological and sub-personal distortion as it is an inversion of relationships involving motive and intention.[25]

Wesley's discussion gives further ground for confusion about his doctrine of sin. It is in the context of sanctification that his frequently quoted definition of sin usually appears: "Nothing is sin, strictly speaking, but a voluntary transgression of a known law of God." [26] Clearly, this definition fails to give expression to

[22] Peters, *Christian Perfection and American Methodism*, pp. 39-47, 58 f., documents these terms in Wesley's writings. Parallel judgments about them may be found in Shipley, "Methodist Arminianism," pp. 180, 297.

[23] Lindström, *Wesley and Sanctification*, pp. 40 f.

[24] Peters, *Christian Perfection and American Methodism*, p. 58.

[25] E. Dale Dunlap, "Methodist Theology in Great Britain," pp. 42 f. and 111: "The Methodists do not view the fall as ontological, but as relational, and recognize that freedom is part of human nature under grace." See also the discussion of this point by Outler ("The Methodist Contribution to the Ecumenical Discussion of the Church"), who asserts that the Methodist heritage holds "a doctrine of original sin and total depravity which maintains that sin is a corruption but not an ontic degradation of human selfhood."

[26] *Letters*, V, 322; IV, 155; see also Peters' helpful discussion of this point, *Christian Perfection and American Methodism*, pp. 39 ff.

his wider and deeper conception of sin as outlined above. Flew writes that the stress on the "conscious and deliberate intention of the agent is the most formidable defect in Wesley's doctrine of the ideal." [27] Hoon rightly suspects that this particular stress comes from demands made by Wesley's doctrine of Christian perfection.[28] It is relatively easy to "perfect" a man whose sin is always conscious and deliberate. Though Wesley's total view is much more perceptive than this suggests, still, on occasion in the context of perfection, he compromises his general view of sin. The use made of such an errant definition of sin must be watched closely when Wesley's successors come under review. They are disposed to regard his specialized conception of sin as characteristic and definitive, and increasingly inclined to ignore his more penetrating and pervasive view.

A final matter must be emphasized. Through the fall man has lost his freedom. His will is now wholly bound, free by inclination only to do evil. "Since the fall, no child of man has a natural power to choose anything that is truly good." [29] In things of "an indifferent nature," Wesley maintains human freedom. Man can dispose as he chooses the motions of his body and the faculties of his soul. But human freedom does not enable him to choose the good; this he can do only as he is assisted by the grace of God. Not only is man totally depraved and guilty, and therefore condemned to eternal death; he labors in such bondage that he cannot take the first step leading him toward release from his fate.

WATSON ON MAN'S
FALLEN CONDITION

Conscious attention to Wesleyan sources and constant regard for the evangelical impact of the Christian gospel both tend to sup-

[27] R. Newton Flew, *The Idea of Perfection in Christian Theology*, p. 333; compare Shipley, "Methodist Arminianism," p. 352.

[28] Hoon, "The Soteriology of John Wesley," pp. 303 f.

[29] *Works*, X, 350; VII, 229.

port an orthodox doctrine of sin in Richard Watson's theology. The challenge of his religious and cultural milieu, his increasing reliance on categories of personal accountability, and his desire to formulate a more integrated statement of Wesleyan theology encourage him to modify that tradition and result in a restrictive scholasticism less exciting and creative than the original Wesleyan theology. It is evident in his rationale for the fall, his denial of original guilt on the basis of man's responsible agency, and his explanation of depravity as being due to a deprivation of the Spirit. His modifications represent new priorities and apologetic interests, not utter insensitivity to the dynamics of faith or perverse distortion of its contents. It is his intention to preserve Wesley's clear-eyed view of man's great need before God. But his implicit modifications, which are not difficult to detect, become more evident in each passing generation.

Man's Primitive Condition and Fall

For Watson, man stands at the pinnacle of the creation narrative. He is made of two essential constituent parts: a body, formed out of the earth, and a living soul, breathed into the body by the inspiration of God. Man is made in God's image, both natural and moral. The *natural* image consists of spirituality, immortality, and intellectual powers. Through his power of rational deliberation, man is capable of knowledge and liberty of will. The natural image in turn becomes the foundation for the *moral* image, which consists in knowing and willing according to law; in knowledge, righteousness, and true holiness; and in the reflection of the moral perfections of his Maker. Original righteousness, correctly understood, regards Adam as "sinless, both in act and in principle"; it holds that his understanding received, retained, and "heartily approved religious truth"; it affirms him to be not merely free from sin but possessed of "positive and active virtues." [30]

[30] The *Institutes*, II, 11-17, contains a detailed discussion of man's primitive condition; see also *Works*, VI, 343; VIII, 418; *Sermons*, I, 49; and *Conversations for the Young*, pp. 26, 36.

Watson insists on the literal sense of the Mosaic account against those who make it only an instructive myth or fable, though he hints also that it has a "mystical and higher sense than the letter," which needs to be explored (II, 19-31). He insists on both original righteousness and original sin, but his literalism, even more than Wesley's, limits him to conventional explanations of the mystery surrounding the appearance of sin in a good world.

Primitive man was in a state of trial to which the power of choosing between good and evil was essential. Unless he could obey, commands were useless; unless he could resist temptation, prohibition was in vain. Adam lived under a universal and comprehensive law suited to a moral agent and under a special injunction —the proscription of the tree of knowledge. His will was subject to external influence, however, by solicitations from intellectual pride, sense, and passion (II, 32). In themselves, these powers were not sinful; indeed, when rightly applied they could produce much good. But their regulation was no casual thing. It required "vigilance, prayer, resistance, and the active exercise of the dominion of the will. . . . An innocent, and in its *kind*, a perfect rational being, is kept from falling only by 'taking hold' on God; and as this is an act, there must be a determination of the will to it" (II, 33). Through "carelessness" or "tampering with desire," Adam was exposed to the wiles of the serpent and subsequently fell.[31]

Watson allows questions about the ultimate ground of evil to go unanswered. For him the serpent is Satan and the real issue concerns the "doctrine of diabolical influence." Watson affirms that man, in both his primitive and his fallen conditions, is exposed to temptations by a "superior, malignant intelligence," but even these must be consented to (II, 38). Like Wesley, he does not probe further the dualism implicit in Satanic temptation. Watson's views on the origin of sin are grounded on three facts: "the necessary finiteness, and, therefore, imperfection in *degree* of created natures";

---

[31] *Sermons*, II, 185 ff., 393; and *Conversations for the Young*, p. 31; "He who perfectly preserves his *senses* under control, and maintains his *reason* in a state of humble subjection to God, cannot sin; and this test called man's virtue into exercise in both respects."

the liberty of choice, which is "essential to rational, accountable beings"; and "the influence of temptation on the will" (II, 33). In man's rationality and accountability Watson finds ingredients for a provisional rationale for man's fall.[32] If fully drawn on these premises, however, this rationale would have called into question elemental realities regarding man's need and God's action about which Watson's orthodoxy would have allowed little doubt.

Results of the Fall

Adam succumbed to temptation, fell, and came under the judgment of death. Watson denies the Pelagian contention that Adam was created mortal and suffered only by being expelled from the garden and made to labor. No more congenial does he find the notion that sin merely exposed human nature to a "greater liability to be corrupted" (II, 45). In actual fact, human nature was corrupted. A total defection from original righteousness resulted, together with a total incapacity to produce any of the effects which lead to conversion. Man's life was dominated by earthly and corrupt dispositions, and his will was so bound as to be free only to make "a universal choice of evil" (II, 77). Watson quotes with approval Calvin's judgment "that man is so totally overwhelmed . . . that no part is free from sin, and therefore whatever proceeds from him is accounted sin" (II, 48). Finally, in consequence of the fall, Adam was punished by the infliction of bodily, spiritual, and eternal death.

Watson had to face the difficult task of explaining the connection between Adam's sin and its consequences in the lives of his descendants. He agrees that Adam is to be thought of not only as an individual but as a *"public man, the head and representative* of the human race" (II, 52). In some manner, then, the race shares in his fall and its results. Watson examines two common explanations of this connection. The *mediate* imputation of sin holds that by virtue of our descent from Adam we receive mortal bodies and

---

[32] *Conversations for the Young*, pp. 35 f.; and *Sermons*, II, 185 ff.

a corrupt nature. Depravity, not guilt, is imputed. But this view, says Watson, by excluding guilt and punishment, does not "appear to go to length of Scripture" (II, 53). The *immediate* imputation of sin maintains that Adam's sin is accounted ours because of our federal relation to him. As part of the human race, consenting to his act, we are guilty with him and justly afflicted by his depravity. But this view, not alien to Wesley, Watson finds quite unsatisfactory.[33] It "obscures that distinct agency which enters into the very notion of an accountable being"; it "makes us stand chargeable with the full latitude of his transgression, and all its attendant circumstances; and constitutes us, separate from all actual voluntary offense, equally guilty with him, all which are repugnant equally to our consciousness and to the equity of the case" (II, 53).

Watson then quotes with approval Dr. Isaac Watts's resolution of the problem. Not Adam's willful disobedience, but the legal consequence of his disobedience (i.e., guilt or liability to punishment) is imputed to his descendants (II, 54). The ground of the entailment of Adam's offense is found in seminal identity; the race was in his loins when he sinned. Consequently, the judicial results of his sin are transmitted to his posterity, subjecting them to bodily, spiritual, and eternal death.[34] Clearly, Watson thinks that he has avoided the inadequacies of both mediate and immediate theories of imputation. Commenting on this issue, John Miley asserts flatly that Watson deceived himself. The imputation of Adam's sin "considered seminally" is subject to all the objections which Watson himself makes to the theory of immediate imputation.[35]

---

[33] Miley quotes several passages from Watson in confirmation of his own denial of original guilt (native demerit) in *Systematic Theology*, II, 508. Leland Scott, "Methodist Theology," pp. 565, 602, shows that both Shinn and Fisk, early in the nineteenth century, deny original guilt in infants since they lack accountability, thus preparing the way for Whedon's thoroughgoing exposition of freedom and accountability.

[34] *Conversations for the Young*, p. 36; *Sermons*, I, 303; and 360: The "sentence of death was passed upon Adam, and upon all his posterity, considered seminally."

[35] Miley, *Systematic Theology*, II, pp. 507-9, 522-24. Though Miley acknowledges that "Watson is still our most honored name in systematic theology," he feels compelled to assert "that the doctrine of original sin which he maintained must lead any Arminian into doctrinal confusion and contradiction" (pp. 507, 523).

Though Watson may have wanted to rid himself of original guilt, which violates voluntary agency, and thus correct Wesley, he succeeded only in implicating himself more deeply in contradiction. His argument that man is unjustly regarded as guilty because of Adam's sin, yet justly exposed to its punitive consequences, is now strangely unconvincing.

Original sin—the Adamic inheritance—is properly understood as a *depravation* of man's nature consequent upon the *deprivation* of God's Spirit (II, 55). The moral condition which results when God withdraws from sinful man is fitly called spiritual death. Watson denies that original sin is a "positive evil, infection, and taint" infused into man's nature (II, 78). Such a view makes God responsible for sin. Much to be preferred is the view which holds the depravation of human nature due to the deprivation of the Holy Spirit, which state of want or absence does in fact produce positive evil.[36] From it "comes inability, the dominion of irregular passions, and the rule of appetite; aversion, in consequence, to restraint; and enmity to God" (II, 79). To contend that man requires the Spirit in order to persevere under the conditions of trial, and inevitably sins when it is withdrawn, however, really begs the question of the original fall from righteousness into sinfulness. Watson fails to meet this problem head-on.

Privation ought not to be equated with the loss of original righteousness unless the definition of righteousness includes the influence and support of the Spirit as necessary to Adam even before the fall. Watson himself does not so define it. The privation of the Spirit

accounts for the whole case of man's corruption. The Spirit's influence in him did not prevent the possibility of his sinning, though it afforded sufficient security to him, as long as he looked up to that source of strength. He did sin, and the Spirit retired; and, the tide of sin once

---

[36] *Works*, VII, p. 234; *Sermons*, II, pp. 291 ff.; and *Conversations for the Young*, p. 38: "The nature of man became wholly corrupt and sinful . . . for when you consider the evils which have in all ages abounded in society, you must conclude that the fountain is most corrupt from which they flow."

turned in, the mound of resistance being removed, it overflowed his whole nature. In this state of alienation from God, men are born, with all these tendencies to evil, because the only controlling and sanctifying power, the presence of the Spirit, is wanting [II, 81 f.].

Thus Watson again compromises his heritage. Active depravity, which for Wesley consumes all human nature in corruption, is surrendered in favor of a less virulent conception of depravity passively elicited by the withdrawal of the Spirit.[37] Though its universality is still affirmed, together with man's inability to free himself from its bonds, an erosion of Wesley's view has taken place.

One of the changes made in Watson's doctrine of man by some later American imitators is worth noting. Following their discussions of sin, and prior to their discussions of the restoration of freedom by prevenient grace, Wakefield, Binney, and Ralston insert sections in their theologies on man's moral agency.[38] Some of the material they use is from Watson; much is derived from American sources, particularly Bledsoe and Whedon. But the change fulfills Watson's tendency to view man's responsible freedom in an anthropological rather than a soteriological setting. Such a change Watson himself was not prepared to make. But the Methodist community had not long to wait for men who regarded this as an essential revision.

MILEY ON MAN'S NEED
FOR REDEMPTION

John Miley's dedication to an Arminian theology closely governed by consistent moral principles finds clear expression in his

[37] *Conversations for the Young,* p. 38; and *Sermons,* II, pp. 81 ff., 291 ff. Dunlap, "Methodist Theology in Great Britain," p. 140, suggests that Watson's analysis tends to mitigate the seriousness and destructiveness of the impact of sin. His contemporary Adam Clarke, he says, is truer to the original Wesleyan position on this point.

[38] Samuel Wakefield, *A Complete System of Christian Theology,* pp. 308-35; Amos Binney, *The Theological Compend,* pp. 111-13; T. N. Ralston, *Elements of Divinity,* pp. 161-76.

doctrine of sin. His logical, systematic mind is nowhere better displayed than in "The Arminian Treatment of Original Sin," appended to the text of his *Systematic Theology*. In it he exhibits an unwavering commitment to the ethical principles of Arminianism and a keen sensitivity to contradictions of and deviations from these principles as they appear in other Methodist theologians. In the denial of "native demerit" or guilt he finds the definitive characteristic of Arminianism. Therefore he rejects original guilt, the punitive imputation of depravity, and the intrinsic guilt of inherited depravity. Yet, consistent with the Wesleyan tradition, he insists on a realistic description of man's depraved condition. At the same time he is curiously blind to the contradiction thus created between his Arminian principle of free accountability and the "justice" he finds in the corruption of innocence by inheritance. It is not surprising that his view of depravity failed to satisfy many many of his contemporaries and most of his successors.

Primitive Man and the Fall

In his treatment of sin Miley feels obligated to comment on several related problems precipitated by the advance of science: the theory of evolution ("mere hypothesis"), the antiquity of the race, the plurality of racial origins, and the reliability of the Genesis record. In each instance, after serious appraisal, he decides in favor of the literal teaching of the Mosaic narrative (I, 358–92).

Miley regards Adam's original endowment as similar to that of his descendants and not greatly superior, as Wesley had believed. Created in the image of God, his "spiritual nature" or "personality is the central truth of man's original likeness to God" (I, 407). It differentiates him from all lower orders of existence. Holiness was implicit in this image of God. The newly created holiness of Adam, before any action of his own, "was simply a subjective state and tendency in harmony with his moral relations and duties" (I, 410). Lacking any ethical element arising from free personal action, his moral rectitude was neither meritorious nor rewardable.

Though holy in nature and tendency, Adam needed the Spirit's help to "retain the good which he might will" (I, 422). Miley includes the presence of the Spirit as an original and abiding element in the holiness of primitive man, but he affirms that the deprivation of the Spirit, after Adam's sin, led to the depravation of his nature. This view he contends is in "full accord with the fact that in the Christian life the Holy Spirit is not only the agent in the primary renewal and purification of the soul, but also an abiding presence in aid of its renewed powers" (I, 422).

In orthodox fashion, Miley sees Adam placed on trial and required to obey the moral law and a particular divine commandment. To account for the defection of this "good" man, Miley posits impulses in his sensibilities adverse to the law of duty. These solicitations were spontaneous, innocent, and consistent with the primitive holiness, but, if "unduly entertained," they could act as impulses toward a voluntary infraction of the law of probation. On the proper mental apprehension of God, love and fear acted to support and restrain man. But temporary diversion of thought clouded his vision of God and the penalties of his justice, and in the absence of restraint man followed his awakened appetencies into disobedience (I, 423–36).

In what sense did God permit the fall? The sophisticated casuistry which Miley offers in partial answer rests on the assumption that "if the punishment of sin is just, the permission of sin cannot be unjust" (I, 437). Further, the fall presupposes responsible freedom; God neither granted man license to sin nor intervened to prevent sin. Miley disputes Wesley's belief that as a result of the fall man is offered even greater glories through the redemptive economy. The attempt to vindicate God in this manner impugns his holiness by making sin necessary to the greatest good.[39]

Native Depravity and Native Demerit

The doctrine of native depravity assumes that by nature man is in a corrupt state, alien from spiritual life and inclined to evil.

[39] For Wesley's view see his *Works,* VI, 295, and IX, 332.

Depravity results, as we have seen, from the withdrawal of God's Spirit. It is a subjective moral state, not distinctively in the will but broadly in the sensuous and moral nature. An evil tendency characteristically follows from it. The reality of depravity is confirmed by Scripture and by the evidence of its universal destructiveness (I, 442–55). It is not rebutted by the so-called "natural virtues." Here Miley reiterates a consistent Wesleyan theme when he ascribes these virtues, not to nature, but rather to the universal prevenience of God's grace (I, 456).

Though the nature of depravity and its origin in the first pair can be readily established, the ground or law of its entailment upon the race is much more difficult to demonstrate. There are but two fundamental theories which attempt to account for the transmission of Adam's sin: the theory of penal retribution and the theory of genetic transmission (I, 467). The first of these theories asserts that all men are subjected to the penal infliction of depravity because of a common participation in the sin of Adam. The generic human nature, often offered as the basis for this common participation, however, makes groundless assumptions and ultimately fails because it lacks the only ground for guilt—free personal agency exercised by each individual (I, 480). The theory of seminal identity, which Watson endorsed, is objectionable for the same reason. Still another version of penal retribution assumes a legal oneness of the race under the federal headship of representation of Adam, on the basis of which God imputes guilt. Such representation, however, is a fiction, entirely incapable of establishing guilt by free, personal participation. The theory must be rejected, further, because it asserts the liability of men to punishment at the same time that it denies their responsibility. Thus Watson had resolved the problem to Miley's discomfort.[40]

[40] Miley insists that Methodists "must eliminate from theology the ideas of ethical character without free personal action," *Systematic Theology*, I, 410. J. W. Mendenhall, reviewing Miley's work in *MQR*, 74 (1892), 496, wrote, "Dr. Miley is on the right ground in his wonderful defense of the Arminian conception of the fall and its consequences, and, in cleansing Augustinianism to the core, elevates man and blots darkness from the Scriptures." Methodist orthodoxy was not without its defenders in this

On any basis, the judicial infliction of depravity must be firmly rejected by knowledgeable Arminians. Depravity is not a punishment; it is an inheritance for which the law of genetic transmission provides an entirely satisfactory explanation (I, 500 ff.). Everything produces its kind. Had Adam continued holy, his offspring would have begun their probation in the same state. Since he sinned, and his nature was depraved following the withdrawal of the Spirit, by natural generation his heirs receive this depravity. Miley holds that his view is supported by Scripture, general Catholic doctrine, and the Articles of the Methodist Church (I, 507 f.). The reality of depravity is not less because it is inherited, rather than inflicted by judicial action. It is just as real and the very same in its own nature as if it were a penal retribution.[41]

Thus Miley accepts common depravity and insists that it comes into being without involving man in guilt or demerit. But might the possession of depravity, by whatever means, be sufficient ground for guilt and punishment? No. Mere nature cannot be the subject of guilt, for guilt requires free personal agency transgressing the law of God. The depraved nature which man inherits gives rise to incitements to sinful action but they are not sin unless and until they are consented to and acted on. Such actual sins alone are the ground of man's guilt and the cause of the divine wrath and punishment (I, 516). If a "sinful" nature is allowed, as it is by

period, however. For example, E. M. Marvin, in *The Doctrinal Integrity of Methodism*, pp. 97 ff., argued that the practical attitude toward human depravity is the starting point of doctrine and its compromise the clearest mark of the abandonment of evangelical theology. He noted two primary "occasions" for missing the truth of depravity: emphasis on the freedom of the will and on the religious nurture of children.

[41] Reviewing Pope's systematic theology, Miley finds confusion in the doctrine of sin which, as expressed, "more properly belongs to Calvinist theology." Miley agrees with Pope on the depravity of human nature and its origin in Adam. But he denies in Pope the derivation of sin by representation, hereditary guilt, penal affliction, and the inherent sinfulness of depravity. See *MQR*, 59 (1877), 400 ff. Olin Curtis, *The Christian Faith*, p. 519, also is critical of Pope's view of sin, especially hereditary guilt: "In the history of Arminian theology there is no position so entirely inconsistent and indefensible." Miner Raymond, *Systematic Theology*, II, 80-98, 315, affirms "depravation by deprivation" also and takes depravity to include the enslavement of the will of the entire race. So severe is man's condition that only God can provide adequate remedies.

some inconsistent Arminians, there is no valid ground on which to deny Calvinist election and reprobation. But if Arminians "keep to their fundamental principle"—native depravity without native demerit—their position is secure. The decisive issue with respect to guilt or demerit is, once again, the issue of freedom.[42]

Definition of Sin

In his defense of depravity, Miley has retreated to the last outpost. What he defends is only a pale image of the mass of corruption, the body of death, that is central to orthodox doctrine. Further, it is difficult to understand how he could square the inheritance of a depraved nature, prior to any action of man, with his Arminian principle of free personal agency. His efforts to do so make depravity represent little more than the possibility of defection required by the freedom of contrary choice. It is no wonder, then, that other Methodists shed his view with such equanimity.

His revision of the character of depravity, as well as his denial of original guilt, stems from his moral intuitions about the nature of sin, guilt, and freedom. To be true to itself, "Arminianism can admit no definition which omits such agency [free, personal] or

[42] Both Miley and Whedon feel that Methodists have often failed on this issue. As they try to relate the guilt of original sin to depravity, Miley charges that Arminius, Wesley, Fletcher, Watson, Pope, and Summers have been forced into contradiction. See Scott, "Methodist Theology," pp. 452, 214, where he indicates that Whedon denies hereditary guilt, allowing only "a hereditary nature personally made guilty," and lists Bledsoe, Raymond, Summers, Merrill, and Miley as agreeing with him. Shipley, "Methodist Arminianism," p. 39, comments that Miley, on logical grounds, repudiated the Wesley-Fletcher doctrine of man and original sin in favor of continental Arminianism. Scott, "Methodist Theology," p. 454, maintains that the ambiguity of early Wesleyans on guilt was not unnoticed or unintended. They were willing to sacrifice strict systematic consistency "in face of what seemed to be the profoundly inescapable tragedy of man's primal participation (or, at least, representation) in the guilt of the Adamic sin. Such a sobering reflection was only relieved in the light of that gracious redemption which had become effective. Miley's interpretive position is subject to criticism, not so much because of its practical limitation of concern to logical consistency, but because of that doctrine of moral responsibility in accord with which exclusive consistency is demanded. It is the insistence on 'guilt' as solely applicable to personal and active agency (excluding any notion of degrees of guilt) which ultimately distinguishes the position of Miley (and Whedon) from that of Wesley, Fletcher and Watson." See also *ibid.*, Appendix 20, "Whedon, W. B. Pope and John Tigert—and 'Hereditary Guilt,'" pp. 624 ff.

includes the guilt of an inherited corruption of nature" (I, 527). Native demerit cannot be affirmed of human nature on the basis of a "want of conformity" between it and the law of God. Conformity pertains to personality, not nature. In addition, there must be a voluntary element in the definition of sin, whether it expresses itself in commission or omission (I, 528). Thus Miley arrives at this definition: *"Sin is a disobedience to a law of God, conditioned on free moral agency and opportunity of knowing the law"* (I, 528). Only such a disobedience involves the liability to punishment.[43]

Despite Miley's insistence on free moral agency based on adequate knowledge, he holds that moral ruin, or native depravity, pervades human life as a grim reality. It is a state of existence alien to spiritual life and "utterly without fitness for a state of blessedness" (I, 529). It makes impossible any power of self-redemption. The fate of children who die in infancy does not negate either inherited depravity or the goodness of God. Christ removes their sinful nature and stands as their justifier against every accuser. Does the denial of native demerit and the retention only of native depravity weaken the practical effects of the doctrine of sin? By no means, says Miley. The only sin which we can really deplore is sin which we have committed (I, 530).

In support of his own, Miley cites Wesley's specialized definition of sin—"nothing is sin, strictly speaking, but a conscious violation of a known law of God"—and finds no substantive difference between the two (I, 528). The similarity in their definitions of sin

---

[43] This definition conforms with his later assertion, *Systematic Theology*, II, 147, that "sin has no real existence apart from the agent in sinning," in which Curtis concurs: "Sin is something which the individual does; it is an act. There is no sin where there is not a sinner" (*The Christian Faith*, p. 200). See also Scott, "Methodist Theology," pp. 621 f., Appendix 19, "Whedon: 'The Doctrines of Methodism.'" Such an estimate of human capacity led William Kelley, in *MQR*, 76 (1894), 837, to observe that Miley presents the soul as an "athlete stripped for the contest." T. O. Summers also differed from the Whedon-Miley view. Summers asserts that sin and virtue are not restricted to voluntary acts. The principle of an act can be sinful and man's condition as well as his acts subjected to moral terms. See Summers' *Systematic Theology*, II, pp. 49 ff.; also Scott's remarks on Summers, "Methodist Theology," pp. 389 f.

and the similarity in their descriptions of depravity convince Miley that he is generally faithful to his heritage. His rejection of native demerit he regards as a purification, not a perversion of Wesleyan Arminianism. His stance in these matters is interestingly poised on both nineteenth- and twentieth-century grounds but came too late to win a receptive hearing in American Methodism. Elements in the doctrine of man for which he made a place become more explicit and increasingly dominate Methodist theology. The full implications of these changes are to be seen in the writings of Albert Knudson.

KNUDSON'S "PRESUPPOSITIONS OF REDEMPTION"

In a recent study of the beliefs of American Methodists, three-quarters of those questioned passed over definitions of man in terms of his sinfulness and marked this as the most appropriate statement: "Man is a rational being capable of knowing God and entering into fellowship with Him." [44] In support of this conviction, they might well have cited Albert Knudson, who characteristically sees man as a free personal being or soul possessed of moral worth. The issues in the doctrine of sin that had occupied Methodist theology—original guilt and depravity, the transmission of Adam's sin and God's condemnation of the entire race—are no longer primary for him. His discussion of man is carried on under the general heading of the "presuppositions of redemption." In it he lists "positive" presuppositions first—the worth of man and the reality of metaphysical freedom. These are required to give meaning in turn to the "negative" presuppositions of redemption—sin and evil. Thus the perspective from which man is viewed changes radically. Related details must be sketched to show the ramifications of this change and hence the end result of a basic transition in Methodist theology.

[44] S. Paul Schilling, *Methodism and Society in Theological Perspective*, p. 279.

Man's Worth and Freedom

Knudson holds the doctrine of man to be of primary significance for theology as well as for the entire view of the universe. It is second in importance only to the doctrine of God and psychologically precedes it (II, 76). A unified and consistent statement of the doctrine requires the subordination of one or the other of "two more or less discordant ideas . . . creation and redemption." The view of man in the first is optimistic and idealistic; in the second it is pessimistic and dualistic. Unequivocally, Knudson chooses the former and makes dominant "those aspects of human nature . . . that are directly implied in the idea of divine creatorship" (II, 77). Unfailingly, he adheres to this choice as he discusses the presuppositions of redemption. But as he subordinates redemption to creation, he decisively sets himself apart from Wesley and makes explicit what Watson and Miley could never approve, even though their modifications, especially those of Miley, tended to move them toward such a position.[45]

Grounded in the goodness of creation, two positive presuppositions of redemption are vital: the worth of man and the freedom of his soul. Despite the probing of the new sciences, a critical examination of the world still permits the conclusions that man is the only known end of creation and that the rest of the world derives its value from its relation to him. The distinct and fundamental element in the Christian view of man is the supreme value it attributes to the human soul or self. This valuation is based on an ethical conviction that man is an end in himself, and on a religious conviction of his capacity for fellowship and his kinship with God (II, 78). But the kinship is neither evident nor demonstrable. It requires faith, the philosophical support for which is found in the conception of God in theistic personalism (II, 89–93).

---

[45] On this point Will observes, "This devaluation of the doctrine of redemption further meant that any theological dimensions which came from taking seriously the Christian doctrine of the fall of man and that point to the distortion of the whole human structure had to be dismissed"; see James Edward Will, "Implications for Philosophical Theology," p. 94. See also Curtis K. Jones, "Personalism as Christian Philosophy," unpublished Ph.D. dissertation, Union, 1944, p. 194.

The ultimate questions with respect to man have to do with his self or soul. The soul is a fundamental presupposition of personalism, even more characteristic than the existence of God. The demonstration of the reality of the soul, says Knudson (in 1933), is "in one sense . . . the deepest need of our time" (II, 92). In the human consciousness or the soul there is a causal agency different from every other form of physical agency by which the mind originates and determines action. Arguments fail to dislodge this as one of the basic human convictions. "Only the belief in a real and active self can save the higher spiritual interests of mankind from collapse; and in spite of all modern attacks upon it, no belief would seem to be better established than it" (II, 113).

Underlying the affirmation of man's "priceless worth and the reality of his soul" is an even more critical affirmation regarding the *freedom* of his soul (II, 113, 120). If the soul is not free, the high estimate placed upon it vanishes. The dignity and unparalleled possibilities of the self reside in its essential power of contrary choice, in which it is uncoerced by, even though subject to, external and internal influences. Denied such freedom, either by naturalistic or by theological determinism, man loses his place in the world and his capacity to cooperate with redemptive forces. Knudson places the highest premium on his "libertarian" doctrine. And, consistent with his position, he defends freedom as prior and indispensable to redemption. For earlier Methodists, freedom with respect to God presupposed a gracious restoration through the redemptive economy. For Knudson, it is redemption that presupposes freedom. Therefore, the chapter on salvation which follows must give renewed and more detailed attention to Knudson's doctrine of "metaphysical freedom."

Suffering and Sin

Human freedom necessarily implies the possibility of "unjust conditions" and "wicked deeds." The plight of the world is in fact much more critical than might seem to be implied by the fact of freedom. Facing this world, the Christian faith must attempt to come to terms both with natural evil and suffering and with moral evil and sin.

Evil is always a thorny problem for idealism, not less so for idealism cast in personalistic categories. Though Knudson discusses the problem at some length, he offers remarkably little by way of an attempted resolution. He surveys the history of man's efforts to come to terms with evil and rejects as wholly inadequate a number of views: Buddhist negation, Old Testament retribution, orthodox depravity, etc. Having cleared the field, he contents himself with a summary of "current Christian teaching" (II, 212–21). He finds general agreement that the problem is on the whole insoluble. A partial theoretical solution may be based on the understanding that pleasure is not the ultimate value in life; that man's standards are not God's; and that pain and suffering serve a positive function, particularly as they lead men to God. A practical solution to the problem is possible, however. Evil is not so much a riddle as it is an enemy to be overcome. In this conquest religion is a strong support (I, 221). Perhaps most revealing in this discussion is the absence of any appeal by Knudson to his personalistic framework. While it renders yeoman service in many areas, in this one it is significantly silent.

Christianity's basic occupation, however, is with moral evil or sin. Its understanding of this reality is complicated by two convictions which seemed opposed to each other. One is the ethical conviction that man is free and therefore responsible for his sins. The other is the religious conviction that man cannot by his own efforts break his bondage to sin. Both convictions are essential to Christian faith, and their reconciliation is one of the basic problems of theology (II, 223–32).

What then is sin? First, it presupposes metaphysical freedom. "Without the power of alternative action there can be no sin in the sense of personal guilt. Sin, guilt, and freedom go together." [46]

[46] *Basic Issues in Christian Thought*, p. 113; see also *The Validity of Religious Experience*, p. 208; Henry C. Sheldon, *A System of Christian Doctrine*, pp. 320-22; Curtis, *The Christian Faith*, pp. 199–206; and Borden P. Bowne, *Studies in Christianity*, pp. 144-46, 179-81.

Second, it is more than a series of acts; it is basic opposition to the all-inclusive virtue of love, in relation to God, man, and self. Third, for accountability, it requires adequate knowledge and relevant standards as judged from God's point of view. Last, the understanding of sin is careful to distinguish between the fact and the feeling of guilt and between the language of devotion and that of theology. There must be no transformation of "a religious metaphor into a metaphysical theory" (II, 415, 233-49).

Thus Knudson arrives at this basic definition of sin: It is "moral imperfection manifesting itself in the defective attitude we take toward God, toward our fellowmen, and toward our own true selves, and also as moral imperfection, for which we are accountable in God's sight" (I, 249). In general, he approves Wesley's voluntaristic definition. The additional realistic elements which he incorporates (sin as basic disposition and judgment from God's point of view) make his position somewhat more comprehensive. Basically, however, there is no sin for him without the misuse of the power of alternative action.[47]

The problem of sin's origin has taxed theological explanation from the beginning. Unequivocally Knudson dismisses all dualistic and necessitarian theories and asserts that sin originates in man's personal freedom (II, 252). There is no other explanation. Neo-orthodox theories implying that sin is necessitation by some extra or sub-volitional force founder on the requirements of responsibility and cannot be saved by their dubious conceptions of freedom.[48]

Original sin in its traditional form is a fiction, and so are all theories that seek to explain its origin by a catastrophic act either in time or out

[47] Paul Ramsey, *Basic Christian Ethics*, p. 287, observes that "Knudson's moralistic definition of sin has the merit of regarding sin as man's own act. However, the word 'sin' becomes merely a class name, a way of grouping particular actions, and the words 'sinful' and 'wilfulness' have no referent at all in human nature. Only the words 'moral tendency' have anything corresponding to them in human nature, and this only on the periphery of the self in its acquired moral nature. Tendency toward evil is never man's own act, but something he has suffered. Knudson's position might be described as a nominalistic interpretation of sin [as] immoral acts."

[48] See *Basic Issues in Christian Thought*, pp. 40 f., 109 ff.; *The Validity of Religious Experience*, pp. 207-11.

of it. There is no such thing as inherited guilt or an inherited moral depravity. Guilt is inalienable, and so are all strictly moral qualities, states and conditions. Apart from the individual will there is neither goodness nor badness. It is in the will, therefore, and its free activity, not in anything extravolitional, that we must seek the origin of sin [II, 257 f.].

Thus, out of hand, Knudson rejects original guilt and original depravity and dismisses the doctrinal expositions of earlier Methodists designed to sustain them. He brings to fulfillment incipient tendencies which had been gaining ground in American Methodism for more than a century.

Knudson also rejects the idea of man's original perfection, in part because it lacks empirical evidence. More conclusive, however, is the fact that righteousness and perfection are moral terms which may be applied only to the achievements of free beings. Human life begins rather on a non-moral plane. Man is endowed with impulses, appetites, and passions which are themselves ethically neutral. Their disproportionate intensity when compared with higher impulses is not to be regarded as sinful either. Such disproportion is the ground of temptation, "but temptation is not sin" (II, 259). Sin does not appear until the will releases its check on wayward impulses. Generally, man does not deliberately choose evil, but rather, and often unaware of the implications of his actions, a lesser good (II, 258–61). Thus, imperceptibly, from mixed motives, partially in disguise, sin enters life. No necessity requires it; it is the result of man's free choice.[49]

[49] Kenneth Cauthen, *The Impact of American Religious Liberalism*, p. 120, notes what Knudson has accomplished by this description. "This continuity between the stage of innocence and the feeble beginnings of sin and between freedom and inevitability enables Knudson to reduce the factor of deliberate choice to the extent that freedom does not appear to be basically corrupt. At the same time, it enables him to retain the idea of freedom sufficiently to speak of accountable guilt. Hence, he is not even conscious of a dilemma because he has overcome it by practically merging the alternatives on the basis of a skillful use of the all-pervading principle of continuity." Jones, "Personalism as Christian Philosophy," pp. 191-95, indicates that personalism denies that there are vital forces in man not amenable to rational enlightenment and also that there is deliberate choice of evil in hostility to God, attenuating thereby both

The universality of sin has been widely affirmed and theories of the fall have been advanced in its explanation. Knudson admits the practical universality of sin but finds the explanation for the fact, not in a non-volitional native tendency to evil, but rather in the "enormous difficulty involved in the task of moralizing the nonmoral impulses, desires and interests with which we are endowed by birth." The moral sense "dawns and develops only slowly" and its nurture requires "ceaseless vigilance throughout life." Psychological and social forces which work against the moral sense are "so numerous and so insistent that yielding to them at some time or other would seem almost inevitable" (II, 265). Sin occurs, "not necessarily, but with such a high degree of probability that few if any escape it" (II, 261). Thus in his discussion of sin Knudson arrives at his explanatory principle by exchanging the bondage of the will for the environmental difficulties in which the will operates. The psychological and theological implications of this exchange are enormous.

What of God's responsibility for the appearance of sin? Knudson maintains that sin is not a part of God's plan. Sin is an absolute evil, not merely a means to the attainment of moral character. In addition, if God wills sin, it is necessary, and inevitable sin is a contradiction. "The only responsibility that God has for sin is in providing for its possibility" (II, 269). This possibility is implied in moral freedom, which to be real must include evil as one of its options. This possibility also represents God's "faith in the power of his own redemptive agency." [50]

One predicate dare not be omitted from Knudson's view of man —his moral character. The character of "moral man" presupposes a personal self, intelligently aware of reality and possibility, free to direct its own life. The various aspects of the doctrine of man must

---

the depth of sin and the merciful grace of God. McCutcheon argues that the personalist anthropology "belies any fundamental division between the human and the divine" and "represents a transition from a category of 'being' to that of 'doing' in the relation of man to God, and thus stresses the moral will as the condition of fellowship with God"; see *The History of American Methodism*, III, 279-80.

[50] *The Doctrine of Redemption*, p. 270; *Basic Issues in Christian Thought*, p. 119.

be subjected to this fundamental conviction. Questions about guilt and depravity, original righteousness and the fall, the origin and universality and the unifying principle and pervasive power of sin—all must be resolved by reference to man's nature as essentially moral. Knudson's unswerving devotion to the idea of moral man and all its implications clearly sets him apart from Wesley, and, in lesser degree, from many of Wesley's successors. While Wesley did not dispute man's moral status, neither did he give much time to its defense. He was far more concerned with man's moral disease and God's ministry of healing. Human goodness was Wesley's goal, not his starting place. On this point a great chasm is fixed between the two men with whom this study begins and ends. And the opposition of their doctrinal views on sin is indissolubly related to their beliefs in nearly every other area of Christian life and thought. Being Christian theologians, they traverse generally the same ground. And precisely for this reason, it is critically important to determine the differences between them, not in order to take sides, but to come as close as possible to the truth.

CHAPTER V
FROM FREE GRACE
TO FREE WILL

From the first, Methodists met in Conference and issued the minutes embodying their deliberations. In the 1745 Minutes, one item contained some basic doctrinal assertions with most controversial implications:

"Q. 23. Wherein may we come to the very edge of Calvinism?

"A. In ascribing all good to the free grace of God. (2) In denying all natural free will, and all power antecedent to grace. And (3) In excluding all merit from man; even for what he has or does by the grace of God."

Other items in these Minutes confirm the conclusion that Wesley and the Methodists had affirmed God's sovereign grace so completely that they found it necessary to inquire if they were "leaning too much toward Calvinism."

In 1770, in the midst of severe controversy with antinomian Calvinists, the Minutes reported out of Conference seemed to make some fundamental concessions to justification by works and caused reverberations throughout the societies. The Conference a year later recorded a clarification of these previous Minutes. "We abhor the doctrine of Justification by Works . . . and as the said Minutes are not sufficiently guarded . . . , we solemnly declare . . . that we have no trust or confidence but in the alone merits of our Lord and Saviour Jesus Christ . . . ; our works have no part in meriting, or purchasing our salvation from first to last, either in whole or in part." [1] At issue in these controversies is one of the knottiest of theological problems—the relationship between God's grace and man's responsibility. It is the focus of interest in our review of the doctrine of grace.

WESLEYAN FREE GRACE

God's Atoning Grace

Wesley's writings are searched in vain for a detailed statement of his belief about the atonement. There is no treatise or sermon devoted to it, perhaps for the reason which Cell assigns, that it is "too comprehensive of the whole meaning of the Gospel to lend itself to a special treatise." [2] As the ground of saving grace, it is critical for Wesley, however, and is constantly referred to throughout his work; "nothing in the Christian system is of greater consequence than the doctrine of the Atonement. It is properly the distinguishing point between Deism and Christianity." [3]

In his excellent study, John Deschner presents a careful, detailed interpretation of Wesley's Christology. For this, he finds the *Notes* to be an unworked mine of most valuable ore. He discusses the work of Christ as prophet, priest, and king, arguing persuasively

---

[1] Minutes of Wesley's Conferences are in the *Works*, VIII (see p. 275); the second quotation is from Luke Tyerman, *The Life and Times of the Rev. John Wesley, M.A.*, III, 100; compare Colin Williams, *John Wesley's Theology Today*, pp. 57-71, on the theological assertions in several of the Minutes.

[2] George C. Cell, *The Rediscovery of John Wesley*, pp. 297, 313-21, argues further that the atonement is not properly subject to the sort of rational support Anselm attempted to give it. However, he finds that Wesley fully shares Anselm's intention.

[3] *Letters*, VI, 297; I, 241; III, 351; *Works*, VIII, 277; *Notes*, Ro. 4:5.

that Christ's sacrificial work as priest is fundamental and determines his prophetic and kingly offices.[4] It is quite generally agreed that Wesley holds the orthodox satisfaction theory of the atonement implicit in the Thirty-Nine Articles of the Church of England.[5]

The atonement expresses both God's justice and God's mercy. His justice is directed toward sin and may be properly termed "wrath." By reason of sin, both his own and that of Adam, man deserves the punishment of death. He stands in infinite debt to God and can render back nothing that is not already due. But God is merciful, as well as just, and seeks to redeem man. He cannot do so in violation of his justice, however, which requires that sin be punished. Therefore, God provides for salvation by sending his Son to suffer the punishment due man's sin. By his suffering and death, Christ pays the debt man owes to God. Wesley refers again and again to what Christ "has done and suffered for us."[6] In the atonement, the justice of God is preserved, his mercy toward man is abundantly declared, and his Son is exalted as head above all.

The atonement of Christ is the sole "meritorious," "procuring,"

[4] John Deschner, *Wesley's Christology*, pp. 77-9, and chaps. IV, V, and VI.

[5] *Ibid.*, pp. 5, 93, 152, 190; Paul W. Hoon, "The Soteriology of John Wesley," p. 145; Harald Lindström, *Wesley and Sanctification*, p. 60; William R. Cannon, *The Theology of John Wesley*, p. 209; Lycurgus M. Starkey, Jr., *The Work of the Holy Spirit*, pp. 118 f. David C. Shipley, "Methodist Arminianism," p. 242, notes that Fletcher also lacks any extended discussion of the atonement but that both he and Wesley "gave tacit approval to the 'satisfaction theory' of the atonement implicit in the statements of the Thirty-Nine Articles."

[6] *Sermons*, II, 430. See Hoon's thorough treatment, "The Soteriology of John Wesley," pp. 54-66, of the attributes of love and holiness in God as they bear on man's redemption in Christ. Wesley's stress on the holiness of God is illustrated in *Letters*, II, 376; V, 284; IV, 321; III, 345; *Works*, VII, 266; *Notes*, Mk. 15:34, Heb. 5:7, John 10:17-18, Matt. 25:34—e.g., Ro. 3:25-26: "The attribute of justice must be preserved inviolate; and inviolate it is preserved, if there was a real infliction of punishment on our Saviour." Wesley's understanding of God's love in salvation is attested to in *Notes*, Matt. 6:9, 10:29, Luke 15:32, I Tim. 1:1, I John 4:19; *Works*, VI, 235, 250, 323. Compare Cell, *The Rediscovery of John Wesley*, p. 342. R. W. Dale, "The Theology of John Wesley," in *Fellowship with Christ and Other Discourses*, p. 232, writes that "in John Wesley's personal discovery of the reality of the Atonement—the synthesis of Justice and Mercy in the death of Christ—he found the inspiration, the force which, under God, created Methodism."

or "efficient" cause of salvation. All merit is in him, none in man. Wesley bluntly insists on this point in correspondence with William Law, whose teaching emphasized the necessity of conforming to the life of Christ in order to gain acceptance. Wesley is reluctant to follow traditional doctrine in affirming the imputation of Christ's righteousness. He fears the poison of antinomianism, in which men passively rely on Christ's work to the neglect of their own righteousness. He stresses instead Christ's passive, not his active, righteousness—that is, his submission and death, which made full satisfaction for the sins of the world and provided the meritorious ground of forgiveness and acceptance.[7]

He frequently refers to Christ as the second Adam and contrasts Christ's healing work with the devastation wrought by the first Adam. The benefits which accrue to mankind through Christ are most significant. The primal sin would have resulted in universal death but for Christ. His gift stays the sentence of death and continues life in Adam and his posterity.[8] Wesley also asserts that the atoning grace of God in Christ cancels the guilt of original sin in infants so that, dying before their time, they are not condemned. This conviction modifies his view of baptism and also undercuts the logic of Calvinist reprobation.[9]

His assertion of the parallel universal influences flowing from Adam's sin and Christ's atonement poses a problem for Wesley. Are adults guilty of the primal sin, or is it canceled by the atonement for them also? On this point, the difficulty of determining Wesley's exact position can be measured by the unending contention about it among his successors. Occasionally Wesley remarks that no man is doomed to eternal death for the sin of Adam; he does not so restrict its consequences regarding temporal and spir-

---

[7] *Letter*, III, 350 ff.; *Sermons*, II, 426 ff.; and *Notes*, II Pet. 1:1, Ro. 1:17. Check J. Brazier Green, *John Wesley and William Law* (London: Epworth Press, 1945), for an extended consideration of the relation of those two men.

[8] *Works*, VIII, 277; *Letters*, VI, 239.

[9] *Sermons*, II, 237-39; *Works*, IX, 303, 462; and Williams, *John Wesley's Theology Today*, pp. 115-22; Starkey, *The Work of the Holy Spirit*, pp. 90-94; Lindström, *Wesley and Sanctification*, pp. 28-30.

itual death, however.[10] But characteristically, apart from prevenient grace, sinful man is condemned eternally. The cancellation of original guilt by the atonement generally seems to be a provisional or emergency measure applicable only to those who die before becoming responsible either for the sin or for the grace that is in them.[11]

The general dispensation of grace won through the atonement extends to the limits of time and space. Thus, when Wesley takes note of pre-Christian figures and distant heathens who display unusual virtues, he is undismayed. Though they do not know the name of Christ, their goodness roots in his universal gift.[12] In them, as in all men, God's goodness precedes human striving. God seeks all men while they are yet far off. This authentic Wesleyan theme leads directly to the heart of the relationship between divine initiative and human responsibility.

Prevenient Grace

God's saving act in Christ is in no sense dependent upon man. What it bestows man cannot otherwise provide. Nor can he earn it. Grace is God's gift freely given. His own inner struggle provided Wesley with unshakable confirmation of this Christian truth. However, to define free grace simply as fixing all merit in Christ does not sufficiently indicate its distinctiveness. In a very famous sermon on "Free Grace," Wesley writes, "The grace or love of God whence cometh our salvation is FREE IN ALL, and FREE FOR ALL." [13] This provides the clue which we shall follow here.

[10] *Works*, IX, 286, 315; X, 236.

[11] *Ibid.*, IX, 268, 273, 303, 476; *Notes*, Ro. 2:14. See Lindström's full presentation of the evidence, *Wesley and Sanctification*, pp. 28-37, 44-50.

[12] Speaking of "natural conscience," Wesley writes, "it is not natural, but a supernatural gift of God, above all his natural endowments. No; it is not nature, but the Son of God, that is 'the true light, which enlighteneth every man that cometh into the world.' So that we may say to every human creature, 'He,' not nature, 'hath showed thee, O man, what is good.' " See *Works*, VII, 188. See also VI, 508-13; VIII, 277-78; *Letters*, VI, 214, 239; *Notes*, John 1:9, Ro. 1:19.

[13] *Works*, VII, 373. Curnock notes, *Journal*, II, 421 n., that Thomas Jackson called the sermon on "Free Grace" "the most powerful and impassioned" of all of Wesley's utterances. Luke Tyerman, *The Life and Times of the Rev. John Wesley, M.A.*,

Grace *for all* is Wesley's answer to Calvinism. The work of Christ is not limited to a specified few who reap its benefits while the greater part of mankind inevitably perishes. God has invited all men to come to him. One by one Wesley marshals his arguments against a limitation of the atonement to the elect and speaks out boldly for free, universal grace. If some men are not saved, the cause must be sought not in divine reluctance but in human resistance. There is perhaps more unanimity on this point than on any other among the successors and interpreters of Wesley.[14]

The grace of God is free *in all*. Each one receives God's gift of prevenient grace, which "waiteth not for the call" of any man but is universally given. There are none who are without it; Christians, Mahometans, Pagans, the vilest of savages "all possess some measure of preventing grace." [15] Only if man has "quenched the Spirit"—that is, so resisted the promptings of prevenient grace that the Spirit has withdrawn—can he be said to be without grace. As an initial gift, prevenient grace is irresistible; man cannot choose not to have it. He may struggle with it, however, and eventually stifle it. Or he may follow its promptings to the presence of Christ.[16]

This original bestowal of grace restores some of the freedom wholly lacking in the bondage of Adamic sin. For Wesley the

---

I, 317, judged it to be "in some respects . . . the most important sermon that [Wesley] ever issued."

[14] *Journal*, II, 71, 177, 223; see also the sermon "On Predestination," *Works*, VI, 225 ff., and the tracts "Predestination Calmly Considered," *ibid.*, X, 204-58, and "What is an Arminian?" *ibid.*, 358-61; *Notes*, John 6:44, Ro. 1:17. George Whitefield and the Calvinist Methodists are an exception to the general Methodist insistence on the universality of grace. They did not become an enduring force in American Methodism, however, though they retained more vitality in Britain. See David C. Shipley, "Wesley and Some Calvinist Controversies," *The Drew Gateway*, 25 (1955), 195-210.

[15] *Works*, VII, 345; and 374: "Whatsoever good is in man, or is done by man, God is the author and doer of it. Thus is his grace free in all; that is, no way depending on any power or merit in man, but on God alone, who freely gave us his own son, and 'with him freely giveth us all things.' " Also *Sermons*, II, 44 n.

[16] John Fletcher, *Works*, III, 442, interprets Wesley thus: "We believe that these benefits were, at first, as gratuitously and irresistibly bestowed upon us as . . . the divine image and favor were at first bestowed upon our first parents. . . . I say irresistibly because God does not leave to our option whether we shall receive a talent of redeeming grace." See Shipley, "Methodist Arminianism," pp. 187-91.

restoration of freedom by grace is not a philosophical idea but a religious reality, expressly soteriological in intention. By it, he argues, man gains a responsible part in salvation; without it, the Calvinist logic is irrefutable. Wesley's affirmation is unqualified: "There is a measure of free-will supernaturally restored to every man, together with that supernatural light which 'enlighteneth every man that cometh into the world.' " [17] Thus, along with freedom, prevenient grace also bestows the light indispensably required by man's corrupted and distorted faculties. His conscience, enlightened by the Spirit, is enabled to know right from wrong. His senses are renewed so that in some preliminary way he is able to see the things of God.

In his sermon "On Working Out Our Own Salvation," Wesley shows the implications of the doctrine of preventing grace. Because God works in every man, man *can* work! Necessity follows from ability.[18] Therefore, God does not save man without regard to his response to the offer of saving grace. And it is prevenient grace which lays the foundation for this response. The problem of the "point of contact" is not thus resolved, however, but only stated.

In general, the problem of relating divine grace and human freedom is solved in one of two ways by Wesleyan interpreters. The

[17] Prevenient grace restores some personal agency to man (see, e.g., *Works*, X, 229 f.; IX, 273, 275, 294; VII, 228; VIII, 52), and a faith-faculty to perceive the Divine (e.g., *Works*, VII, 188, 345; VI, 512; VIII, 106; *Notes*, John 1:9, Ro. 2:14). J. Weldon Smith III, in "Some Notes on Wesley's Doctrine of Prevenient Grace," *Religion in Life*, 34 (1964), 79 f., concludes that prevenient grace has a double meaning. As *imputed* grace it covers the guilt of Adam's sin but *"in no way leads to faith"*; as *active* grace it becomes effective in "an existential encounter with Christ." This is a useful insight but it leaves unclear the relation between active grace and faith.

[18] *Works*, VI, 513; in VIII, 373, Wesley writes, "For the preventing grace of God, which is common to all, is sufficient to bring us to Christ, though it is not sufficient to carry us any further till we are justified." Hoon, "The Soteriology of John Wesley," p. 102, observes, "In order to magnify the power and love of God, to exalt the merits of Christ and to humble man, Wesley yields to his Calvinist leanings in so far as to insist that in salvation God is everything, man is nothing. On the other hand, in order to place a responsibility on man, to make him aware of the state of crisis he is in, he allows that man can and must work together with God." And Starkey, *The Work of the Holy Spirit*, p. 122, suggests that Wesley's assertion of human responsibility grounded in grace enables him to escape the errors both of Lutheran antinomianism and of Catholic justification by works.

most prevalent position affirms that on the basis of prevenient grace man is able to will God—or at least offer repentance, if not faith, toward his justification. Man shares responsibility in his own salvation, not by nature, but by grace. Or, more subtly, because it lies within man's power to make of non-effect the prevenient grace with which he has been endowed, it is said that man has a positive role in salvation as he chooses not to resist. Thus there is in Wesley a genuine synergism, or perhaps better, with Starkey, an "evangelical" synergism, in which man's reponse is based on prior grace.[19]

However, this "solution" may well attribute more to man than does Wesley, who is understood here to say that, even on the basis of prevenient grace, man cannot will God or take the decisive step toward salvation. In justification, man is passive. He is not saved until he despairs completely of his own efforts toward salvation and relies wholly on God's grace. As he ceases to resist, God is able to have sway. No longer depending on himself, he is set free to depend on God. Thus the purpose of prevenient grace is not to enable man to will God; rather it is to produce a radical self-knowledge, a conviction of sin and helplessness, which drives him to despair so that God can have full course in his life. To use Cushman's phrase, "the inactivation of the will through despair" is the secret of it all.[20] For Wesley, this is the essence of repentance,

[19] Starkey's section on "The Holy Spirit and the Human Will: Evangelical Synergism (Co-Operation)," *The Work of the Holy Spirit*, pp. 116-23, makes clear that Wesley's synergism is based on grace and asks, "Can we not say that the Wesleyan position supersedes the synergistic controversies of the past in the recognition that *both* God *and* man work under the ultimate aegis of God's redemptive purpose and will" (pp. 122 f.). Throughout his study, however, Starkey holds to the term "evangelical synergism." For a detailed presentation of synergism in Wesley see Cannon, *The Theology of John Wesley*, chap. V; compare Umphrey Lee, *John Wesley and Modern Religion*, pp. 161-73; S. Paul Schilling, *Methodism and Society in Theological Perspective*, pp. 50-52; Lindström, *Wesley and Sanctification*, pp. 93, 214; and Maximin Piette, *John Wesley in the Evolution of Protestantism*, p. 362.

[20] Robert E. Cushman, "Salvation for all: Wesley and Calvinism," in *Methodism*, ed. William K. Anderson, p. 114. Cushman elaborates, "Freedom from the will to evil can never be effected by the operation of that will. . . . The will must die, subsiding in the despair of exhaustion" (p. 115). "Despair is the neutralization of man's perverse volition wherewith human causality ceases to resist so that divine causality

through which, by the sole grace of God, man is brought to salvation. In their traditional signification, the terms "synergism" and "monergism" do not touch Wesley. This is in part his lasting contribution to the theological understanding of the religious life.

For Wesley, works meet for repentance are proximate causes, not the necessary cause of justification. Saving faith does not necessarily accompany repentance. Man's importunity does not command God. Both the "what" and the "when" of the bestowal of grace are in God's hands. "Sooner or later the power of the Lord will be present," Wesley writes, to impart faith and justification. A person may continue in the throes of despair "till God, in the manner that pleases Him" gives answer to his plea.[21] The uncontrolled, unpredictable, sovereign character of grace is to be noted

---

effectually can begin to operate" (p. 108). The inactivation of the will through despair "is not the work of man, but the death of man's working. In the last resort Wesley is not a predestinarian because he rejects the practically absolute disjunction between nature and grace—that philosophical and theological ineptitude of the Reformation" (p. 115). "The decisive difference between Wesley and the Calvinists is that he viewed the process of faith from an empirical vantage point as well as from a speculative one; they from a predominantly scholastic and rationalistic one" (p. 105). Cell, *The Rediscovery of John Wesley*, p. 251, argues that freedom in Wesley's theology is never used "to refute or to compromise or to qualify the early Reformation doctrine of saving faith." For Wesley, "monergism means that there is no energy of moral goodness in man outside our total dependence on God" (p. 257). "The Wesleyan doctrine of saving faith . . . is a complete renewal of the Luther-Calvin thesis that in the thought of salvation God is everything, man is nothing" (p. 271). See also Shipley, "Methodist Arminianism," pp. 277 f., who describes man's concurrence with initial redemptive grace (prevenient grace), in repentance and faith, as an "absence of opposition"; and pp. 184, 218-23. Hildebrandt also supports a monergistic interpretation of Wesley. "The humanist among the Reformers could not help inquiring into the measure of freedom which is left to human will and reason in man's response to God. . . . Such subtle 'synergism' had to be firmly and finally banished from the Lutheran book of Confessions. But it is not quite so commonly recognized that it is equally alien to Wesley. His 'Arminianism' rightly defies the Calvinist errors on predestination; with the *liberum arbitrium* of Erasmus or even of Melanchthon it has nothing whatever to do" (*From Luther to Wesley*, p. 173; see also section on "The Edge of Calvinism," pp. 91-99).

[21] *Letters*, VII, 202; *Sermons*, I, 258. Shipley notes that though man believes, and receives God in faith, he does not command God—in "Methodist Arminianism," p. 115. Hoon, "The Soteriology of John Wesley," p. 88, writes that for Wesley grace is all-powerful but not irresistible; there is irreconcilable variation in its operation. See also *Works*, VI, 280; *Sermons*, I, 185; II, 52; *Letters*, IV, 32, 321; VII, 202, 298.

throughout Wesley's writings. After prevenient grace has produced the despair which neutralizes man's perverse volition, it is God's good pleasure to will and to do. Easy assurances about the simplicity of the road to salvation are alien to Wesley. He knows too much about the soul's agonizing struggle with God to speak about it with the bland confidence characteristic of some of his successors.

Justifying Grace

For Wesley, as for the Reformers, Augustine and St. Paul, there is no doctrine of grace side by side with other doctrines. The doctrine of the grace of God in Jesus Christ is identical with the whole of the gospel of salvation. Grace is not impersonal or objectively mediated by sacramental hierarchies. It is God in action, giving "nothing apart from himself." [22] Grace is the disposition of God to pardon and reconcile men in spite of their sin, to declare them just and no longer subject to wrath and punishment. It is also an immanent, subjective healing and empowering work of God in the soul, which stems from divine love applied by the working of the Spirit. Grace for Wesley is both pardon of the guilt of sin by the transcendent favor of God and power to conquer the depravity of sin by the immanent working of the Holy Spirit. The two foci of salvation, justification and sanctification, are rooted in Wesley's understanding of this dual character of God's disposition toward man and reflect his understanding of sin as involving both guilt and depravity.[23] The entire work of God, salvation is by

[22] H. L. Goudge, "Some Notes on Grace," in *The Doctrine of Grace,* ed. W. T. Whitley, p. 323; N. P. Williams, *The Grace of God* (New York: Longmans, Green and Co., 1930), pp. 22 f. E. Dale Dunlap, "Methodist Theology in Great Britain," p. 38, contends that in the Wesleyan tradition, "strictly speaking, one does not speak of the grace of God; grace is God in the soul of men. Grace is thus not something mediated by 'means' apart from itself."

[23] See *Works,* VI, 509: "By justification we are saved from the guilt of sin, and restored to the favour of God; by sanctification we are saved from the power and root of sin, and restored to the image of God." "The people called Methodists take care not to put asunder what God has joined together . . . the doctrine of free, full, present justification, on the one hand, and of entire sanctification both of heart and life, on the other; being as tenacious of inward holiness as any Mystic, and of outward

grace alone. From Aldersgate to the end, Wesley affirms this key-note of the Reformation.

Man receives God's grace through faith, which is itself a gift. If faith were man's own work, he would trust himself rather than Christ and think himself "to be justified by some act or virtue that is within" his power. But "true and living faith in the merits of Jesus Christ" is a gift of grace, conveyed by the Holy Spirit.[24] It is a restoration of man's spiritual senses enabling him to see the things of God and be convinced by their evidence. "Faith is that divine evidence whereby the spiritual man discerneth God." It implies "a kind of spiritual *light* exhibited to the soul and a super-natural *sight* or perception thereof." [25] Faith is also "a sure trust and confidence in God," a reliance upon the merits of Christ. It means to renounce all merit in self and accept God's mercy mani-fest in him. In faith, the work of Christ becomes direct and per-sonal; the sinner sees that Christ died for him.[26]

Through such faith man is justified, his sins are pardoned, and he is restored to God's favor. This for Wesley is the plain, adequate account of justification. Man is not made righteous in justification; it is the forensic act whereby guilt is canceled. Justification is most certainly not for those who have become righteous; it is for sinners who seek righteousness. Man cannot earn it or achieve it. Justifica-tion is the free gift of God, as he pardons man's sin and accepts him as though righteous for Christ's sake.

Sanctifying Grace

Wesley denies that the imputation of Christ's righteousness through faith actually makes the sinner righteous. Christ is not

---

as any Pharisee" (*ibid.*, VII, 205). See also *Sermons*, I, 41-45; II, 226 f. Starkey care-fully summarizes the twofold character of grace in Wesley's thought, *The Work of the Holy Spirit*, pp. 34-37, as does Shipley, "Methodist Arminianism," pp. 398-405.

[24] *Works*, VIII, 361, 362; *Notes*, Ro. 4:5, and John 6:44; *Letters*, I, 239; II, 46; IV, 110, 220.

[25] *Works*, VIII, 4; *Sermons*, II, 448.

[26] *Sermons*, I, 284 f. Perhaps the essence of Wesley's Aldersgate experience is to be found in this new dimension of faith: "I felt I did trust in Christ, Christ alone for salvation; and an assurance was given me that He had taken away my sins, even mine, and saved me from the law of sin and death" (*Journal*, I, 476).

righteous in our stead but provides the ground whereby we may become righteous under the power of the divine Spirit.[27] According to Wesley, we are forgiven because of what Christ has done *for* us; at the same time we are made holy for what Christ through the Spirit does *in* us. Thus, we see that grace is both *pardon* and *power*.

Not to be distinguished in time from justification is the work of grace in sanctification (regeneration, or the new birth). In the same act of faith, man is not simply declared righteous (free from guilt and condemnation) but made righteous, that is, renewed in the image of God. Often interpreters of Wesley take sanctification to be the determining aspect of his entire theology.[28] It scarcely can be denied that Wesley drew on Catholic sources for his understanding of the life of God in the soul of man, that he placed great stress on the life of holiness, and that he felt commissioned to spread scriptural holiness throughout the land. But Williams' contention holds: Little illumination is given to Wesley's mature thought by the assertion that to a Protestant understanding of salvation he joined a Catholic emphasis on character and works. Wesley's Catholic concern for morality and perfection is always in process of conversion by his Protestant understanding of grace. The remark-

[27] See *Works*, VIII, 49: "As all merit is in the Son of God, in what he has done and suffered for us, so all power is in the Spirit of God. And therefore, every man, in order to believe unto salvation, must receive the Holy Ghost." See also the sermon on "The Lord Our Righteousness," *Sermons*, II, 423 ff.

[28] Thus Lindström's excellent study, *Wesley and Sanctification*. See his review of the literature on this subject, *ibid.*, pp. 7-16, in which he finds that interpreters who stress Wesley's Arminianism tend to accentuate his conception of sanctification—Leger, Piette, Rattenbury, Petri, Lee, and, of course, Lindström himself. It is instructive to note that more recent studies of Wesley's theology tend to find a dual stress on justification and sanctification (Williams), or find an underlying unity lodged in the doctrines of the Holy Spirit (Starkey) or Christ (Deschner). Hildebrandt, *From Luther to Wesley*, p. 24, acknowledges that "it is probably correct to say with Lindström that the central place which justification holds in the teaching of Luther is for Wesley occupied by sanctification." But, he warns, "it is well not to exaggerate what is essentially a mere difference of approach," and not to "divide the Gospel against itself and by one part of it to overthrow the other." See Wesley's sermon "Satan's Devices," *Sermons*, I, 199; also *Letters*, VII, 55: "How admirably pardon and holiness are comprised in that one word 'grace'! Mercy and Strength! So are our justification and sanctification woven together."

able thing is how consistently his stress on grace prevails at every critical turn.[29]

Thus the new birth, regeneration, sanctification, entire sanctification, Christian perfection all have this in common—they are the fruit of faith, the product of God's love, depending fully on the atonement for their appearance, continuation, and fulfillment.[30] "Scriptural holiness" is in fact a primary Wesleyan concern. The adjective points to the source of power and to the manner in which holiness is accomplished—the grace of God freely and fully given through the scriptural scheme of salvation. Only on this basis does Wesley's insistence on entire sanctification and perfection cohere with his total position. Holiness is not a moral achievement; righteousness must be ascribed to God, not man. And, because arbitrary limits to God's grace cannot be set, entire sanctification is possible both in this life and before the hour of death. Thus still another predicate of free grace is the fullness or completeness of its operation.[31]

In the new birth, the power of sin is broken. Though sin continues, it does not reign. Its presence requires "evangelical repentance" and further faith. Progress in sanctification is dependent on the receptivity of faith to further gifts of grace. But entire sanctification, the end toward which salvation moves, is not the end product of progressive sanctification nor is it produced by human striving. It results from a further act of faith, freely given. Thus in all its stages, sanctification is never a static possession; rather it is

[29] Williams, *John Wesley's Theology Today*, pp. 174-76; see also Deschner, *Wesley's Christology*, pp. 197 f.

[30] *Works*, VII, 41: "Whoever improves the grace he has already received . . . will surely retain it. God will continue, yea, will give it more abundantly: Whereas, whoever does not improve this talent, cannot possibly retain it. Notwithstanding all he can do, it will infallibly be taken from him." See also XI, 380; *Notes*, John 3:3, Acts 2:19, Ro. 2:9.

[31] Starkey, *The Work of the Holy Spirit*, p. 162: "John Wesley's understanding of the Christian life in terms of God's possibilities rather than man's incapacities, of God's promises rather than man's fears, of God's victorious presence here and now in the Holy Spirit for guidance, comfort and strength, rather than in some future age; needs to be reasserted today." John Peters, *Christian Perfection and American Methodism*, p. 185, enters the reminder: "Realistic as Wesley was in his estimate of the nature of man, he nevertheless refused the arbitrary dictum that the grace of God can go only so far and no farther in its redemptive efficacy."

maintained moment by moment in a personal relationship between God and man. "We feel the power of Christ every moment resting upon us, whereby we are enabled to continue in spiritual life and without which, notwithstanding all our present holiness, we should be devils the next moment." [32]

At the end of life man is rewarded according to the works of faith. "God hath joined from the beginning, pardon, holiness and heaven"—all is of grace from end to end.[33] The initiative rests with God; at every stage in the order of salvation the effective agent is his grace. Salvation is never conceived of in a mechanical or impersonal way, however. The Spirit of God is breathed into each life, which, to retain the Spirit, must breathe it back to God in prayer and praise and service.

In summary, "free grace," as an interpretative key to Wesley's theology, has the following distinguishable characteristics. (1) Grace is a gift—grounded in God's free act in Christ. (2) Grace is free for all—the atonement contains a universal invitation. (3) Grace is free in all—prevenient goodness leads and strengthens every man. (4) Grace is free in salvation—independently of any merit or work, man is saved by grace through faith. (5) Grace is free to accomplish full salvation—consummated in entire sanctification and Christian perfection. While Wesley did not explicate the dimensions of free grace in exactly these terms, doing so inflicts no violence on his understanding of salvation. It will prove illuminating to observe how these characteristics are treated by his heirs.

[32] *Sermons*, II, 393; I, 95, 292; II, 217, 235, 382. See Hildebrandt's contention, *From Luther to Wesley*, pp. 182-95, that perfection is by grace alone—it is not man's achievement, but Christ's gift, continuously bestowed; and Peters, *Christian Perfection and American Methodism*, pp. 181-88, and 218, where he states that Asbury, like Wesley and Fletcher, considered perfection a day-to-day gift: "He never measured today's possession by yesterday's experience. . . . One day's profession, therefore, became the next day's petition. It was not vacillation but aspiration." And *Letters*, V, 26, 69, 138, 188; VI, 91, 241, 339.

[33] *Sermons*, II, 202; *Works*, X, 307, 320, 388, 431, 444; *Notes*, Matt. 12:37, Ro. 2:11, I Cor. 1:7, Heb. 4:2; Shipley, "Methodist Arminianism," pp. 259-68; Deschner, *Wesley's Christology*, 177-86.

WATSON ON "THE ATONEMENT
AND ITS BENEFITS"

From Richard Watson's writings, impressive support can be derived for the claim that the atonement of Christ is the central doctrine of Wesleyan theology.[84] Its formal treatment occupies nearly one-fifth of the *Institutes*, and the discussion of its extent receives more space than any other theological issue. If this prominence reflects Wesley's own view, it reflects also the apologetic demands which Watson faced. He is more concerned to refute the denial of the atonement by the Socinians and its limitations by the Calvinists than he is to set forth systematically and clearly his own position. But he leaves no doubt about the benefits derived from the atonement. Explicitly he makes God's work through Christ central, preeminently so in justification, sanctification, and eternal life. His doctrine of grace enables him to affirm that the man who is depraved and bound in sin is also responsible for accepting or rejecting God's offer of salvation. Beneath his apologetic concerns for the doctrine of grace, Watson is essentially true to Wesley.

Universal Atonement

Richard Watson's views on the nature of the atonement are commented on by John Miley, who observes, "We cannot accord to him any very clear view."[85] What then distresses Miley is Watson's failure to provide a clear and steady assertion of the rectoral or moral government theory of the atonement, and his

[84] Dunlap, "Methodist Theology in Great Britain," p. 100, observes that the entire theological enterprise of early Methodists "was motivated by an evangelical zeal. The salvation of souls was their passion, and salvation rooted firmly in the reality and efficacy of the Atonement. The Atonement was the heart of their theology; it was the theme of their preaching; and it was the practical ground of their Christian living and hope of glory"; and see also pp. 214 f. See Outler, "Lecture in Methodist Polity," at Yale, 1951, pp. 4-7; Deschner, *Wesley's Christology*, pp. 3-5; and Watson, *Sermons*, I, 348: "The death of Christ, as an expiatory sacrifice, is the glory of the true Christian." It is "the keystone of the Christian arch; and it therefore becomes us to hold it in its place."

[85] Miley, *Systematic Theology*, II, 166.

frequent lapse into variants of the satisfaction theory. Miley's bias prevents him from seeing that the satisfaction, not the governmental theory, has priority in Watson.

Watson sets the atonement in the context of God's moral government, which presupposes, first, a divine law, directing man to his true end (compliance with the will of God) and, second, human freedom (enabling man to follow or disobey its injunctions). God sought to prevent man's violation of the law by supplying motives to obedience, the most severe being the penalty of death. As man falls into sin, he is deflected from his true end and subjected to this penalty. Though mercifully unwilling that man should perish, to sustain his justice God must uphold the moral government by punishing sin (II, 91–94).

God has provided the ground for man's restoration. Christ becomes the provisional substitute for the penalty due man's transgression. Words used to describe this transaction, such as "propitiation," "reconciliation," and "redemption," indicate that there is a mutual hostility between God and man, that God's anger must be turned aside or atoned, and that, to this end, a "ransom or redemption price" had to be "exacted" and "paid" (II, 123). Thus Watson stresses the objective bearing of the atonement on God's justice and the authority of the divine law. In the face of the violation of the law, Watson sees the alternatives as the disruption of moral government, the personal punishment of every offender, or the "acceptance of the vicarious death of an infinitely dignified and glorious being, through whom pardon should be offered, and in whose hands a process for the moral restoration of the lapsed should be placed" (II, 139). In this view of the atonement there is no major departure from Wesley.

Watson is also true to his heritage when he insists that Christ's active righteousness does not relieve man of the necessity of obedience to the law (by the imputation or substitution of Christ's acts for man's) (II, 140 f.). Again, with Wesley, he denies that in the atonement the punishment of the guilty was unjustly laid upon the innocent. In his vicarious suffering, Christ was a willing substitute for condemned and helpless man.[36]

To whom is Christ's work available? Watson gives this question extensive consideration. He affirms the universality of Christ's offer and seeks to refute every Calvinist contention in favor of its limitation. His appeal is chiefly to the Scriptures, which "manifestly assert" that Christ died "for the sins of the whole world." There is no "text whatever to be adduced, which declares as literally, that Christ *did not* die for the salvation of all, as those which declare that he did so die" (II, 288 f.). Properly understood, he argues, the scriptural terms used by Calvinism—election, calling, foreknowledge—support the universality, not the restriction, of God's offer of salvation (II, 289–361). Thus, for nearly two hundred pages in the *Institutes* Watson contends for the universality of God's offer of grace.

Watson gives even greater prominence to the universality of the atonement than did Wesley, who appealed to man's freedom restored by prevenient grace as well as to the universality of Christ's work. Though Watson gives prevenient grace less significance, by no means does he ignore it.

Grace and Freedom

Certain general benefits of the atonement are conferred by the Spirit on all men without their desire and without exception. This divine influence, or prevenient grace, is the ground of all dispensations of general and particular providence and the so-called "natural virtues." It checks the folly of unregenerate men; it visits sinners and often improves their lives. It kept Adam from suffering immediate death and enables men to avoid the penalty of bodily death in immediate consequence of their sins. It insures persons dying in infancy against eternal damnation. It is the foundation of

[36] *Sermons*, II, 180, 190-99; I, 332-37; *Works*, VIII, 428 ff., 538 ff. Compare Dunlap, "Methodist Theology in Great Britain," pp. 108-10, who says that Watson followed Anselm, stressing the substitutionary sacrificial death of Christ; the "crucial part of the Atonement, is the expiation of human sin."

man's restored freedom, enabling him, despite his corrupt state, to accept or reject the offer of salvation.[37]

To understand Watson, as well as Wesleyan theology generally, it is imperative to ascertain the way in which prevenient grace is related to that further grace which justifies and sanctifies. Methodists are one, and not different from Calvinists, says Watson, in asserting that fallen man is free only to sin. But that man can choose the good, under the gracious influence of God, is the view of Scripture, which in its "whole tenor" upholds the "doctrine of human accountability." [38] If prevenient grace is faithfully complied with, it may lead to that further grace which brings salvation. If it is resisted, the Spirit may be ultimately provoked so as to "withdraw his aid" and permit a lapse into a state even "more guilty and dangerous" (II, 87; I, 221).

Watson recognizes that at times grace is irresistible and that man is merely passive under its power. There is, then, some evidence for a doctrine of irresistible grace. The general influence of the Spirit (prevenient grace) is given to each man without his desire or seeking. Moreover, in the initial reception of saving grace, man is passive and God works without hindrance. But always, as in the case of Paul, a point is reached where "the irresistible influence is terminated and where [man's] own agency recommenced" (II, 448). In this assertion of man's passive reception of saving grace, Watson is not far from Wesley's deepest insight.[39]

More consistently, however, Watson contends that prevenient grace does not override man's freedom. It works by persuasion, not by coercion. Good desires, resolves, and aspirations, produced by the Spirit, may be resisted. Yet man has "the power of complying with them though still in the strength of grace which . . . neither wills nor acts for him, nor even by him as a passive instrument" (II, 448 f.). God gives the power which enables man to will the good, but he does not will for him. "The free use and application of this

---

[37] *Works*, VII, 227, 237, 346 f.; *Sermons*, I, 361, 415; II, 56 f., 87, 362 f.; also *Institutes*, II, 207, 83 ff.

[38] *Works*, VII, 255; *Sermons*, II, 110-12, 312-14.

[39] *Works*, V, 411 ff., 434 ff.; VI, 354; *Sermons*, II, 314, 418.

power is that which constitutes man accountable. . . . upon this hypothesis the sinner is no more the author of his own salvation, than the man's stretching out his withered hand at the command of Christ made him the author of his own cure." In a mysterious manner, God is able to combine his power with "the freedom of human agency, . . . without destroying its moral nature." Devout men will require no more of the resolution of the "disputed point of divine help and human agency"; this account is adequate "not philosophically, but authoritatively and practically." [40]

Man's efforts in the life of faith are not displaced by God's grace (I, 223). On the contrary, divine influence is the only true encouragement to effort, for without it "effort would be hopeless." With it, man works out his own salvation with fear and trembling. Prevenient grace does not lessen the alienation of sinful man from God, nor does its exercise count as merit in man's behalf. Through it, God strives with man in the midst of his guilt and depravity to bring him to repentance and faith. [41]

Therefore, freedom-in-grace stands as a bulwark against Calvinism. It is the foundation of the conditional factor in salvation to which the Scriptures and experience abundantly attest. It preserves the righteous character of God, upholds the necessity and efficacy of the work of Christ, and makes men capable and accountable in salvation. At the same time, it denies all merit to man and makes salvation entirely a matter of grace freely given. In his affirmation of human freedom based on the grace of the atonement, Watson sounds a genuine Wesleyan note.

Though prevenient grace is more often identified by Watson as the "influence of the Spirit," no departure from Wesley's basic conviction is represented by this change. However, the provision of light and sight for things spiritual by prevenient grace is not as prominent as in Wesley. And, while prevenient grace has sub-

---

[40] *Sermons*, II, 112; I, 392; II, 128. Dunlap, "Methodist Theology in Great Britain," p. 151 n., contends that "cooperant" grace in Watson "rests on prevenient grace and is not to be misunderstood as Melanchthonian synergism."

[41] *Sermons*, I, 449, 140; II, 238; *Works*, VII, 253-55; *Conversations for the Young*, p. 239.

stantially the same meaning for both men, its appearances in Watson are less frequent, suggesting that it is less determinative for his theology as a whole. Closer study amply confirms this suggestion.[42]

Salvation by Grace

In the discussion of salvation proper, Watson is most faithful to his heritage. The first movement toward God in repentance stems from "the work of the Holy Spirit in the heart." Watson is regularly insistent that man cannot repent apart from the grace of God, yet holds also that repentance is not willed for him; it is not without his consent. The Spirit strives with man until, seeing his lost condition, in despair man cries out "for help from another." [43] But repentance is only preliminary to acceptance and cleansing. Forgiveness and new life, on the basis of repentance alone, would utterly subvert Christian salvation, for which faith is the one indispensable condition (II, 96-102).

Watson follows Wesley closely in his description of the nature of faith. Two elements are noted, "the first, that of assent or persuasion; the second, that of confidence or reliance" (II, 243). The first element becomes more rationalistic in Watson, for whom faith is an assent to the truths of revealed religion. But he adds that this act of the intellect must be supplemented by a work of the heart. "True faith, then, is a personal trust in the atonement of Christ, and in the promises of God . . . and if this faith is not added to our general belief in the truth of Christianity, the fault is in our

[42] Dunlap, "Methodist Theology in Great Britain," pp. 477 f., concludes that the theology of Watson and Clarke "does differ from that of Wesley" on the "crucial Wesleyan doctrine of prevenient grace. While it is true that the fact of prevenient grace is assumed, the taking of it for granted has the effect of rendering it less central than it was for Wesley. Related to, but more serious than this light treatment of prevenient grace is a distinct tendency on the part of both Clarke and Watson to shift the emphasis from prevenient to cooperant grace. This is seen in their larger stress on man's free will and his 'doing.' There is evidence of a subtle shift in emphasis from divine grace and initiative to the human agency and role in the economy of salvation. In neither man is this tendency pushed to the danger point, but it does open the door to Pelagianism, Socinianism, and a humanistic-moralistic perspective"; and see pp. 150 f.

[43] Works, VI, 346; see 339-46; Sermons, II, 356 f., 399, 409.

own hearts." [44] Faith is not a natural response of man to God but is intellectual assent applied by the Spirit to the heart and conscience. "The office of faith in justification," writes Watson, is one of "those points on which we have the greatest accordance" with the Calvinists.[45]

Based on faith, justification is the pardon and remission of sins by exemption from the penalty which they rightly entail. It is that "act of God by which he remits all past sin, receiving the sinner into his favour, and treating him as a just or a righteous man." [46] This understanding rules out the mistaken idea that in justification man is made just and righteous by the imputation of Christ's righteousness. The imputation of faith for righteousness means only that, through faith in Christ, man's offenses are pardoned and that he is restored to God's favor (II, 213–42). Thus Watson is fully consistent with Wesley. Together both lay the ax to the root from which stems antinomian unrighteousness.

Justification is pardon and acceptance, forgiveness and adoption (II, 212). It is a change of man's objective relation to God from that of a sinner to that of a son. The same act of faith which justifies also begins the renewal of man's inmost nature (II, 267). Justification takes away the guilt of sin and the penalty attached to it; regeneration marks the restoration of God's Spirit to man. The return of the Spirit breaks the hold of depravity and empowers man to live a life of progressive holiness. Regeneration is both deliverance from the bondage of sin and the power to do all things which are pleasing to God.[47] Obviously, such a re-creation of man's nature can be attributed only to God.

[44] *Sermons*, II, 387-90, 109; I, 120, 337; *Works*, V, 414.

[45] *Works*, VII, 195, 223 ff.

[46] *Sermons*, I, 289; *Conversations for the Young*, pp. 59, 231.

[47] Regeneration "is the mighty change in man, wrought by the Holy Spirit, by which the dominion which sin has over him in his natural state, and which he deplores and struggles against in his penitent state, is broken and abolished, so that, with full choice of will and the energy of right affections, he serves God freely" (*Institutes*, II, 267; see also *Sermons*, II, 33, 413 f.). Dunlap "Methodist Theology in Great Britain," p. 133, summarizes the meaning of the atonement for Watson and early Methodists thus: "The centrality of the Atonement for the Methodists lay not

Watson consistently recognizes that regeneration or the new birth only begins the process of sanctification. "The former corruptions of the heart may remain" but they are not man's "inward *habit*"; they now "have no *dominion*" (II, 269). The power of sin is broken though the root of sin remains. By a further work of God's grace, man is delivered "from all spiritual pollution, all inward depravation of the heart [and] indulgence of the senses" (II, 450). Sanctification is both a gradual process and the "fruit of an act of faith in the Divine promises" (II, 455). Both the process of growth and the instantaneous act are the work of grace received in faith.[48] Entire sanctification does not render the work of Christ of non-effect, for it proceeds from his work with the Spirit as its agent (II, 269, 456).

The end toward which salvation moves is eternal life. Those who accept Christ have the promise of the immediate reception of their souls into a state of blessedness, after death, until the general resurrection to eternal life (II, 457). That one who has been justified and sanctified should be brought to glory is the final gift of grace. Man is rewarded then only "secondarily and subordinately" for his works; the indispensable ground of his reward is the work of Christ which he has received by faith (II, 263 ff.).

MILEY ON THE DIVINE
ACTIVITY IN REDEMPTION

The changes in the doctrines of grace in nineteenth-century American Methodism are nowhere more clearly and systematically summed up than in John Miley's theology. Raymond and Ralston show considerable openness to the rectoral theory of the atonement;

---

in what it does to God, but what it does in man. The fundamental significance of the Atonement was not as it related to justification, but as it related to sanctification. The Atonement is relational—its end is the bringing of man back into his created filial relationship to God. It is itself that relationship. Its purpose is sanctification and perfection."

[48] In his study of Christian perfection, Peters, *Christian Perfection and American Methodism*, p. 109, concludes that Richard Watson, though he "does not deny the Wesleyan emphases," by his stress on the gradual tends "to merge sanctification with the doctrine of regeneration."

Whedon and Bledsoe, Raymond and Wakefield display the full range of Methodist innovations regarding man's moral agency; in nearly all Methodist theologians from 1840 to 1890 the treatments of justification and sanctification have basic identities. But in Miley all these developments meet and are logically related and consistently expressed. He is the last of the front-line Methodist theologians to endeavor consciously to hold to the Wesleyan-Arminian heritage and at the same time to maintain some rapport with the currents of a new age. In the end, his success in both endeavors proved to be limited.

"The Atonement in Christ"

- In 1879 Miley published *The Atonement in Christ*, his first book in systematic theology. It received widespread notice and was placed on the Course of Study in 1880 and in substance continued to 1908. Such was the consistency and comprehensiveness of his theology that this volume on Christology was fitted into his complete *Systematic Theology* with scarcely a change when the latter was published in 1894. Scott notes that Miley's study of the work of Christ "was to prove the most uniquely significant of any of his works." Summers, Tigert, and Kelley in the southern church, and Whedon, Warren, and Raymond in the north all responded to it. Some gave it wholehearted endorsement.[49] Others demurred, noting that his theory of the atonement "does leave us with the wish that it had a little more weight and content." [50]

Miley is greatly concerned for a logically consistent governmental theory of the atonement, which he contends is one of the significant developments in Methodist theological literature (II, 166–69). He is critical of the compromise of the atonement within Methodism and holds that only two theories are possible and that

[49] Scott, "Methodist Theology," pp. 426, 436, and Whedon, MQR, 62 (1880), 184.

[50] William Kelley, MQR, 76 (1894), 836; see also J. J. Tigert, MQRS, 40 (1894), 260; Henry C. Sheldon, A *System of Christian Doctrine*, p. 400. S. McChesney, in "The Methodist Doctrine of Atonement," MQR, 76 (1894), 268-73, levels a blast at Miley for deserting the satisfaction for the governmental theory of the atonement. He finds Watson to be much more normative for Methodism than Miley, that is, Arminian, and not Grotian.

they are mutually exclusive (II, 112). The necessity of the atonement must be located in God's governmental justice, not his commercial justice or personal wrath. Along with their primary satisfaction theories, even Watson and Summers hold that the righteousness of God is sustained by his attention to moral government.[51] But, continues Miley, in "consistent Arminianism" there is no place for penal satisfaction, and he proceeds to purge all its elements (II, 146–48).

The satisfaction theory rests on the necessity of penalty for sin, a penalty which man cannot pay. The theory depends on Christ's substituted punishment and substituted obedience (II, 134). As one of Miley's enthusiastic reviewers agreed, however, "If there be any such thing as a moral axiom, it is that guilt and penalty are untransferrable." [52] The satisfaction theory must be put aside in favor of one which finds the necessity of Christ's atonement in God's justice and concern for the welfare of human beings. There is in God no absolute justice which must punish sin, for his punitive disposition is counterbalanced by his loving compassion. Man must be punished, not because of the demerit of his sin, but in order to protect the rights and interests of others in the divine economy. In this way God reveals his "profound regard for the sacredness of his law, and for the interests which it conserves" (II, 180). The atonement of Christ meets all these ends: "The vicarious sufferings of Christ are an atonement for sin as a conditional substitute for penalty, fulfilling, on the forgiveness of sin, the obligation

[51] Sheldon observes, "Changes in Theology Among American Methodists," *American Journal of Theology*, 10 (1906), 41, "The established theory of Methodism was a moderate satisfaction theory—a theory which paid respects to the governmental bearing of Christ's work, but at the same time contended that in and through that work a tribute was rendered to the ethical nature of God, and not merely to the requirements of his governmental position." By the time of Miley, this theory had given way largely, though not entirely, to the governmental one. Compare Wade C. Barclay, *History of Methodist Missions*, Vol. III, *Widening Horizons, 1845-95*, p. 70; and Scott, "Methodist Theology," pp. 429-32.

[52] Whedon, MQR, 62 (1880), 185. In a review of Pope's systematics, MQR, 59 (1877), 406-9, Miley takes Pope to task for overstressing elements of satisfaction in the atonement because they compromise the free personal character of guilt and righteousness.

of justice and the office of penalty in moral government" (II, 68).

In Miley there is a decided weakening of the demands of the divine holiness and justice as seen in Wesley and, to a lesser extent, in Watson. Miley restricts the categories which he applies to the God-man relation: first, by his stress on an extremely individualistic conception of moral responsibility; second, by his contention that the necessity of the atonement is rooted solely in the requirements of moral government; and third, by his insistence that there are only two doctrines of the atonement possible, depending on which view of justice is stressed.[53] There is warrant for suggesting that Miley purchases consistency at the price of obscuring and rejecting some of the deeper realities of Christ's work which his more "inconsistent" Wesleyan predecessors had retained. His theory makes logical sense, but it fails to probe deeply into the relation between man's sin and bondage and God's righteousness and mercy.

In keeping with the broad Methodist tradition, Miley asserts that the atonement is universal in extent, revealing both the true sovereignty of God and the state of evil and need common to all men (II, 193, 217–39). Not simply the justice of God but also his holiness, wisdom, and goodness require that the atonement be extended to the "uttermost circle of humanity" (II, 224). However, universal atonement receives far less stress in Miley than it had received in Watson. This change in accent reflects both growing Calvinist concessions to general election and a shift in the basic issue with them from the extent of the atonement to the freedom of the will.

Miley is carefully explicit in his discussion of the benefits of the atonement. Its *immediate* benefits accrue to all men without any condition. They are prior and preparatory to actual salvation. Here Miley faithfully articulates the Wesleyan tradition as he lists four immediate, unconditional benefits of the atonement: the fact of present life, which would have ceased under the law of Adam's punishment; gracious help for all evidenced by the moral and re-

[53] Scott, "Methodist Theology," pp. 434 f.

ligious tendencies among unconverted men; provision of a capacity for probation; and the salvation of infants, who, though born in depravity, at death are spiritually regenerated through Christ to salvation (II, 242–48).

A second group of *conditional* benefits—which constitute and help realize actual salvation—are attainable only on specified and appropriate action. Salvation is "not an immediate benefit of the atonement, nor through an irresistible operation of divine grace, but is attainable only on a compliance with its appropriate terms" (II, 249). The great facts of salvation are each of them conditional: justification, faith, regeneration, perseverance, and future blessedness. Each is conditioned by man's free personal action. As a consequence of these convictions Miley must face the problem common to Wesleyan soteriology—how to relate man's free personal agency, an immediate unconditional benefit of the atonement, to God's conditional offer of salvation mediated through faith in Christ (II, 252 f.).

Gracious Motives Freely Chosen

As Miley sees it, the logical alternative to Arminianism—making man's free personal response a condition to salvation—is the system of Calvinism (II, 254). Therefore, man's freedom to choose salvation is the "profoundest question of psychology," of "supreme importance" in ethics, and "the cardinal question" in theology (II, 274, 283). In Miley's systematics, the chapter on "Freedom of Choice" stands between chapters on the general benefits of the atonement and justification by faith. Methodologically, as well as doctrinally, he makes freedom of choice decisive. It is for him the most fundamental principle of Arminianism and "chiefly determines the cast of our doctrinal system" (II, 275; I, 523).

Miley follows Whedon rather closely in his discussion of freedom. Both men stress the axiomatic principle that ability is essential to responsibility, a principle which they find confirmed by the universal intuitions of the moral sense. In this the influence of common-sense philosophy is clearly evident. However, Miley introduces greater emphasis on the rational character of choice.[54] Freedom has to do with the power of rational self-action. A psychological analysis of choice discloses four elements: an end, a motive, a judgment, and an elective decision. In choosing, the rational agent reflects on ends and motives, weighs them in judgment, and then, in elective decision, determines his action with respect to the ends (II, 286). A particular end is chosen for a reason mentally apprehended and approved—the motive of the choice. Without a motive, choice would be capricious, that is, without any "reason" (II, 288).

Further, the mind must have occasion to deliberate on the motives presented to it. If there is no place for reflection and judgment between the motive impulse and the volition which it determines, there is no place for rational life. But such reflection and deliberation are possible, says Miley, through a "rational suspension of choice," enabling the mind to consider the motives, and the ends to which they are related, and then to form a judgment concerning them (II, 291–96). As the personal agent brings to mind the end of a motive or dismisses it, he controls the motive state connected with that end. Thus he has power over motives and can judge whether or not they will condition his choice.[55]

Sufficient motives are required if choices are to be truly free. Since Miley approves a doctrine of native depravity, which asserts

[54] See above, chapter II, and Scott, "Methodist Theology," p. 619, Appendix 18, "Whedon: The Self-Conscious Reality of the Will's 'Alternative Freedom.'" The concerns of both Miley and Whedon are evident in Bledsoe's earlier work, *Theodicy*, p. 131, in which he criticizes all schemes of necessity as void of moral character: "Virtue and vice lie not in the passive state of the sensibility, nor in any other necessitated states of the mind, but in acts of the will and in habits formed by a repetition of such free voluntary acts."

[55] See *Systematic Theology*, II, 301 f.: "Over the impulsions of appetite and passion we may enthrone the rational and the moral. . . . We are not helplessly passive under any one spontaneous impulse or any stronger or strongest impulse in the coincidence of two or more of opposite tendency. We have no immediate power of volition to prevent or repress such a motive state; but we have immediate power to defer any volition or deed toward its end. Then through reflection and judgment we may realize the motives of reason and conscience, and direct our life from them." Scott, "Methodist Theology," p. 459, relates the rational suspension of choice in Miley to its antecedents in Bangs, Fisk, Shinn, and Whedon.

that good motives cannot arise from a corrupt source, he must somehow account for the existence of moral and religious motives. To do so, he invokes the doctrine of prevenient grace. Motives to the good are graciously granted fallen humanity through the universal atonement of Christ. Yet, having traced these motives to God's grace, Miley adds equivocally that "for the question of moral freedom, it is indifferent whether this capacity be native or gracious. For the consistency of Scripture truth it must have a gracious original" (II, 304). Thus, the deep sense of gratitude for God's gift, characteristic of Wesley and not lacking in Watson, is seriously compromised in Miley. The testimony of faith to prevenient grace is overshadowed by a predilection for moral intuitions of responsibility. Rather than experiential conviction, deference to Scripture appears to prompt Miley's formal allegiance to this basic Wesleyan tenet.

Miley argues further that moral and religious motives, based on grace, are subject to the command of a rational agent just as are all other motives. But this power to command is alleged to be a gracious endowment itself. The Spirit is a constant aid in the choice of motives to the good, "often active as a light in the moral reason and a quickening force in the conscience" (II, 305). However, the choice of the good and the attainment of the good are two separate and distinct facts. It is through the help of divine grace and a proper use of man's spiritual agency that such a choice can be made—this is the sphere of synergism. The realization of the new life that is chosen can be effected only through the work of the divine Spirit—this is the sphere of strict monergism (II, 336).

In Miley, freedom becomes a distinct doctrine, which he discusses systematically as the point of contact between the atonement and justification. Ostensibly freedom is set in a context of grace; God supplies spiritual motives which make possible the choice of the good. However, even in depraved man, personal agency can choose freely among the motive objects presented to it.[56] Essential to the exercise of this agency is the "rational suspension of choice," a conviction of Miley's which places high premium on rationality (II, 291–96). He ascribes even greater power to rationality in his assumption that motives come and go as the ends to which they are related are approved or dismissed by the mind. Such facile control of the non-rational side of man does scant justice to the reality of sin and belies the testimony both of Scripture and of the Wesleyan heritage. Miley's view is consistent with his episte-mology, his doctrine of sin, and his allegiance to immediate moral intuitions of free agency and responsibility. But the consistency may be too dearly won.

As the source of good motives, prevenient grace is given a limited place, but almost incidentally, as a reflective consideration. Grace can be so lightly taken only where sin has failed to receive its due. Surely such is the case when the basic defect of personal agency is located in the lack of moral and religious motives. Miley struggles to formulate an Arminian doctrine of freedom-in-grace to mediate between man's depravity and his responsiveness. But his careful work achieved limited success. Practically, it left man's personal agency free and unimpaired. Historically, the refinement about gracious motives was easily put aside. Realistically, the propensity

[56] See *Systematic Theology*, II, 306 f.: Rational freedom "is the freedom of personal agency, with power for required choices. It is sufficient for the sphere of our responsible life. Spontaneous impulses often tend toward the irrational and the evil, and the more strongly in many instances from previous vicious indulgence; but as rational and moral agents we have a gracious power against them. We can summon into thought and reflection, and into the apprehension of conscience and the moral reason, all the counter motives of obligation and spiritual well-being as they may arise in the view of God and redemption and the eternal destinies. With these resources of paramount motive, and the light and blessing of the Holy Spirit, ever gracious and helpful, we may freely choose the good against the evil. This is the reality of freedom in choice." Kelley, *MQR*, 76 (1894), 837, enthusiastically endorses Miley's "really great chapter on man's 'Freedom of Choice.'" Miner Raymond, *Systematic Theology*, II, 316, has substantially the same view of freedom; compare Scott, "Methodist Theology," p. 311. Even the generally more orthodox Pope in his *Compendium of Christian Theology*, II, 364, denies that prevenient grace is needed to "restore to the faculty of will its power of originating action: that has never been lost. But it is needed to suggest to the intellect the truth on which religion rests and to sway the affections of hope and fear by enlisting the heart on the side of that truth."

of reason to choose the better part, once known, could not be sustained.

Justification and Regeneration

For Miley, man's participation conditions each of the great facts of salvation; at the same time each is "entirely from the divine Spirit." In the work of moral regeneration, God operates according to the "doctrine of the most rigid monergist" (II, 305). When he comes to discuss justification, faith, regeneration, and sanctification, however, Miley is hard pressed to demonstrate his claim to strict monergism.

In Wesleyan fashion, he interprets justification as pardon or forgiveness of sins. It removes man's amenability to punishment on the ground that Christ suffered provisionally in his stead, thereby upholding the interests of God's moral government and making forgiveness possible on the condition of faith in him (II, 309, 317). But justification cares solely for the guilt of man's own sins; its bearing on the guilt of Adam's sin is explicitly denied (II, 316). Thus, rooted only in the need for governmental justice, and applied only to actual sins, forgiveness in Christ becomes more mechanical and less exacting than it was in Wesley.[57]

The understanding of faith is also subject to revision. Faith for Miley requires a "mental apprehension" whose "truth must have a ground in evidence" (II, 321). Contrary to the Wesleyan stress on the necessity for a gracious restoration of spiritual senses, divine truth here commends itself to man's natural reason. God's objective truth includes the promise of needed help and an assurance that

[57] Shipley, in "Theology of American Methodism," p. 262, appraises Miley thus: His "moralistic revisionism of the doctrine of salvation and the analysis of the human predicament is far too shallow and psychologically inadequate—if not contradictory—to retain a place as a creative contribution to theology." It led "to the necessity of revising the Methodist emphases in the doctrine of the atonement toward a morally rationalistic construct [in which] the meaning of the Incarnation and the saving work of Christ has to do primarily with enhancing the good motives amenable to unimpaired human free will, and thus actualizing divine moral government essentially through man's rationalistic choice of the good."

this promise is trustworthy. Thus, on the basis of evidence centered in Christ, man believes.

Faith also presupposes a "true state of repentance . . . because only in such a mental state can the proper faith be exercised" (II, 323). Repentance is one of the "requirements of our own agency," though it requires divine assistance (II, 102). Though faith is held to be the one condition of justification, yet repentance is "always presupposed" (II, 323). Thus, to repentance Miley imputes a necessity which Wesley refused. Further, Miley specifically denies "the view that faith is itself the gift of God"; rather its interpretation "must accord with the nature of faith as a free personal act" (II, 252). Usually he remembers to add that this personal agency rests on gracious influences, but, both in repentance and in faith, he stresses man's contributing capacity.

In several places Miley affirms that regeneration is the sphere of "strict monergism." However, as it is dependent on the same act of faith as is justification, it too is conditioned by man's free personal agency. Only after regeneration has been elected does its realization come entirely from God (II, 305, 336). But surely this view of "strict monergism" has little support in the history of Christian thought.[58] Nor does Miley's discussion of sanctification strengthen his case. Wesley's stress on sanctification as a moment-by-moment relation, sustained in faith, does not appear. Sanctification is attributed to the Spirit, which progressively subdues man's depravity, but scant mention is made of faith as the means whereby the Spirit is received. Entire sanctification, understood as a "second blessing," dependent on a decisive act of faith, is largely denied in favor of the progressive realization of regeneration (II, 362–71). Though Wesleyan motifs are generally present in this statement of sanctification, their basic orientation has been modified.[59]

[58] Raymond's view of regeneration, *Systematic Theology*, II, 355, 358, is basically the same as Miley's but he identifies it more accurately. "The work of regeneration," he says, "is synergistic and not monergistic, as is affirmed by the Augustinian anthropology."

[59] Peters, *Christian Perfection and American Methodism*, pp. 159-61. Miley writes, *Systematic Theology*, II, 365, "The reality of sanctification concerns us far more deeply

Lastly, Miley views final blessedness as conditional; there can be no "faithfulness unto death, without free personal action" (II, 253). However, neither the spirituality of man's mind nor the merit of his works ensures eternal salvation. Man is wholly dependent on God and finds "no immortality without his pleasure" (II, 427).

Miley seems determined to have the best of two worlds—that of Wesleyan evangelicalism and that of logical moralized theology. He gives formal recognition to the gracious origin of the power which enables man to perform the conditions of salvation. He alleges that salvation depends wholly on God. But the general tenor of his discussion admits only wavering recognition of such dependence. His commitment to man's free personal agency is decisive at every turn, not only in his doctrine of sin, but also in his doctrine of grace. With its severe restrictions placed on the role of prevenient grace, and its imposing claims made for the freedom of rational man, his theology of salvation represents a reluctant but decided departure from original Wesleyanism.

KNUDSON ON CHRIST AND REDEMPTION

The modifications in the doctrine of grace which are suggested in Watson and evident in Miley receive precise formulation in Knudson. The principles underlying these modifications are openly acknowledged and carefully explicated: the continuity between God and man evidenced in the oneness of religious and general knowledge, the unimpaired reality of contrary choice, and the transforming power of the "revelation" of the divine nature. In the place of the Wesleyan heritage, these principles rule the reconstruction of theology and result in a great simplification. The doctrines of redemption are reduced to repentance and faith. Salvation is no longer the rescue of an otherwise helpless man; it is his free

---

than any question respecting the mode of the work within the soul. Sanctification, whether in part or in whole, is in the measure of the incoming and power of the Holy Spirit. It is entire when through his presence and power the evil tendencies are subdued and the dominance of the spiritual life is complete."

resolve to improve his condition, divinely assisted in its fulfillment. Man is not "saved" but in process of "being saved." Toward this end, God's disclosure in Christ is the most salutary impetus eliciting the wholehearted response of man and effecting his moral and spiritual transformation. In Methodism, the reconstruction of theology guided by the spirit and principles of liberalism reached its zenith in Knudson's personal idealism. Both the theologians of transition who preceded him and the theologians of orthodoxy who followed him were less accommodating to the demands of culture and more committed to the historically defined demands of Christ than was Knudson.

God in Christ

Man's need for redemption is evident, asserts Knudson. The magnitude of the difficulties he faces, the imperious call of the ideal, and the limitations on his freedom preclude the possibility that man can save himself (II, 406). He must be redeemed by a power outside himself, which, in a way altogether unique, Christians link to the person and work of Christ (II, 282 f.). Christ stands between God and man as a perfect revealer of the Father and as a redemptive power in human life. For Knudson, there is no sharp cleavage between the person and the work of Christ. Indeed, in critical places in his discussion of the atonement he declares that "the incarnation is the guarantee of the atonement," more its essence than its presupposition (II, 378).

Christ is a unitary being whose divinity is to be found not in a divine nature but rather in a "unique dependence on God," caused by an unprecedented interaction between Christ and the Divine Spirit, producing a "powerful God-consciousness." Thus Jesus is both an ideal man and a clear revelation of God.[60] The incarna-

---

[60] *Basic Issues in Christain Thought*, pp. 140-48; compare *The Validity of Religious Experience*, pp. 220 ff. Kenneth Cauthen, *The Impact of American Religious Liberalism*, pp. 122 f., observes that "no part of Knudson's theology is more typically liberal than his Christology." His view of the person of Christ presupposes the doctrine of immanence. The two realities, incarnation and immanence, merge in Christ. Incarnation is extended by Knudson to all men and to the natural world. "At no point, then, is a

tion is well thought of as a particularized expression of divine immanence. Viewed thus, the incarnation renders inadequate all theories of the atonement which are "abstract" or "impersonal" and limit "God's free relation to men" (II, 366–69). Only the moral theory remains as acceptable. It recognizes that the obstacle to reconciliation always lies in man, never in God, who eternally stands ready to redeem. Because God was in Christ, his death reveals the sacrificial nature of the divine love and provides a profoundly moving example of absolute faithfulness. "The presence of God in Christ gives immediate revelational value to his death, and the sacrificial love of God thus revealed awakens an answering love in the hearts of men. This is the only way in which sinful men can be redeemed, namely, through moral and spiritual transformation. No other kind of redemption would be truly Christian." [61]

Atonement has no objective bearing on God, nor is it addressed to man's guilt. In his response to it, man seems not to be hampered by depravity of any sort. Though Wesley might term this "agreeable doctrine," he would judge it to be only tenuously related to that unique, indispensable act by which God in Christ provides the conditions for salvation and enables man to meet them. Confined to Knudson's terms, Wesley would find it most difficult to account for the anguish of the convicted sinner as well as for the joy of the sinner accepted for Christ's sake.

---

radical break or gulf to be found in this scheme. Nature, ordinary men, Christ and God are all parts of one organic whole."

[61] *Basic Issues in Christian Thought*, p. 148; see also "A Doctrine of the Atonement for the Modern World," *Crozier Quarterly*, 23 (1946), 51-64. Curtis K. Jones, "Personalism as Christian Philosophy," pp. 192, 195, contends that "this moral theory of the work of Christ can be called an atonement only by courtesy, as Bowne perceived. . . . It is a work of revelation from the divine side resulting in a work of regeneration on the human side." It suggests "a rather superficial moralism which does justice neither to the depth of sinfulness in man nor to the merciful grace of God." Cauthen, *The Impact of American Religious Liberalism*, p. 125, suggests that Knudson's moral influence theory assumes the continuity of holiness and love in God, "making objective atonement unnecessary." The implicit suppression of God's holiness is related to a weakening of the view of man's sin. Not the objective reconciliation of God is required of Christ, but, rather, the moral empowering of man, "in order to overcome the drag of nature on a free and virtuous but weak spirit."

Metaphysical Freedom and Divine Grace

The freedom of man and the personality of God are the "two most fundamental doctrines of the Christian faith." [62] As we have seen, in his doctrine of man Knudson asserts that man's "metaphysical freedom" is part of his created nature; he calls it a "positive presupposition of redemption." For Wesley, the religious dimensions of freedom require its consideration within the redemptive order; for Knudson, logical and theological considerations require its location within the created order. Therefore, to compare Knudson and Wesley on freedom, it is necessary to uproot the relevant discussion of one or the other from its normal systematic context. This shift reveals a significant theological transition.

The freedom of the soul is a critical conviction for Knudson. "There is in man a self-directing power, to which different courses of action are really open and which is able to decide for itself what particular course it will take. This power of contrary choice is the essence of metaphysical freedom" (II, 123). Only "closet logic" will attempt to maintain that freedom, or indeterminism, implies causeless, motiveless, and, therefore, capricious action. Guided by motives from his own nature, the free agent is the cause of his own actions. By his own volition, man imparts value and attractiveness to his motives, and choice follows (II, 123–25). He is more dependent on the hidden forces of his being and the surrounding world than he realizes, but for all this, man is "the captain of his own soul, the determiner of his own destiny" (II, 160). The whole Christian conception of man as worthy and capable of saving is dependent on his freedom, self-control, and power of contrary choice. [63]

[62] *Basic Issues in Christian Thought*, p. 51. These two doctrines are closely related and interdependent: "The personality of God is intelligible to us only through our own experience of personality, and the freedom of man can be satisfactorily explained only by assuming the free creative activity of a personal God" (p. 51).
[63] *The Principles of Christian Ethics*, pp. 64, 82. See *Basic Issues in Christian Thought*, pp. 60, 76: "Over and above these molding influences [environment and heredity] there is within us a self-directing power which enables us to choose among different possible courses of action." "Without freedom man would not be a moral

Knudson lists three "decisive reasons" why metaphysical freedom, or the power of alternative action, is true to the nature of reality. It is "the overwhelming testimony of common sense; . . . there can be no true morality or spirituality without" it; "the pursuit of knowledge presupposes" it.[64] Finally, he gives curt treatment to determinism, both naturalistic and theological. In their consequences for metaphysical freedom they are the same (II, 143–58).

Specifically, how is man's freedom related to God's grace in redemption? Knudson denies that the Christian life is solely the work of divine grace, insisting instead that grace must be combined with human activity. Though, for polemic reasons, the divine side is often given precedence, a proper balance needs to be kept between them: "Both the divine and the human, both the religious and the ethical, both worship and work, need to be recognized as essential elements in Christian experience." [65] Knudson hastens to add that the measure of freedom which man possesses does not make him independent of God. It is so limited, and the conditions of life are so difficult, that he is constantly in need of divine aid. Nor does man's freedom endanger the doctrine of divine providence. Both grace and providence presuppose man's ability to receive and cooperate with them (II, 152). Finally, man's freedom does not encourage Pharisaic pride or lessen his devotion to God. The power of contrary choice is a gift of creation to be exercised with gratitude.[66]

No sharp cleavage exists between human freedom and divine grace. Man's exercise of freedom does not exclude but draws upon grace. Grace does not negate the human factor but is its highest expression. The position of theological synergism, which upholds the reciprocal relation between the divine and human factors in

and responsible being." Compare similar valuations of freedom in Olin Curtis, *The Christian Faith*, pp. 40-42, and Sheldon, *A System of Christian Doctrine*, pp. 294-96.

[64] *Basic Issues in Christian Thought*, pp. 77-79, 59-61; see also "The Theology of Crisis," MQR, 111 (1928), 529-43, 549-60.

[65] *Basic Issues in Christian Thought*, p. 164, and *The Validity of Religious Experience*, pp. 201 ff.

[66] *The Validity of Religious Experience*, p. 213; *The Principles of Christian Ethics*, p. 82.

Christian experience, must be maintained in any rational account of the Christian life, insists Knudson.[67] In his judgment, Wesley did more than any other man to gain acceptance for this view.[68] In one context, Knudson says that the power of contrary choice belongs to man's essential nature (II, 158–60). In another, he affirms that freedom is a gift of grace (II, 164–68). But examination discloses that in fact freedom is a "gift" of creation. It is not graciously restored by the redemptive economy, as is generally asserted in the Wesleyan tradition. Even Miley, torn as he was between his attachment to free, personal agency and his allegiance to the traditional insistence on grace, gave formal recognition to the latter as the ground of freedom. Only by the most gratuitous reinterpretation can Knudson claim Wesley in support of his position.

The Christian Life

Knudson gives relatively brief consideration to the distinctively religious aspects of the operation of divine grace in "conversion." Conversion generally is regarded as having both a divine and a human side. The human side is represented by repentance and faith, and the divine side by justification and regeneration. Men are summoned to "repent" and "believe"; they are not called to "justify," "regenerate," or "sanctify" (II, 407). Repentance and faith are basically human acts even if divinely assisted; justification, regeneration, and sanctification are manifestly acts of the divine.

[67] *Basic Issues in Christian Thought*, p. 165: "There is in man a native capacity for God; we are made for him; and it is only because this is so that there can be a divine factor in our human experience. The divine in man is not the negation of human nature, but its crown. In other words, God manifests himself in human life at its highest level. At this level there is a reciprocal interaction between God and man. On the one hand we seek God and find him, and on the other hand he speaks to us and we answer. This mutual relationship is the heart of Christian piety. Such is the teaching of theological synergists as distinguished from monergists." See also *The Validity of Religious Experience*, p. 204: "We have a limited power of contrary choice. On this power the Arminian bases both moral responsibility and the possibility of moral redemption."

[68] *The Validity of Religious Experience*, p. 212; *Basic Issues in Christian Thought*, p. 166.

The comprehensive attitude of the Christian toward God may be summed up in one word: faith (love is an admirable equivalent). Faith is more than mere belief or simple emotional trust. It includes the right direction of the will. It is "a whole-hearted devotion to God because of what he is believed to be and because of our trust in him" (II, 404). Repentance is the preface to faith, though it is impossible without the binding ideal of faith. Repentance may be regarded as the "negative counterpart of faith"; it is faith viewing the past in sorrow and contrition and turning away from it. In its forward aspect, faith consists in wholehearted devotion to God—the profoundest act of which man is capable (II, 408). Thus, faith is given a place of primacy in Christianity.

Knudson denies that faith is a unique gift of God, qualitatively different from all other human experience.[69] Its relative distinctiveness resides in its moral depth and inwardness; it is the "profoundly inward and ethical act or experience" of the free man. It is distinctive also in the nature of the object: "the God and Father of our Lord Jesus Christ. The object of faith in the last analysis determines subjective faith, and imparts to it whatever illuminating and redemptive character it may possess" (II, 409 f.).

While faith and repentance, the human side of conversion, are to be understood literally, the terms which designate the divine side are simply metaphors drawn from the law court, family relations, and ritual worship. If the metaphors are transformed into doctrines, confusion, disappointment, and distress result. These figures point to the divine agency in the various phases of Christian experience; they do not describe the actual processes that take place (II, 410–16). Interpreted figuratively and empirically, "they denote the subjective effects of the divine graces, such as joy, peace, trust and assurance, rather than mysterious objective divine acts." The divine agency itself is not a "miraculous incursion into the stream of consciousness" but "enters into the orderly processes

[69] *The Validity of Religious Experience*, p. 216: Knudson asserts that, for Wesley, faith is "a human as well as a divine act"; it is an "ethical conception." He voices his firm conviction that "faith is a free and at bottom a moral act."

of the human mind." It is not an unusual or alien factor in the Christian life but "takes the form of a more thorough moralizing and spiritualizing" of that life.[70] It is limited to man's conscious moral and spiritual experience and is free from all traces of magic and "soul-enslaving fatalism." Perfection is a "theological provincialism" for Knudson, yet he finds positive meaning in it and in sanctification if they are taken to imply "a completely integrated moral life." [71]

It is instructive to note that though Knudson makes much of the self or soul, and its reality and freedom, he refuses to ascribe natural immortality to it. Despite the many considerations which tend to support belief in its continuation after death, the soul has no "metaphysical claim to immortality. The one basis of our hope is the divine grace and the divine rationality; and other ground than this we do not need" (II, 497). Whether his position on immortality represents a concession to Christian tradition and a compromise of his underlying personalism is an open question. Perhaps his hesitation in affirming natural immortality is chiefly an expression of his "epistemological realism," which regularly requires him to posit faith in order to move beyond the predicament of egocentric isolation.[72]

Knudson's view of man as a creature worthy and capable of redemption makes explicit basic assumptions which had appeared with increasing frequency through the latter half of the nineteenth century. Metaphysical freedom, based on the power of contrary choice, essentially unimpaired by sin, became central in the doctrine

---

[70] *Basic Issues in Christian Thought*, pp. 169, 175, 153. "The principle of continuity dominates the liberal conception of salvation," writes Cauthen, *The Impact of American Religious Liberalism*, pp. 120 f. For Knudson, salvation is "both religious and ethical, individual and social, present and future. The terms of these pairs are bound up with each other and are harmoniously related to each other." It is Cauthen's judgment that the continuity thus evident is, at every point, at variance with contemporary orthodoxy exemplified, for example, by Reinhold Niebuhr.

[71] *The Validity of Religious Experience*, p. 217; see also *The Principles of Christian Ethics*, chap. VI, "The Principle of Perfection."

[72] *The Philosophy of Personalism*, p. 326. Most personalists leave the assurance of the truth of immortality "to faith in God. The reality of the self, they hold, does not necessarily imply its immortality" (p. 75).

of man. Traditional Wesleyan theology had insisted that free-dom-for-God was lost in the fall and that the possibility of its restitution, in even a limited way, rested on the provisions of the redemptive economy. But Knudson's argument for freedom appeals primarily neither to Scripture nor to tradition, but rather to moral sensitivity and, essentially, to the basic postulates of personal idealism.

In his theology, man's free response in redemption assumes an importance qualitatively different from that given to it by Wesley. Knudson's drastically revised doctrine of sin paves the way for his magnification of man's freedom in salvation. Or, better perhaps, both are decisively influenced by his chosen point of departure—the reality, integrity, and responsibility of the self. If the free self is the primary intuited datum which "explains" all else, significant modifications in the doctrines of sin and salvation are inevitable. As it rounded off the sharp edges of stubborn realities in order to fit them into a two-dimensional mosaic, this theology seemed relevant and appealing to the optimistic and scientific age which gave it birth. But in this mosaic, though the heights and depths of the Wesleyan theology, its tensions and discontinuities, occasionally appear in the distant background, in the basic composition they find little essential place.

CHAPTER VI
TOWARD A PRACTICAL APPLICATION

One of the doctrinal norms of historic Methodism, *The Standard Sermons of John Wesley,* may also serve as authority for a final practical consideration. Though Wesley's sermons carried doctrinal explication to surprising lengths, he expected his simple, unlettered hearers and readers to give his words the most serious attention and to apply them to their lives. In his preaching, a common pattern is to be discerned: toward the end of his sermons he might declare, "I design to close these considerations with a plain, practical application"; or, again, "we may now draw some plain inferences with regard to our own practice"; or yet again, "it remains only to apply the preceding considerations to all who are here before God." [1] Wesley's intention in this pattern, though not unique, is nonetheless clear and consistent with all his life and thought. Preaching must be related to practice; abstract theory

---

[1] These quotations are taken from the *Sermons,* I, 94; II, 101 and 415. Compare similar statements in I, 173, 382, 451; II, 25, 105, 237, 426, and 434.

must have bearing on concrete existence; theology must be joined to evangelical reality. The suggestions which follow about the theological implications and practical applications of this study, therefore, are consistent with the Wesleyan homiletical habit.

A PROFILE OF TRANSITION

American Methodism's theological pilgrimage through the years from Wesley to Knudson has received only scant attention until quite recently. Seen against the broader perspectives of Christian thought, its claims to distinction are modest. Nevertheless, the study of this strand of theological history helps to fill a gap in American Christian thought and may assist contemporary Methodism's search for identity. It may even contribute to the general understanding of the dynamics of theological history.

Now that the story has been told, it may be wise to summarize briefly. Certain guideposts have marked the way. First, Wesley's theology has been made normative in the description of continuity and change, respecting his desire and supplying a steady frame of reference. Second, "Methodist peculiarities" have been put aside in order to concentrate on three "fundamental doctrines," revelation, sin, and grace. Third, the study has centered on the theology of Wesley and three of his representative heirs, Richard Watson, John Miley, and Albert Knudson, who worked a generation or so apart.

A broad survey of the theological developments beginning with Wesley and ending with Knudson has been offered as an interpretative background for the story. The century and a half covered divides simply into three periods at 1840 and 1890. The period from 1790 to 1840 was marked by the scholastic inclinations of influential British Methodists and by independent American theological essays reflecting the demands on the New World. The period from 1840 to 1890 was distinguished by the progressive "moralization" of theological categories and their integration in explicitly American systematic theologies. The period from 1890 to 1935 shows the widespread impact of new cultural forces and an extensive reconstruction of theology according to "liberal" criteria.

The main body of the discussion has been occupied with the major transitions that have occurred in the three doctrines basic to the Wesleyan theology of salvation: revelation, sin, and grace. The first transition, "from revelation to reason," began with Wesley's conception of scriptural, experimental religion and moved through Watson's efforts to authenticate Scripture, and Miley's arguments for the scientific certitude of theology, to Knudson's rational justification of faith by means of personal idealism. Increasing importance was attached to reason, natural theology, and philosophical demonstration, as priority shifted from the revelatory encounter, and its description, to the reasons for and the reasonableness of that which was revealed.

"From sinful man to moral man," the second major transition, delineated the change from Wesley's classical view of the nature and consequences of sin to an ethical redefinition of sin in terms of free moral agency. The guilt of original sin was placed in doubt very early and eventually denied, along with any inheritance of depravity. The realities which Wesley attributed to prevenient grace were gradually incorporated into man's created nature, depreciating his estrangement and helplessness apart from God. Sin ceased to be the presupposition of every human act and came to specify only those voluntary acts which violate known obligation.

The third major change in Methodist theology, "from free grace to free will," began with the Wesleyan doctrine of grace as free for all and in all and as the sole power of salvation. Steadily the areas of achievement assigned to man's freedom were increased. The atonement ceased to be the indispensable means of salvation objectively required by God and man. Instead, it found its ground in governmental necessity and finally was valued primarily for its subjective moral influence. Repentance and, eventually, faith came to be considered essentially human acts, not God's gifts, and salvation proper became man's divinely assisted effort to moralize and spiritualize his life.[2]

Thus scriptural revelation was compromised by reason's concern for evidence and logical implication; man was identified in terms of his moral capacity rather than by his captivity in sin; and the sovereignty of God's grace in salvation was qualified by man's intrinsic freedom.

In addition to these internal modifications in the doctrines of revelation, sin, and grace, some of the broader relationships among them and their deeper meanings call for attention. In the next section, they prompt observations on the sequence or chronology of change and, in the section following, on the interdependence

---

[2] Compare the developments in these three doctrines with the more broadly based characterizations of American Methodist theology in Scott's summary of his dissertation in *Religion in Life*, 25 (1955), 87-98. He specifies the "emergent characteristics" of nineteenth-century Methodism in terms of "gracious ability"—its basic soteriological contribution; a "transition in primary theological orientation" which found the uniqueness of its position in man's "intrinsic, absolute freedom of contrary choice"; an evident tendency "toward religious moralism in doctrines of Christian life"; an "uncertainty in religious authority," involving a fluid combination of "Scriptural, moralistic and empirical stereotypes"; and a "conservative adaptability in theological method" which was "qualified pragmatically by a sustained evangelicalism." His conclusions confirm the more restricted doctrinal interpretations proposed in this study.

Similar changes occurred in British Methodism, according to E. Dale Dunlap, "Methodist Theology in Great Britain," pp. 484 ff. Soon after the passing of Wesley, "an unimaginative scholasticism began to develop," which continued "until the advent of W. B. Pope who recaptured the spirit of Wesley." At the end of the nineteenth-century there were "stirrings" of a "liberal ferment" which gave promise of changes to come: "the weakening of ties of authority by Biblical criticism and the reconciliation of science and religion, the liberalizing attitude toward the Atonement and universalism, the emerging interest in natural theology, [and] the shifting from prevenient grace to co-operant grace in a drift toward humanism."

In his concluding comments on the *causes* of change in nineteenth-century Methodist theology, *London Quarterly and Holborn Review*, 28 (1959), 262-64, David C. Shipley observes that "the problem of methodology and apologetics [was] central to each representative Methodist theologian." A new statement of natural theology was needed which would enable people to endure in their struggle with nature and its new scientific understanding. Further "the concern for human responsibility" in salvation became "confused with 'the will to live' " necessary in the New World environment and "perverted into a false sense of human ability." These, he says, are "the formal causes for the *temporarily* characteristic American theological mood of self-reliance which appears so patently to be in rebellion against the sovereignty of God, and which, in most cases, unquestionably is."

of various doctrines. Then, on the basis of the total study, some comments are offered on the prospects for the Methodist theological tradition.

THE SEQUENCE OF TRANSITION

In retrospect, it is tempting to offer some observations on the anatomy and meaning of theological transition, beginning with a question about the order in which these changes take place. Is there a sequence in time according to which theological changes seem to occur? The history of Methodist theology suggests that there is: The chronological order by which a tradition undergoes basic modification seems to correspond to the logical order in which revelation, sin, and grace are discussed in systematic theology. That is, both move from epistemology, to anthropology, to soteriology. A brief glance at the characteristic preoccupations of Watson, Miley, and Knudson in turn provides evidence to illustrate this supposition.

In the main, Watson's theology is consciously Wesleyan. His doctrine of sin shows minor deviations from his heritage, some of which root in Wesley's own ambiguities. His doctrine of salvation is Wesleyan with scarcely an exception. However, his understanding of revelation and reason and his theological methodology disclose radical departures for which little warrant can be found in Wesley. His preoccupation with "evidence" and "authentication" led him to compile a body of material and to exhibit a way of thinking which are almost wholly foreign to Wesley. Clearly, in the first period of American Methodist history, under the influence of the writings of the British Methodists, the most significant modification of the Wesleyan heritage occurred in its handling of revelation.

Miley agrees that Wesley's methodology needed a major overhaul, but, not too pleased with Watson's suggestions, he offered some of his own. They differ from those of Watson, however, more in detail than in principle. Miley's most passionate interest is apparent in his discussion of the doctrine of sin. He eschews Watson's timid modifications of Wesley's anthropology and decisively rejects all suggestions of guilt and responsibility apart from free personal action. Inconsistently, he retains a belief in man's inherited depravity, although he ascribes no guilt to it. When he comes to grace, though he amends the description of the atonement out of preference for a strict governmental theory, his treatment reveals general willingness to accept Wesley's position and less desire to offer qualifications. Thus, in the second period of the history of Methodist theology, the most substantial theological revisions were made in the doctrine of sin.

In his effort to provide a more comprehensive and defensible position for reason, Knudson was willing to dismiss all lingering attachments to revelation as historically understood. He completed Miley's revision of the understanding of sin, denying depravity and original sin of any sort. He regarded man's freedom as intrinsic to his created nature and its exercise in salvation as essentially unimpaired. In effect, he fulfilled changes which, in principle, already had been accomplished. He broke new ground, however, in his drastic restatement of the doctrine of grace. He divested the atonement of its objective bearing on God and replaced the doctrines of justification and sanctification with more inclusive doctrines of repentance and faith predicated on man's metaphysical freedom. These changes in the doctrine of grace are the most distinctive emergents in the third period.

Thus the sequence of modification in the Methodist theological tradition proceeds from revelation to sin to grace.[3] Perhaps transition follows this sequence because matters of authority and method

---

[3] Whether the same dynamics prevail in the modification of other theological traditions is a subject for further study. So also is the relationship between this sequence and a more generally recognized pattern in which scholasticism follows reform, to be succeeded in turn by pietistic moralism (or moralistic pietism), itself finally rationalized to become culturally acceptable. Among many interpreters, John Dillenberger and Claude Welch, in their *Protestant Christianity,* identify this general pattern of theological succession in several different traditions and historical contexts. The survey of Methodism's theological history in Chapter II above presents clear evidence that changes in Methodist theology exhibit this pattern.

seem peripheral to the central reality of evangelical life, and their modification, therefore, seems unlikely to imperil it. Or perhaps it does so because apologetic theology in its concern for the "mind" of the world tends to offer concessions to it. Or perhaps transition follows this sequence because the free spirit of man cannot long endure the risks of radical dependence and must seek external support.

The reality of the chronology of change, however, does not depend on the validity of these speculations about its causes. Nor is its denial required by the probability that broader changes in the view of man's nature and possibilities first dispose theology toward epistemological and methodological revision, or by the further probability that changes in the view of man are related to a decline in the experience of grace. All that is intended here is an observation about the order in which basic modifications appeared. Alterations in the doctrine of revelation, once admitted, cleared the way for open expression of the modified view of man. This, in turn, finally required the reconstruction of the doctrines of redemption. Grace in salvation, the inner citadel of Christian theology, was guarded longest and best. But after its more remote outposts had fallen, eventually it too had to succumb.

THE DYNAMICS OF TRANSITION

The nature of the systematic interrelationships among the doctrines in theological transition is another important issue which invites comment. Is it possible to observe any pattern of reciprocal influence among these basic doctrines? Such interdependence can be identified, and it seems to be both more obvious and more significant for theology than the preceding observations about the sequence of transition. The critical relationships which demand examination are those between revelation and reason and between sin and grace.

These pairs of doctrines both root in the initiative of God in his relation to man. In the interpretation of Wesley's theology adopted here, the accent falls at just this point: Wesley consistently refused to compromise the sovereign character of God's relation to man; his view was so thoroughgoing that sometimes he was reprimanded for denying that logic required him to endorse election and reprobation, which were, in fact, upheld by his Methodist colleague Whitefield.

God's sovereignty is basic not only because of God's nature but also because of man's need. Sovereign love is constitutive in God's overtures to man both in revelation and in grace; both reveal his outgoing redemptive disposition toward his creation. But in addition, the character of man's existence *requires* this initiating love. For Wesley, the distortions to which man's reason is subject and the pretensions by which they are covered cannot be clarified or removed apart from God's healing revelation. Further, man's existence in bondage renders it wholly impossible for him to cross over the chasm fixed by sin between himself and God, except as God first comes to him. To this issue Wesleyan theology speaks a distinctive word, as has been pointed out. Thus the divine-human relationship is predicated upon man's existence in pride and slavery as well as upon God's character as holy love.

Another characteristic of this relationship produces the most difficult problems for life and thought. Man is in contention with God. Man does not want to be renewed and set free—at least he does not want to accept the humiliation and privation intrinsic to his release. Therefore, inevitable tension prevails between man and God—that is, between reason and revelation, and, again, between sin and grace. These tensions are determinative in Wesley's theology; the degree of reluctance with which they are maintained portends the transitional tendencies in the theology of his heirs.

Evidence for this assertion runs throughout the pages of our study. For present purposes it should suffice to review briefly several of the most salient aspects of the relaxation of the tensions between revelation and reason and follow with a review of the lessening tensions between sin and grace. First, in Wesley's theology, revelation is self-authenticating, based on Scripture, and confirmed in evangelical experience. External validation is of secondary importance. In essence, revelation is saving encounter, not truthful propositions (as it became in Watson and Miley), upon which reason is required to pass judgment. Drastically departing from Wesley, Watson assumed that the evidence for revelation must be rationally convincing before it can be existentially efficacious. Thus he strove to prove the "authenticity" of Scripture. Similarly, Miley endeavored to establish the "requisite certitude" for "theological science," and Knudson, by means of personal idealism, tried to furnish a rational justification for faith. The result is that revelation was subordinated to the external supports which reason provided, and the critical tension between them was glossed over.

Second, Wesley's successors tended to diminish the intrinsic opposition between revelation and reason by extending the significance of reason. In Wesley, revelation and reason are often antagonistic. In the resolution of their antagonism, reason is required to make submission. In Watson, the propositions of revelation never contradict divine reason, though they may contradict human reason. In Miley, human and divine reason are cognate and compatible, neither involving any contradiction with the truths of revelation. Revelation is not a substantive reality in Knudson and therefore cannot vie with reason. For him religious truth has no special source or standing; it is derived from common human experience and is subject to the usual tests of reason.

Finally, Wesley's theology of revelation possesses only token elements for a natural theology. In Watson, natural theology achieves some prominence, and his methodology becomes largely rationalistic. Miley further restricts the place and role of revelation in theology while he expands that given to nature and reason. Knudson denies the distinction between natural and revealed theology and disavows all two-story theological structures. The unitary structure for which he contends, however, belongs almost wholly to the domain of reason, in which revelation has become a naturalized citizen.

Between sin and grace the areas of tension are even more revealing of the transitions in Methodist theology than are the tensions between revelation and reason. First, Wesley affirmed that both guilt and depravity are integral to original sin. Depravity he depicted as utterly real. It is a corruption or sickness which is mortally infectious. Watson and Miley both affirmed the reality of depravity also but denied its positive character, insisting that it stems rather from a deprivation of the Spirit. Knudson accounted depravity an unethical, impossible notion. Turning to guilt, Wesley conceived it as adhering to original sin and entailing eternal death. Original guilt for Watson did not imply individual responsibility but only a liability to punishment. Miley and Knudson rejected Watson's compromise as an immoral contradiction. Thus the Wesleyan tradition begins its understanding of the doctrine of sin by asserting guilt and depravity; it ends by denying both, and original sin, altogether.

Second, Wesley's theology contains frequent references to "natural man," a phenomenon he describes as indeed far removed from original righteousness. The phrase implies man's condition apart from grace or, perhaps, after he has stifled and driven out the gracious Spirit. Wesley's uneasy commentators make clear, however, that "natural man" is only an abstraction; no man exists solely in a state of nature, entirely apart from divine grace. It is revealing that this concept is completely lacking in Wesley's successors. It is not rejected, but simply disregarded, as though a category for the interpretation of an abstract state were so much excess baggage. But its abandonment weakened the stress on man's corruption and helplessness, thus obscuring the dialectical tension between the assertions of sin and the promptings of grace.

Third, in somewhat similar fashion, Wesley's heirs gradually relinquished his doctrine of prevenient grace. This doctrine was of greatest importance for Wesley, as it expressed his belief in the universality of God's saving intention and supplied the foundation for his insistence on man's responsible participation in salvation. But soon this grace, given from the beginning to all men, ceased to be distinguished from the human nature with which it strove. Is it just a minor point, whether what man does in fact, he does by nature or by grace? Though it may be a fine distinction it can make a tremendous difference. As a result of its compromise, increasingly, the Methodist tradition magnified man's part in salvation in terms of his intrinsic freedom and consequently blurred the essential opposition between sin and grace.

Fourth, Methodist modifications of the doctrine of the atonement have also steadily reduced the distance between God and man. Wesley's satisfaction theory assumed an infinite distance between them and an irreconcilable contradiction, apart from God's costly act in Christ. The Grotian, governmental theory, which gained in popularity until its conquest was complete in Miley, assumes far less antagonism between God's holiness and man's sin. In it the atonement promotes the general moral welfare of mankind; it is not intrinsic to man's release from guilt and bondage. Atonement, understood as moral influence, presupposes no chasm between God and man; in it man is free to respond to the ennobling example set forth in Christ. Thus the changes in the doctrine of the atonement tend to provide in a simpler, less costly fashion for the reuniting of God and man.

Wesley's heirs did not maintain his high view of God's sovereign initiative as the indispensable foundation of revelation and grace. Their relaxation of the tension between revelation and reason ends in the assertion that "reasoning faith" and "faithful reason" amount to the same thing. Their relaxation of the tension between sin and grace ends in the assertion that man's created, not his sinful, nature defines his relation to God. These pairs of realities are contrapuntal, their terms so inescapably dependent on each other that changes in one side necessarily entail changes in the other. Thus it is that the transitions under discussion began with terms widely disparate and end with these opposed realities reduced to a common denominator. Man is the enlightened-rational, and the free-moral, creature.[4]

The temptation to escape the uneasy and difficult tensions in Christian thought and life has presented itself to every generation. Very often temptation has prevailed. The simplification of theology which results may be distressing, but the implicit simplification of the realities of the redemptive life seems to be more critical. If, in actuality, ineluctable tension exists between man's sinful ways and the Way of God, can theology ignore it except by paying a price?

Thus simplified, theology may try to veil its liberation from the burden of tension. Repressing man's loneliness, it may devote itself to "Christian beliefs" rather than to the encounter with God. By-passing the reality of sin, it may assert man's freedom rather than acknowledge his helpless estrangement. Suppressing the inadequacy of man's life, it may affirm his goodness and sufficiency rather than encourage his painful openness to the unpredictable invasion of grace. But in each of these ways, as theology conceals man's true condition, it acts to withdraw him from that encounter, acknowledgment, and openness which God uses for his own good purposes.

Honesty about the dismaying realities of life, about the sovereign character of grace, and about the tension between the two is fundamental. If such is the case, does it not follow that the theology which deals most faithfully with all the tensions between man and God is most to be commended? This is why Wesley's theology continues to be important for Methodism, and why, in several ways, the history of American Methodist theology is a tragic history.

[4] The inevitable tensions in Christian theology are discussed also with reference to the principles of continuity and discontinuity. Two enlightening studies which interpret the work of a number of twentieth-century American theologians may be consulted for elaboration of this theme: *Man as Sinner in Contemporary American Realistic Theology,* by Mary Frances Thelen, and *The Impact of American Religious Liberalism,* by Kenneth Cauthen.

THE INEVITABILITY OF TRANSITION

Can this exercise in theological history propose suggestions for the promotion of theological vitality? Serious concern for Christian life and faith prompts such a question and waits expectantly for an affirmative answer which would imply exciting possibilities for the church and its theology. Though a decided majority within Methodism finds its prospects encouraging and expansive, evidence supporting a more sobering estimate may be found in the 150-year history of its theology.

Rather than unequivocally undergird a buoyant optimism, one view of this history warns us, first, not to hope too much from the study of the lessons of the past and to scrutinize the motives behind our expectations. Second, it witnesses to the inevitability of theological transition, which it finds to be largely indifferent to man's control. Third, it cautions that the very determination to secure relevance for theology may entail tragic compromises with the world. And fourth, it acknowledges the hard necessity for a recovery of the past, more existential than intellectual, as a first step toward renewal. But beyond these sobering reflections about the future, the Methodist theological heritage points to the sovereign God as the continuing object of its theology and the Lord of its history despite all compromises and defeats.

The desire to turn the study of history and theology to practical profit may be more devious and less commendable than it appears at first glance. Just because this desire is legitimate and important, the distortions which it fosters are all the more difficult to detect. Therefore, those who would seek to revitalize theology need to inquire whether, and in what ways, their undertaking might be a compromise, not a consequence, of faith. Three quite obvious temptations in the use of history arise which may lead the Christian to betray his trust.

First, the impulsion to apply the lessons of theological history to contemporary life may spring from a desire to possess the fruits of Christianity by intellect and contrivance, rather than to accept the redemptive necessities imposed by the gospel. Christian faith and history, however, counsel that no study, whether of history or of theology, can discover secret knowledge or radical measures enabling man to direct or divert the course of spiritual development. Put most simply, no short or easy way exists which will enable a man or an age to become Christian. Gnosticism of every sort must be rejected, including the quest for prescriptions that will preserve theological vitality.

Second, the pursuit of theology in order to enhance Christian reality may conceal man's willful determination to supply his own needs when he is not able to trust God to do so. Underneath his apparent confidence in God may lie unacknowledged helplessness and hopelessness; thus out of fear and despair, not faith and hope, he may exact a willful claim on God's action. A basic dimension of faith, however, is its ability to wait patiently before God; obedience often dictates trusting expectation rather than feverish activity. This reminder is essential for us when we are determined to turn the lessons of the past to redemptive ends, for our insistence may subtly invert the divine-human relationship by requiring God to execute our fear-ridden commands.

Third, the effort to improve the future by lessons learned from the past may be a covert stratagem to escape the demands of the present. The Christian gospel is always and appropriately addressed to man's existing need for redemption. Any pursuit, therefore, which allows man to evade his dismaying blindness and bondage is, for the moment at least, an artful dodge. Preoccupation with the problems and failures of the past or with the plans and hopes of the future must not be employed to avert confrontation with the present, the dimension which truly levies life's imperative demands. It is in the present that the evangelical encounter with the living God takes place. This encounter gives rise to and must not be obscured by the theological enterprise.

If the quest for theological integrity in the service of religious reality can be so unwittingly and variously corrupted, we are cautioned not to entertain false hopes about the future. It is true, of course, that the pursuit of theology cannot be cynically written off merely as a subtle effort to possess Christian faith by intellectual contrivance, or a willful claim on God's support grounded in man's fear, or a stratagem to escape the evangelical demands of the present by hiding in the past or future. Theology does have bearing on legitimate expectations for religious renewal and assists in their actualization. Man does have a responsibility in each generation to formulate Christian truth as carefully and effectively as he can. But the service of the Christian and theologian is strengthened, not diminished, by being set free from false confidences and expectations. Thus these warnings about the dangers of theological pragmatism seem to be in order.[5]

Wary of lurking temptations, the inquirer into Methodism's theological prospects needs next to survey relevant evidence from historical experience. Such evidence gives limited support to two possibilities regarding theological transition. At best it offers uncertain ground, both for the hope that theological decline can be arrested or reversed by man's efforts, and for the hope that theology can be concretely related to the problems and demands of its environment without tempting it to compromise its integrity. Between the demand for theological integrity and the demand for theological relevance inevitably there seems to be dialectical tension. In Methodism, both demands have had their servants.

The proponents of theological integrity are conservatives in the exact sense of that term. They want to retain a truth which they feel has been given and is now present. They resist every apparent denial of that truth and prophetically call defectors to return to it. Because of Methodism's experiential and evangelical interests, it lacked the extensive prosecution of orthodoxy common in most traditions. Concerted efforts were frequently made, however, to

[5] For further remarks on the general character and role of theology see the Introduction. These fragmentary observations undoubtedly imply a particular view (or views) of the nature and function of theology and perhaps raise more questions than they settle. It is not my purpose here, however, to attempt to relate and answer them. They receive continuing consideration by many others who write with great insight and helpfulness in this area.

retain or recapture fundamental Wesleyan emphases. These conservative apologetics have figured at length in the present study and now need only be illustrated. We will look in turn at the supporters of more orthodox views of revelation, sin, and grace.

Within the Methodist family, Richard Watson sought to prevent the encroachment of Adam Clarke's rationalism on the statement of revelation. Daniel Curry saw in Whedon's adoption of commonsense epistemology a compromise of the uniqueness of Christian revelation. Miley and Mendenhall rejected most of the findings of biblical studies out of a reverence for the literal word of the Bible. Still later, Harold Sloan and George Wilson stood aghast at the boldness of Bowne and the liberal theologians who sought to conform revelation to the canons of reason and to expose the Bible to "destructive" critical study. But this struggle for the doctrine of revelation was destined to lose far more ground than it won.

Against moderating tendencies, Watson maintained a view of man's depravity at one with that of Calvin and Wesley. Daniel Steele felt that Whedon and Miley had undermined the doctrine of original sin by their stress on the philosophical doctrine of responsible freedom and guilt. Miley labored to enforce the fact of man's depravity after he had rejected all possibility of guilt apart from free action. Thomas Neely and John Faulkner charged that Wesley's understanding of sin was hopelessly subverted by most of the books on the 1916 Course of Study. Thus the contention in behalf of the Wesleyan view of man and sin ran through the generations. Its single most consistent feature, however, was its failure to accomplish its avowed purpose.

Against Reformed and humanist extremes Watson contended for universal responsibility in salvation based on a gracious restoration of freedom. Bangs and Fisk carried the same assertion to their Calvinist opponents. In mid-nineteenth century some Methodists denounced dependence on the intuitions of ability in commonsense philosophy and decried the substitution of romantic and enlightenment convictions for evangelical conversion. Whedon, Raymond, and Miley inveighed against revisionist Calvinism on the grounds that its doctrine of natural ability attributed to man what only God could supply. Against Knudson and the dominant liberal theologians of his day, George Croft Cell and Edwin Lewis summoned Methodism to return to a theology of salvation stressing God's initiative and sovereign grace. Though somewhat more slowly, Methodism's doctrine of grace also underwent a steady declension.

Thus were battles waged over each threatened point in Wesleyan theology. Repeatedly, predictions of decay and disaster were sounded and prophetic calls issued for a return to orthodoxy. Periodically, theology was subjected to agonizing review and laborious efforts were devoted to reconstruction. If, however, the conservation of the substance of the "fundamental doctrines" in the Wesleyan heritage was the goal, then the Methodist history surveyed in this study fails to provide much heartening evidence of success. The conservatives seem regularly to be engaged in a losing battle.

The evidence of history has bearing on a second mandate laid upon theology. Theology must establish its relevance to human society as well as maintain its authenticity. Thus Christian individuals and communities are required to wrestle endlessly with the divergent demands of Christ and culture.[6] In so doing, they seem inescapably to confront a tragic choice between an aloofness which will protect their integrity (but deny their mission) and an involvement which will establish relevance (but compromise their integrity). Faithfully, as the church seeks to be all things to all men, it must risk the integrity of its life and message by involvement in the world. What light does Methodist history throw on the possibility that theology can sustain relevance with its environing culture without at the same time subverting the gospel? We will note some instances in which men endeavored to gain a wider hearing for revelation, sin, and grace in order to advance vital piety.

[6] One of H. Richard Niebuhr's invaluable books, *Christ and Culture*, is a most suggestive study of the relation between the dual demand for Christian integrity and relevance. Related themes are distinctively developed by Paul Tillich in essays collected in two volumes, *The Protestant Era*, and *Theology of Culture*.

To authenticate scriptural revelation, Richard Watson used many of the arguments of the deists and often addressed himself to them. Whedon and Miley, in an effort to correct Watson, utilized the epistemology of common-sense philosophy and attempted to demonstrate a congruence between it and more traditional views of revelation. Warren, Sheldon, Knudson, and the evangelical liberals appropriated the findings of critical biblical study, incorporated variously the methodological suggestions of the philosophies of Schleiermacher, Ritschl, and Hegel, and took cognizance of the stress in science on evidence and empirical demonstration. Usually Methodist theology gained a wider hearing among those to whom its revisions were addressed; usually, too, its revisions meant the surrender of some earlier theological point or emphasis.

In the early American environment, pioneer independence and individualism subtly invited a less pessimistic view of man. Whedon and Miley responded to widely approved demands for moralistic and rationalistic revisions in their statements on sin, guilt, and accountability. Warren argued for the retention and restatement of the evangelical doctrine of sin in terms compatible with scientific and philosophical tenets. Bowne, Knudson, and others accepted many of the implications of Darwinism which lent support to belief in man's ascent but not his fall. Thus, as Methodist theology secured an expanding audience in American society, it gradually shifted its emphases in the doctrine of sin.

Sympathetic response to the demands of the frontier and revivalism led Methodism to reduce the fullness of the gospel to the elements of evangelical appeal. Bangs, Fisk, Whedon, and Dempster stressed the importance of theological education and demanded a respectable interpretation of faith for an intellectually enlightened age. Its competition with popular revisionist Calvinism encouraged Methodism to eliminate all theological irrationality and ethical ambiguity. An optimism which pervaded the entire culture exerted strong pressure on it for a reappraisal of the nature, means, and ends of salvation. Methodist theology established points of contact for its doctrine of grace, but in so doing it offered a series of concessions which, step by step, produced a different doctrine.

Thus Methodism succeeded only indifferently in maintaining the gospel as phrased in Wesleyan accents in the course of its engagement with the world. The forms which it adopted often failed to bear the full weight of Wesleyan doctrine; perhaps some were chosen just because they permitted a difference in accent. Still it is quite likely that the change in diction and vocabulary saved Methodist theology from isolation outside the mainstream of American life and also made Christianity a possibility for many despite the antithetical pressures of a complex and baffling world. Yet the struggle to find a language the world understood entailed a tragic necessity. To the degree that they were victorious, those who carried on this struggle faced the prospect of defeat. The translation of the gospel into the idiom of the day involves the risk of objectification, controversy, and loss. This appears to be one of the edifying lessons offered by Methodist history.

Inquiry into the prospect for Wesleyan theology turns appropriately from a review of the probabilities indicated by experience to a consideration of those realities of the past which still live in the present and thus shape the future. What response do such realities require? In far-reaching ways, the future of Methodism may depend on its recovery of the past. Within its corporate memory there is a great range of experience, some of it vital and self-effacing, some of it ineffective and vain. Its times of greatness and power are inspiring and reassuring. In fact, Methodism's memories are often limited to a few proud and frequently cited accomplishments. Quite different levels of fact and meaning also live on in the Methodist tradition, many of them little understood, suppressed, or lost to recall. It can be argued that the necessity for seeing and accepting all this legacy is axiomatic for Methodism's spiritual life—as elemental as the need for and practice of confession, to which, indeed, it is closely related.

The recovery of the guilt and glory of the past serves man and his tradition in several indispensable ways. It enables him to understand what he remembers, to remember what he has forgotten, and to appropriate what thus he learns.[7]

First, two facts about man's understanding of the past are initially evident and disturbing: the widely variant interpretations which he gives to common historical recollections, and the resistant forces which preclude his agreement on a common interpretation of these recollections. What makes the past so elusive? Might the explanation of man's inability to understand what he remembers root primarily in spiritual resistance rather than in intellectual confusion? If this supposition is true, it appears that coming to understand the past is essentially a spiritual problem, its solution dependent on divine illumination. That is, God's revelation is required to clarify the inner meaning of events which otherwise appear mundane and insignificant.

Second, much that has been forgotten needs to be recovered. Wider study of the details and broad meanings of our tradition should help recall what has been lost. But more is required. Historical-theological knowledge is inadequate because it can neither penetrate to nor deal with the largely hidden inner structures fashioned in our past and still exerting massive power. These enduring structures include unresolved guilt, which enslaves and paralyzes; repressed failure, which compels constant defense and rationalization; and unacknowledged pretension, which stubbornly denies the need to purge the past.[8] These realities must be brought to light if their demonic power is to be broken.

Third, that which has been brought to light needs to be re-

---

[7] See H. Richard Niebuhr's *The Meaning of Revelation*, pp. 109-21. In chap. 2 he elaborates a distinction between external and internal history which is also directly related to the theme developed above. The entire book is immensely provocative for insights into the study of the meaning of history.

[8] Though it requires little skill, it also yields little profit to identify failures and pretensions in the Methodist tradition for those who do not already see them or perhaps do not wish to see them: its loss of the intimate context of grace in the class and society meetings; its wavering surrender of the high promises of Christian perfection; its unabashed glorification of man's ability as a mask for the erosion of evangelical reality; its indulgent habit of veiling evangelical ineffectiveness by compulsive activism. Gaining freedom from the dominion of such principalities and powers is a matter of first magnitude for Methodism with decisive bearing on its future.

sponsibly accepted. Viewed not simply as objective external history, it needs to become our own personal internal history. This act of appropriation must include the dual streams of sin and faith which course through our history. And, since sin and faith have no bounds, their appropriation joins us to the companions of our past both within and beyond our particular traditions. It enables us to achieve community with mankind as well as unity of self. When memory is converted, when its destructive and divisive forces are recalled and accepted, they lose their power and new possibilities emerge. Thus the conversion of the past is prelude to the possession of the future.

The recovery of the secrets of the past is the work of God's grace. Without his support man cannot face, let alone accept, his burden of guilt and failure. Consequently, the deepest meaning of his personal and corporate past remains opaque to him until God casts on it the light of truth enabling him to apprehend it. This is such a disquieting admission that we strive to avoid it by rejecting the past—a habit which mere admonition will not break. But until we desire in all seriousness to apprehend the full significance of our personal and corporate past, we are not likely to possess unified and complete identities.

It is no easy counsel, therefore, which bids us recover the past. Such counsel imposes, rather, the hard necessity for disruptive, humiliating confrontation with our private and collective history. It can scarcely succeed on the strength of human determination alone. In God's grace, however, there is a way to gain release from the past and the way is open. But, specifically, the difficulties and demands of the road seem to belie the assurance of a comfortable prospect to the Methodist tradition.

THE ETERNAL CONSTANCY

It is strange that Christians who claim acquaintance with the hardness of the human heart are so often disconcerted, if not defeated, when confronted by the ambiguous prospects of their traditions. And, since it contradicts their conviction that these traditions are sustained by the redemptive goodness of God, their distress is stranger still. For God's goodness is eternal; it cannot be escaped or dismissed, predicted or controlled. It performs a continuous ministry to mankind which occasionally becomes widely evident in periods of revival. It is an enduring reality which men of faith may embrace with utmost confidence.

God's redemptive grace should be evident to Methodists when they recall the history of their beginnings in a great Evangelical Revival. Their very existence as a separate tradition bears witness to God's gracious action and gives cause for the most secure confidence in his continuing providence and transforming power. This confidence should save Methodism from bleak anxiety about the future as well as the burdensome certainty that it holds its destiny in its own hands. As it remembers its providential past, therefore, Methodism may reaffirm its faith in the graciousness of God and confirm its hope in his everlasting sovereignty over its history.

Again, the freedom of God's redemptive design may be discerned in the developments in Methodist life and thought in the present generation. In fact, the single most significant reversal of the dominating theological transitions of the last century and a half has taken place since 1935. The fundamental doctrines of Wesley have received sympathetic expression and acceptance by increasing numbers of teachers, clergymen, and laymen. This theological renaissance has been accompanied by hopeful signs of evangelical renewal in local congregations. Both movements have been supported by more widespread parallel tendencies throughout the Christian world. Though it is too early to assess the permanent value of these developments, it seems clear that in this generation Methodism confronts "openings" which imply new accessions of vitality.[9]

[9] For a careful exposition of Methodism's reaction to European crisis theology in the 1930's, see McCutcheon's "Praxis: America Must Listen," *Church History*, 32 (1963), 452-72; for a summary of recent developments see his section "Since 1939—Methodist Theology Today," in *The History of American Methodism*, III, 315-27. Refer also to the discussion of the question "Is there a Neo-Wesleyanism?" in *Reli-*

In addition, Methodism's theology of salvation is a powerful witness both to the imperative necessity for grace and to its effective reality. The doctrines of this authentic version of Christian theology have been confirmed in the concrete experience of present salvation. If they underscore man's inadequacy, they also underscore God's sufficiency. Indeed, the Methodist heritage distinctively proclaims God's grace to be unusually full and free. At the same time, it denies that its "optimism of grace" is an endorsement of "cheap grace" and insists that the bestowal and appropriation of grace exacts a price. Wesley held it necessary, under God, that the old man must die in order that the new man might come to life. His pervasive concern was Christian salvation. His heirs reveal fidelity to their theological heritage when they hold intact this same concern and speak out against its compromise and distortion.

Finally, if it is sobering to contemplate the future in terms of the transitions in 150 years of Methodist theology, it is ultimately reassuring to behold the sovereign God to whom these years and all of history belongs. If the record of their achievements is neither impressive nor promising, honest men may yet be saved from despair by the vision of a lordship which transcends their province. In the sovereignty and redemptive grace of God they find the best news and deepest reassurance. Methodists might well reread Wesley's *Journal* to learn anew that this fact was absolutely central for him.

And, at length, just as Wesley was "surprised by joy," so his heirs may discover, almost incidentally, that the renewal which they seek comes most surely when they live in obedient trust and cease to struggle cheerlessly to attain it. True, not to pursue a detailed program for the future is dangerous and frightening and may seem to be a cynical surrender of faith and hope. However, to trust God and live in daily obedience is neither to deny him nor

---

gion in Life, 29 (1960), 491-539. The appendix below, on "Methodist Theological Literature," describes many relevant books and studies of Wesleyan and American Methodist theology completed since 1935.

to accept defeat. It may well reflect the surest faith and promise the most enduring hope of all.

Behind and beyond the vicissitudes of religious life and theological formulation, men of faith discern the eternal constancy of God. Sustained by this vision, they are delivered from the pride of achievement and the futility of despair. Thankful to God for his gifts through their heritage, they face firmly toward the future, assured that great goodness shall yet come from his hand.

APPENDIX
METHODIST THEOLOGI-
CAL LITERATURE

A review of the literature relevant to the several aspects of this investigation will provide guidance for those who wish to pursue its theses. It will also supply a brief descriptive history of the more important contributions to this area of research.

There is an abundance of primary source material for an analysis of Wesley's theology. His important statements are scattered throughout the more than thirty volumes of his complete writings, all of which have been available for this study. Following Wesley's direction, the author has given priority to the *Standard Sermons* and *Notes upon the New Testament*. References are to the accepted editions of the *Sermons, Works, Letters,* and *Journal* by Sugden, Jackson, Telford, and Curnock. Quotations from the *Notes* are identified by Scripture references and can be found in all editions.

An increasing number of admirable studies of Wesley's theology are now available. Some of the more useful in the development of this study and more in keeping with its general perspective will be briefly noted. One of the earliest and still one of the finest studies in contemporary Wesley scholarship was done by George Croft Cell in 1935. Unyielding in its protest against misinterpretations of Wesley, it strikingly pictures Wesley as Luther translated into English, separated from Calvin by only a hair's-breadth.

Several first-rate, thorough doctoral studies have been completed since Cell's book. One of the most comprehensive and judicious is by Paul W. Hoon (Edinburgh, 1936). Its treatment of Wesley's doctrine of God and the dual character of the doctrine of salvation are outstanding. Another, by David C. Shipley (Yale, 1942) on Wesley's theological commentator, John Fletcher, breaks new ground in its critical examination of the "Arminian" antecedents of Wesleyanism. Unfortunately, neither of these insightful early studies has been published.

Among those studies which are now in print, Harald Lindström's work on sanctification (1946) is of first importance, especially valuable for its treatment of Wesley's views on sin, the law, love, and Christian perfection. A related study by William Cannon (1946) analyzes the doctrinal antecedents, parallels, and implications of the doctrine of justification. These two books provide an interesting contrast as each contends for a different doctrine as the interpretative key to Wesley's theology. More recently, John Deschner's perceptive interpretation of Wesley's Christology (1960), based primarily on the *Notes,* adds new dimensions to the understanding of this critical doctrine and its determinative bearing on the whole of his theology. Colin Williams' (1960) general survey of Wesley's thought illuminates a number of issues and relates Methodism's historic theology to its current ecumenical interest. In his balanced exposition of the doctrine of the Holy Spirit, Lycurgus Starkey (1962) also draws the implications of this doctrine for Wesley's general theological position.

From overseas have come several significant books on Wesley's thought, among which Henry Carter's (1951) is one of the best; it is inclusive, considerate, and suggestive in its ecumenical reflections. Franz Hildebrandt, a former Lutheran pastor, in convincing fashion explicates the essential continuity between Reformation and Wesleyan theology in two volumes (1951, 1956). The works of Rattenbury, Simon, Bett, Piette, and Yates have contributed to a lesser extent. Two essays by Robert E. Cushman are most provocative for the theses adopted in this study. Two papers by Albert C. Outler, privately circulated, also lend assistance.[1]

Ample primary material exists for the exacting examination of the theology of Wesley's three successors. Watson's collected works, which have been consulted, comprise thirteen volumes. Citations from the *Institutes* and *Sermons*, however, are from more readily available American editions. Miley's earlier theological writings consist of several articles and a book on the atonement. Most of this material is incorporated in his *Systematic Theology*, which is so comprehensive and clear that there is little cause for uncertainty about his views. Knudson wrote more than a dozen volumes directly and indirectly related to theology and many articles and reviews. A bibliography of his work, complete to 1943, is available in a symposium dedicated to him. All relevant materials from his writings have been utilized.[2]

Interpretative studies of each of these men are also available. Scott (Yale, 1954) gives consideration to Watson in several contexts and carefully and thoroughly summarizes Miley's thought. Dunlap (Yale, 1956) presents a comprehensive review of Watson's theology. Kenneth Cauthen, in his recent volume, reviews Knudson's theology in the context of religious liberalism. McCutcheon (Yale, 1960) includes Knudson in his study of Methodist theology between the world wars. Jones (Union, 1944) and Will (Columbia, 1962) refer frequently to Knudson's thought in their discussions of personalism. These sources may be consulted for more ordered summaries of the theology of Watson, Miley, and Knudson.

Only a very modest literature is devoted to the history of Ameri-

---

[1] Robert E. Cushman, "Salvation for All: Wesley and Calvinism," in *Methodism*, ed. William K. Anderson, pp. 103-15; and "Theological Landmarks in the Revival under Wesley," *Religion in Life*, 27 (1957-58), 105-18. Albert C. Outler, "The Methodist Contribution to the Ecumenical Discussion of the Church" (n.d.), and a Lecture to a Class on Methodist Polity, Yale, 1951, both mimeographed and privately circulated.

[2] *Personalism in Theology*, ed. Edgar S. Brightman, pp. 249-57.

can Methodist theology. John Peters' published doctoral dissertation (1956) discusses many of the men and much of the literature of American Methodism to 1900 but confines its interest to the doctrine of Christian perfection. Paul Schilling's work (1960) pursues the particular interests of its sponsor, the Methodist Board of Social and Economic Relations. It largely ignores developments in the years between Wesley and the end of the nineteenth century but contains a useful survey of theological developments in the first half of this century. Also in print on the history of Methodist theology are articles by David C. Shipley, Leland H. Scott, William J. McCutcheon, Paul S. Sanders, and the writer.[3]

A new three-volume *History of American Methodism,* edited by Emory S. Bucke and published in 1964 by Abingdon Press, supplies a long-felt need for such a complete and up-to-date work. Its contributions are uniformly of high quality; it is comprehensive and detailed and contains extensive bibliographies. Along with many briefer references, three of its chapters are largely given over to a treatment of the history of American Methodist theology: "The Message of Early American Methodism," by Leland Scott; "The Theology and Practices of Methodism, 1876-1919," by Gerald O. McCulloh and Timothy L. Smith; and "American Methodist Thought and Theology, 1919-60," by William J. McCutcheon. Scott also contributes a section on "The Concern for Systematic Theology, 1840-70."

Four doctoral projects have produced substantial references. An outstanding contribution by Leland Scott, "Methodist Theology in America in the Nineteenth Century" (Yale, 1954), is a detailed, careful, judicious survey of the leading men and movements

---

[3] David C. Shipley, "Historical Theology—Postscript and Prospect," *The Garrett Tower,* 29 (1953), 3-5; and "The Development of Theology in American Methodism in the Nineteenth Century," *London Quarterly and Holborn Review,* 28 (1959), 240-64. Leland H. Scott, "Methodist Theology in America in the Nineteenth Century," *Religion in Life,* 25 (1955), 87-98. William J. McCutcheon, "Praxis: America Must Listen," *Church History,* 32 (1963), 452-72. Paul S. Sanders, "The Sacraments in Early American Methodism," *Church History,* 26 (1957), 355-71. Robert E. Chiles, "Methodist Apostasy: From Free Grace to Free Will," *Religion in Life,* 28 (1958), 438-49.

of the century. It is important for its picture of cultural and historical factors, for the relationships and developments it traces from generation to generation, and for the general interpretations and conclusions it proposes.

Paul S. Sanders' "An Appraisal of John Wesley's Sacramentalism in the Evolution of Early American Methodism" (Union, 1954) is a thorough review of the period to 1844. Two chapters carefully survey theological developments. Helpful insights are offered on the cultural setting and the important forces in Methodism's theological evolution. The theological foundations for the church and sacraments are fully elaborated.

E. Dale Dunlap's "Methodist Theology in Great Britain in the Nineteenth Century" (Yale, 1956) parallels Scott's study. It reviews in detail the theology of Richard Watson, Adam Clarke, and William Burt Pope and offers surveys of lesser men and movements in British Methodism. It prompts interesting comparisons and contrasts with related developments in American Methodism and generally supports several basic conclusions presented here.

William J. McCutcheon's "Theology of the Methodist Episcopal Church during the Interwar Period, 1919-1939" (Yale, 1960), is an intensive study of Methodist theology set against the cultural and religious forces of the time. It provides a helpful analysis of Methodist liberalism, both of major systematic theologians and of the "creators of popular piety," and includes an illuminating account of the Methodist reaction in the thirties to the increasing influences of European crisis theology.

The literature on American Christianity has been enriched recently by two fine general works, *American Christianity*, by H. S. Smith, R. T. Handy, and L. A. Loetscher, and *Religion in American Life*, by J. W. Smith and A. L. Jamison. They give pattern and perspective to an understanding of the wealth of materials produced in this country since colonial times and sure guidance to a vast secondary literature. Selected from these and other materials, the books on American and Methodist history and theology which have contributed most helpfully are listed in the Bibliography.

BIBLIOGRAPHY

The following books are listed in four groups: Works by Primary Men, Works on Wesley's Theology, Works on Methodist Doctrine and History, and General Works. They are selected from an extensive literature and generally have been the most useful in this study. Books containing bibliographies particularly helpful for further research are marked thus (*).

WORKS BY PRIMARY MEN

Knudson, Albert C. *Basic Issues in Christian Thought*. Nashville: Abingdon Press, 1950.

_____. "The Christian Doctrine of Man," in *Theology and Modern Life*. Edited by Paul A. Schilpp. Chicago: Willett, Clark and Company, 1940.

_____. *The Doctrine of God*. New York: The Abingdon Press, 1930.

_____. *The Doctrine of Redemption*. New York: The Abingdon Press, 1933.

_____. *Personalism in Theology, A Symposium in Honor of Albert Cornelius Knudson, by Associates and Former Students*. Edited by E. S. Brightman. Boston: Boston University Press, 1943.*

————. "A Personalist Approach to Theology," in *Contemporary American Theology*. Edited by Vergilius Ferm. New York: Round Table Press, 1932.

————. *The Philosophy of Personalism*. New York: The Abingdon Press, 1927.

————. *Present Tendencies in Religious Thought*. New York: The Abingdon Press, 1924.

————. *The Principles of Christian Ethics*. Nashville: Abingdon Press, 1943.

————. *The Validity of Religious Experience*. New York: The Abingdon Press, 1937.

Miley, John. *The Atonement in Christ*. New York: Phillips and Hunt, 1879.

————. *Systematic Theology*. 2 vols. New York: Eaton and Mains; Hunt and Eaton, 1892, 1894.

————. *Treatise on Class Meetings*. Cincinnati: Methodist Book Concern, 1851.

Watson, Richard. *A Biblical and Theological Dictionary*. 14th ed. London: Wesleyan Conference Office, 1868.

————. *Conversations for the Young*. New York: G. Lane and O. P. Stanford, 1841.

————. *Remarks Upon the Eternal Sonship of Christ and the Use of Reason in Matters of Revelation*. London: T. Cordeux, 1818.

————. *Sermons and Sketches of Sermons*. 2 vols. New York: Carlton and Porter, 1851.

————. *Theological Institutes*. Edited by J. M'Clintock. (Copious index and an analysis by J. M'Clintock.) 2 vols. New York: Carlton and Porter, 1850.

————. *The Works of the Rev. Richard Watson*. 5th ed. 13 vols. London: John Mason, 1847–48.

Wesley, John. *Explanatory Notes Upon the New Testament*. 1st American ed. Philadelphia: Prichard and Hall, 1791.

————. *The Journal of the Rev. John Wesley, A.M.* Edited by Nehemiah Curnock. 8 vols. London: Robert Culley, 1910.

————. *The Letters of the Rev. John Wesley, A.M.* Edited by John Telford. 8 vols. London: The Epworth Press, 1931.

————. *Minutes of Several Conversations between Rev. John Wesley, A.M., and the Preachers in Connection with Him, Containing the*

Form of Discipline Established among the Preachers and People in the Methodist Societies. London: G. Whitefield, 1779.

————. *A Survey of the Wisdom of God in the Creation: or, A Compendium of Natural Philosophy.* 3rd American ed. 2 vols. New York: N. Bangs and T. Mason, 1823.

————. *Wesley's Standard Sermons.* Edited by S. H. Sugden. 2 vols. Nashville: Lamar and Barton, ca. 1920.

————. *The Works of the Rev. John Wesley, A.M.* Edited by Thomas Jackson. 3rd ed. 14 vols. London: John Mason, 1829.

WORKS ON WESLEY'S THEOLOGY

Bett, Henry. *The Spirit of Methodism.* London: The Epworth Press, 1943.

Burtner, Robert W., and Chiles, Robert E. (eds.). *A Compend of Wesley's Theology.* Nashville: Abingdon Press, 1954.

Cannon, William R. *The Theology of John Wesley.* Nashville: Abingdon Press, 1946.*

Carter, Henry. *The Methodist Heritage.* Nashville: Abingdon Press, 1951.

Cell, George C. *The Rediscovery of John Wesley.* New York: Henry Holt and Company, 1935.

Dale, R. W. "The Theology of John Wesley," in *Fellowship with Christ and Other Discourses.* New York: A. C. Armstrong and Son, 1892.

Deschner, John. *Wesley's Christology.* Dallas: Southern Methodist University Press, 1960.

Green, Richard. *The Works of John and Charles Wesley—A Bibliography.* London: Charles H. Kelley, 1896.*

Hildebrandt, Franz. *Christianity According to the Wesleys.* London: The Epworth Press, 1956.

————. *From Luther to Wesley.* London: Lutterworth Press, 1951.

Hoon, Paul W. "The Soteriology of John Wesley." Unpublished Ph.D. dissertation, Edinburgh, 1936.

Lee, Umphrey. *John Wesley and Modern Religion.* Nashville: Cokesbury Press, 1936.

Lindström, Harald. *Wesley and Sanctification.* Stockholm: Nya Bokforlags Aktiebolaget, 1946.*

Outler, Albert C. (ed.). *John Wesley: A Representative Collection of*

His Writings. New York: Oxford University Press, 1964.

Pennington, Chester A. "The Essentially Wesleyan Form of the Doctrine of Redemption in the Writings of Emil Brunner." Unpublished Ph.D. dissertation, Drew University, 1948.

Piette, Maximin. *John Wesley in the Evolution of Protestantism.* Translated by J. B. Howard. New York: Sheed and Ward, 1937.

Rattenbury, J. Ernest. *The Conversion of the Wesleys.* London: The Epworth Press, 1938.

————. *Wesley's Legacy to the World.* London: The Epworth Press, 1928.

Shipley, David C. "Methodist Arminianism in the Theology of John Fletcher." Unpublished Ph.D. dissertation, Yale, 1942.*

Simon, J. S. *John Wesley and the Religious Societies.* London: The Epworth Press, 1921.

Starkey, Lycurgus M., Jr. *The Work of the Holy Spirit: A Study in Wesleyan Theology.* Nashville: Abingdon Press, 1962.*

Watson, Philip S. *The Message of the Wesleys.* New York: The Macmillan Company, 1964.

Williams, Colin. *John Wesley's Theology Today.* Nashville: Abingdon Press, 1960.*

Yates, Arthur S. *The Doctrine of Assurance.* London: The Epworth Press, 1952.

WORKS ON METHODIST DOCTRINE AND HISTORY

Anderson, William K. (ed.). *Methodism.* Nashville: The Methodist Publishing House, 1947.

Asbury, Francis. *The Journal and Letters of Francis Asbury.* Edited by E. T. Clark and J. M. Potts. 3 vols. Nashville: Abingdon Press, 1958.

Bangs, Nathan. *The Errors of Hopkinsianism Detected and Exposed.* New York: John C. Totten, 1815.

————. *A History of the Methodist Episcopal Church.* 4 vols. New York: T. Mason and G. Lane, 1839.

Barclay, Wade Crawford. *History of Methodist Missions.* Part One, *Early American Methodism, 1769-1844.* Vol. I, *Missionary Motivation and Expansion;* Vol. II, *To Reform the Nation.* Part Two, *The Methodist Episcopal Church, 1845-1939.* Vol. III, *Widening Hori-*

zons, 1845-95. New York: The Board of Missions and Church Extension of The Methodist Church, 1949, 1950, 1957.*

Binney, Amos. *The Theological Compend.* Cincinnati: Swormstedt and Poe, 1858.

Bledsoe, Albert T. *A Theodicy.* New York: The Methodist Book Concern, 1853.

Bowne, Borden P. *Metaphysics.* New York: Harper & Brothers, 1882.

_____. *Studies in Christianity.* Boston: Houghton and Mifflin, 1909.

_____. *Theism.* New York: American Book Company, 1902.

Brailsford, Edward J. *Richard Watson, Theologian and Missionary Advocate.* London: Charles H. Kelly, n.d.

Bucke, Emory S. (ed.). *The History of American Methodism.* 3 vols. Nashville: Abingdon Press, 1964.*

Butler, Joseph. *The Analogy of Religion, Natural and Revealed, to the Constitution and Course of Nature.* New York: Harper and Brothers, 1857.

Cameron, Richard M. *The Rise of Methodism.* New York: Philosophical Library, 1954.

Clarke, Adam. *Christian Theology.* Edited by Samuel Dunn. New York: Carlton and Porter, 1835.

Comfort, Silas. *An Exposition of the Articles of Religion of the Methodist Episcopal Church.* New York: The Conference Office, 1847.

Crooks, George R. (ed.). *The Present State of the Methodist Episcopal Church: A Symposium.* Syracuse: Northern Christian Advocate Office, 1891.

Curry, Daniel. *Fragments; Religious and Theological.* New York: Phillips and Hunt, 1880

Curtis, Olin. *The Christian Faith.* New York: Eaton and Mains, 1905.

Du Bose, Horace M. *A History of Methodism.* Nashville: The Publishing House of the Methodist Episcopal Church (South), 1916.

_____. *The Symbol of Methodism, Being an Inquiry into the History, Authority, Inclusions and Use of the Twenty-Five Articles.* Nashville: The Publishing House of the Methodist Episcopal Church (South), 1907.

Dunlap, Elden Dale. "Methodist Theology in Great Britain in the Nineteenth Century." Unpublished Ph.D. dissertation, Yale, 1956.*

Duvall, S. M. *The Methodist Episcopal Church and Education up to*

1869. New York: Bureau of Publications, Teachers College, Columbia, 1928.

Edwards, Maldwyn. *Adam Clarke.* London: The Epworth Press, 1942.

Faulkner, John A. *Modernism and the Christian Faith.* New York: The Methodist Book Concern, 1921.

Fisk, Wilbur. *Calvinist Controversy.* New York: Phillips and Hunt, 1880.

Fitzgerald, O. P. *Dr. Summers, a Life Study.* Nashville: Southern Methodist Publishing House, 1885.

Fletcher, John. *The Works of the Rev. John Fletcher.* 9 vols. London: T. Cordeux, 1815.

Foster, Randolph S. *Objections to Calvinism.* Cincinnati: The Methodist Book Concern, 1850.

Hendrix, E. R. *If I Had Not Come.* New York: The Methodist Book Concern, 1916.

Hodgson, Francis. *An Examination of the System of New Divinity or New School Theology.* New York: Mason and Lane, 1839.

Holdich, Joseph. *Life of Wilbur Fisk.* New York: Harper and Brothers, 1842.

Hurst, John F. *The History of Methodism.* 7 vols. New York: Eaton and Mains, 1902.

Jackson, Thomas. *Memoirs of the Life and Writings of the Rev. Richard Watson.* New York: T. Mason and G. Lane, 1836.

Jimeson, A. A. *Notes on the Twenty-five Articles.* Cincinnati: Applegate and Company, 1853.

Joy, James R. (ed.). *The Teachers of Drew, 1867-1942.* Madison, N.J.: Drew University, 1942.

Kern, Paul B. *Methodism Has a Message.* Nashville: Abingdon Press, 1941.

Lee, Jesse. *A Short History of the Methodists in the United States of America, 1766-1809.* Baltimore: Magill and Clime, 1810.

Lee, Luther. *Elements of Theology.* Syracuse: Samuel Lee, 1861.

Lewis, Edwin. *A Christian Manifesto.* New York: The Abingdon Press, 1934.

M'Clintock, John, and Strong, James (eds.). *Cyclopedia of Biblical, Theological and Ecclesiastical Literature.* 12 vols. New York: Harper & Brothers, 1867-87.

McConnell, Francis J. *Borden Parker Bowne*. New York: The Abingdon Press, 1929.

McCutcheon, William J. "Theology of the Methodist Episcopal Church During the Interwar Period, 1919-1939." Unpublished Ph.D. dissertation, Yale, 1960.

Marvin, E. M. *The Doctrinal Integrity of Methodism*. St. Louis: Advocate Publishing House, 1878.

Merrill, S. M. *Doctrinal Aspects of Christian Experience*. Cincinnati: Jennings and Pye, 1882.

The Methodist Quarterly Review, 1818-1931. From 1818 to 1830 called *The Methodist Magazine;* from 1830 to 1840 called *The Methodist Magazine and Quarterly Review;* from 1841 to 1893 called *The Methodist Quarterly Review;* from 1894 to 1931 called *The Methodist Review*. Replaced by *Religion in Life* in 1932. Referred to as MQR, variations in title ignored.

Mims, Edwin. *History of Vanderbilt University*. Nashville: Vanderbilt University Press, 1946.

Mossner, Ernest C. *Bishop Butler and the Age of Reason*. New York: The Macmillan Company, 1936.*

Neely, Thomas B. *Doctrinal Standards of Methodism*. New York: Fleming H. Revell Company, 1918.

————. *Present Perils of Methodism*. Philadelphia: E. A. Yeakel, agent, Methodist Book Store, 1920.

Norwood, Frederick A. *Church Membership in the Methodist Tradition*. Nashville: The Methodist Publishing House, 1958.

Olin, Stephen. *Sermons, Lectures and Addresses*. 2 vols. New York: Harper & Brothers, 1852.

Overton, J. H. *The Evangelical Revival in the Eighteenth Century*. London: Longmans, Green and Company, 1886.

Peters, John L. *Christian Perfection and American Methodism*. Nashville: Abingdon Press, 1956.*

Pope, William B. *A Compendium of Christian Theology*. 3 vols. New York: Phillips and Hunt, 1881.

The Quarterly Review of the Methodist Episcopal Church, South, 1847-1930. (Publication suspended from 1861 to 1879.) From 1847 to 1886 published under this title; from 1886 to 1888 called *The Southern Methodist Review;* from 1889 to 1902 called *The Methodist Re-*

view; resumed original title from 1903 to 1930. Referred to as *MQRS,* variations in title ignored.

Rall, H. F. *A Faith for Today.* New York: The Abingdon Press, 1936.

————. "Theology, Empirical and Christian," in *Contemporary American Theology.* Edited by Vergilius Ferm. New York: Round Table Press, 1933.

Ralston, Thomas N. *Elements of Divinity.* Nashville: Redford, 1847.

Raymond, Miner. *Systematic Theology.* 3 vols. Cincinnati: Hitchcock and Walden, 1877-79.

Roy, James. *Catholicity and Methodism, or the Relation of John Wesley to Modern Thought.* Montreal: Burland Desbartas Company, 1877.

Sanders, Paul S. "An Appraisal of John Wesley's Sacramentalism in the Evolution of Early American Methodism." Unpublished Ph.D. dissertation, Union (New York), 1954.*

Schilling, S. Paul. *Methodism and Society in Theological Perspective,* Vol. III of *Methodism and Society.* Edited by the Board of Social and Economic Relations of The Methodist Church. Nashville: Abingdon Press, 1960.

Schilpp, Paul A. *Theology and Modern Life: Essays in Honor of Harris Franklin Rall.* Chicago: Willett, Clark and Company, 1940.

Scott, Leland H. "Methodist Theology in America in the Nineteenth Century." Unpublished Ph.D. dissertation, Yale, 1954.*

Sheldon, Henry C. *History of Christian Doctrine.* 2 vols. New York: Harper & Brothers, 1886.

————. *A System of Christian Doctrine.* Rev. ed. New York: Eaton and Mains, 1912.

Shinn, Asa. *Essay on the Plan of Salvation.* Baltimore: Neal, Wills, and Cole, 1813.

Simpson, Matthew (ed.). *Cyclopedia of Methodism.* 4th rev. ed. Philadelphia: Louis H. Everts, 1880.

Sloan, Harold P. *Historical Christianity and the New Theology.* Louisville: Pentecostal Publishing Company, 1922.

Smith, Henry B. *Faith and Philosophy, Discourses and Essays.* New York: Scribner, Armstrong and Company, 1877.

Steele, Daniel. *The Holy Spirit, the Conservator of Orthodoxy.* Boston: McDonald and Gill, n.d.

Stevens, Abel. *History of the Methodist Episcopal Church in the United States of America.* 4 vols. New York: Eaton and Mains, 1864-67.

_____. *The Life and Times of Nathan Bangs.* New York: Carlton and Porter, 1863.

Summers, Thomas O. *Systematic Theology.* Edited by John Tigert. 2 vols. Nashville: Publishing House of the Methodist Episcopal Church, South, 1888.

Sweet, W. W. *Methodism in American History.* Rev. ed. Nashville: Abingdon Press, 1953.*

_____. *Religion on the American Frontier, 1783-1840.* Vol. IV, *The Methodists.* Chicago: The University of Chicago Press, 1946.*

Tappan, H. P. *The Doctrine of the Will.* New York: Wiley and Putnam, 1840.

Telford, John. *The Life of John Wesley.* 3rd ed. London: Robert Culley, 1910.

Terry, Milton S. *The New and Living Way.* New York: Eaton and Mains, 1902.

Tigert, John J. *A Constitutional History of American Episcopal Methodism.* 6th ed. Nashville: Publishing House of the Methodist Episcopal Church, South, 1916.

Tillett, Wilbur F. *A Statement of Faith of World-Wide Methodism.* Nashville: Publishing House of the Methodist Episcopal Church, South, 1906.

Tipple, Ezra S. (ed.). *Drew Theological Seminary, 1867-1917.* New York: The Methodist Book Concern, 1917.

_____. *Francis Asbury, The Prophet of the Long Road.* Cincinnati: The Methodist Book Concern, 1916.

Townsend, W. J., Workman, H. B., and Eayrs, George (eds.). *A New History of Methodism.* 2 vols. London: Hodder and Stoughton, 1909.

Tyerman, Luke. *The Life and Times of the Rev. John Wesley, M.A.* 3 vols. New York: Harper & Brothers, 1872.

_____. *Wesley's Designated Successor.* London: Hodder and Stoughton, 1882.

Wakefield, Samuel. *A Complete System of Christian Theology.* Cincinnati: Cranston and Stowe, 1869.

Whedon, Daniel D. *Essays, Reviews, and Discourses, with a Biographical Sketch.* New York: Phillips and Hunt, 1887.

―――. *The Freedom of the Will as a Basis of Human Responsibility and a Divine Government.* New York: Carlton and Porter, 1864.

Wheeler, Henry. *History and Exposition of the Twenty-five Articles of Religion of the Methodist Episcopal Church.* New York: The Methodist Book Concern, 1908.

Wickenes, Stephen B. *The Life of Rev. Richard Watson.* 3rd ed. New York: Lane and Scott, 1851.

Wilson, George. *Methodist Theology vs. Methodist Theologians.* Cincinnati: Jennings and Pye, 1904.

GENERAL WORKS

Aulén, Gustaf. *The Faith of the Christian Church.* Translated by E. H. Wahlstrom and G. E. Arden. Philadelphia: Muhlenberg Press, 1948.

Baillie, John. *The Idea of Revelation in Recent Thought.* (Bampton Lectures at Columbia, 1954.) New York: Columbia University Press, 1956.

Brauer, Jerald C. *Protestantism in America.* Philadelphia: The Westminster Press, 1953.

Brunner, Emil. *Revelation and Reason.* Philadelphia: The Westminster Press, 1946.

Cauthen, Kenneth. *The Impact of American Religious Liberalism.* New York: Harper & Row, 1962.*

Clark, Elmer T. *The Small Sects in America.* Rev. ed. Nashville: Abingdon Press, 1949.

Cole, Stewart G. *The History of Fundamentalism.* New York: Richard R. Smith, 1931.

Commager, Henry S. *The American Mind.* New Haven: Yale University Press, 1950.*

DeWolf, L. Harold. *The Case for Theology in Liberal Perspective.* Philadelphia: The Westminster Press, 1959.

Dillenberger, John, and Welch, Claude. *Protestant Christianity.* New York: Charles Scribner's Sons, 1954.

Ferm, Vergilius (ed.). *Contemporary American Theology.* 2 vols. New York: Round Table Press, 1932, 1933.

Flew, R. Newton. *The Idea of Perfection in Christian Theology.* London: Oxford University Press, 1934.

Foster, Frank H. *A Genetic History of the New England Theology.* Chicago: The University of Chicago Press, 1907.

Gabriel, Ralph H. *The Course of American Democratic Thought.* New York: The Ronald Press Company, 1940.

Hudson, Winthrop S. *The Great Tradition of the American Churches.* New York: Harper & Brothers, 1953.

Johnson, Charles A. *The Frontier Camp Meeting.* Dallas: Southern Methodist University Press, 1955.*

Jones, Curtis K. "Personalism as Christian Philosophy." Unpublished Ph.D. dissertation, Union (New York), 1944.*

Mode, P. G. *The Frontier Spirit in American Christianity.* New York: The Macmillan Company, 1923.

Nash, Arnold (ed.). *Protestant Thought in the Twentieth Century.* New York: The Macmillan Company, 1951.

Niebuhr, H. Richard. *Christ and Culture.* New York: Harper & Brothers, 1951.

_____. *The Kingdom of God in America.* New York: Harper & Brothers, 1937.

_____. *The Meaning of Revelation.* New York: The Macmillan Company, 1946.

Niebuhr, Reinhold. *The Nature and Destiny of Man.* 2 vols. New York: Charles Scribner's Sons, 1941, 1943.

Osborn, Ronald E. *The Spirit of American Christianity.* New York: Harper & Brothers, 1958.*

Ramsey, Paul. *Basic Christian Ethics.* New York: Charles Scribner's Sons, 1959.

Randall, John Herman. *Making of the Modern Mind.* Boston: Houghton Mifflin Company, 1940.*

Rupp, Gordon. *Principalities and Powers.* London: The Epworth Press, 1952.

Schneider, Herbert N. *A History of American Philosophy.* New York: Columbia University Press, 1946.

Smith, H. Shelton. *Changing Conceptions of Original Sin, A Study in American Theology since 1750.* New York: Charles Scribner's Sons, 1955.*

Smith, H. Shelton, Handy, Robert T., and Loetscher, Lefferts A. *Amer-

ican Christianity. 2 vols. New York: Charles Scribner's Sons, 1960-63.*

Smith, James Ward, and Jamison, A. Leland (eds.). *Religion in American Life.* 4 vols. Vol. I, *The Shaping of American Religion.* Princeton: Princeton University Press, 1961.*

Smith, Timothy L. *Revivalism and Social Reform in Mid-Nineteenth-Century America.* Nashville: Abingdon Press, 1957.*

Soper, David W. *Major Voices in American Theology.* Philadelphia: The Westminster Press, 1953.

Sperry, Willard L. *Religion in America.* New York: The Macmillan Company, 1946.

Sweet, W. W. *Religion in the Development of American Culture 1765-1840.* New York: Charles Scribner's Sons, 1952.

————. *The Story of Religion in America.* Rev. ed. New York: Harper & Brothers, 1950.

Thelen, M. F. *Man as Sinner in Contemporary American Realistic Theology.* New York: King's Crown Press, 1946.*

Tillich, Paul. *The Protestant Era.* London: Nisbet and Company, Ltd., 1951.

————. *Systematic Theology.* 3 vols. Chicago: The University of Chicago Press, 1951, 1957, 1963.

————. *Theology of Culture.* Edited by Robert C. Kimball. New York: Oxford University Press, 1959.

Van Dusen, Henry P. *The Vindication of Liberal Theology.* New York: Charles Scribner's Sons, 1963.

Weisberger, Bernard A. *They Gathered at the River.* Boston: Little, Brown and Company, 1958.*

Whitley, W. T. (ed.). *The Doctrine of Grace.* London: Student Christian Movement Press, 1932.

Wieman, H. N., and Meland, B. E. *American Philosophies of Religion.* Chicago: Willett, Clark and Company, 1936.

Will, James Edward. "Implications for Philosophical Theology in the Confrontation of American Personalism with Depth Psychology." Unpublished Ph.D. dissertation, Columbia University, 1962.*

Willey, Basil. *The Eighteenth Century Background.* New York: Columbia University Press, 1941.

Williams, N. P. *The Ideas of the Fall and of Original Sin.* London: Longmans, Green and Company, 1938.

INDEX

Numbers in italics refer to
references found in footnotes

Acceptance, 147, 163

Adam, 84, 116-18, 124-27, 130-33, 147, 160
first, 147
second, 118, 147

Adoption, 164

Age of Reason, 82, 87, 89

Agnew, Theodore L., *43*

Agnosticism, 114

Ahlstrom, Sydney E., *50, 54, 64*

American context, 39, 42-43, 49, 52, 55, *187*, 201

American Revolution, 23, 38

Analogy (Butler), 35, 40-41

Anderson, William K., *23*

Anglicanism, 19, *28*

Anselm, *145, 160*

Anthropology, 45, 60, 188-89; see also Man, Sin

Antinomianism, 144, 147, *150*, 164

A Priori categories, 107-8

Arguments for God, 84, *85*, 94-95, 98,

Arguments for God—*cont'd*
102-3, 107-9, 109-11; see also Evidence

Arminianism, 19, 34, 49, 55, 58-61, 129-30, 133-34, *152, 155*, 166, 167, 172

Arminius, James, 59

Asbury, Francis, 42, *157*

Assurance. *See* Witness of Spirit

Atonement, 17, 27, 145-48, 158-60, 166-69, 176-77, 186, 189, 194
conditional benefits, 162, 169
governmental (rectoral, Grotian), *54*, 60, 158-59, *165*, 166-69, 186, 189, 194
moral influence, *56*, 176-77, 186, 194
satisfaction, *54*, 146-47, 159-60, *166*, 167, 194
substitutionary, *53, 56*
unconditional benefits, 147, 150, 160-61, 168-69
universality, 158-60, 168

227

Atonement in Christ, The (Miley), 58
Augustine, 60, 118, 153, *174*

Balch, William M., *63*
Bangs, Nathan, *33*, 34, 44, *61*, *170*, 199, 201
Bangs, W. M., *94*
Baptism, 147
Barclay, Wade Crawford, 24, *33*, *51*, 57, 59, *63*, 67, *167*
Barnes, Albert, 45
Basic Issues in Christian Thought (Knudson), 73, 106
Baxter, Richard, *33*
Beecher, Lyman, 45, 53
Benson, Joseph, *33*, 34, 39, 41
Bertocci, Peter A., 64, 65
Bible. *See* Scripture
Biblical criticism, 50, 51, 61, 62, 66, 67, 68, *70*, 99, *187*, 199, 201
Biblical and Theological Dictionary (Watson), 46
Biblical and Theological Library (Crooks and Hurst), 56
Binney, Amos, 48, 54, 129
Bledsoe, Albert T., 47, 52, 59, 61, 129, *134*, 166, *170*
Book of Common Prayer, 84
Bosley, Harold, *25*
Boston University School of Theology, 35, 55, 63, 64, 66, 67, 72, 73
Bowne, Borden Parker, 35, 36, 64-65, 66, 67, 70, 104, 108, *109*, *139*, 199
Brailsford, Edward J., 47
Brauer, Jerald C., *43*, *51*
Brightman, E. S., 64
British Methodism, 23, *33*, 38-42, 60, 185, 188
Bucke, Emory S., 24, 212
Buckley, J. M., *59*

Bushnell, Horace, 49
Butler, Joseph, *33*, *35*, 40-41, *50*

Calvin, John, *85*, 119, 126, *152*, 199
Calvinism, 39, 40, 43-46, 51, 52-53, 56, *61*, 66, 69, *133*, 134, 144, 147, *149*, 150, 158, 161, 164, 168, 169, 199, 201
  New Divinity, 52, 53
  New School, 45
  Old School, 45
Calvinist Controversy (Fisk), 45
Cannon, William R., *33*, *118*, 119, *146*, *151*, 210
Carlyle, Thomas, 67
Carter, Henry, 23, *30*, 210
Catholic spirit, 23, 26
Catholic tradition, 84, 133, 155
Cauthen, Kenneth, 73, 74, *105*, 108, *141*, *176*, *177*, *182*, *195*, 211
Cell, George Croft, 23, *31*, 68, 69, 80, 81, *85*, *118*, 145, *152*, 200, 210
Certainty, 97-101, 186, 192
Chandler, Douglas R., *33*
Chaplain, J .F., *59*
Checks to Antinomianism (Fletcher), 40
Chiles, Robert E., 212
Christian Advocate, 42, 50, 68
Christian apologetics, 13-14, 198-200
Christian Manifesto, A (Lewis), 69
Christian perfection, 17, 30-31, 62, 156, *165*, *182*, *203*; *see also* Sanctification
Christian tradition, 79, 84, 86
Christmas conference, 24, 38
Christology, 145-48, 158-60, 166-69; *see also* Atonement
Church of England, 27, 146
Church Fathers, 84, 86
Civil War, 49, 51, 62

Clark, E. T., 70

Clarke, Adam, 33, 34, 39, 41-42, 70, 72, 97, *163*, 199, 213

Class meeting, 56, 86

Class Meetings (Miley), 58

Classical Christianity, 16, 19, 31, 87

Cocker, B. F., *94*

Coke, Thomas, *33*

Cole, Stewart G., *71, 99*

Coleridge, Samuel Taylor, 49

Comfort, Silas, 54

Commager, Henry Steele, 62

Commentary on the Old and New Testament (Clarke), 72

Common-sense philosophy, 50, 52, 94, 169, 199, 201

Compendium of Natural Philosophy (Wesley), 78, 84

Complete System of Christian Theology (Wakefield), 48

Conscience, 150

Conservative reaction, 56-58, 69-72, 198-200

Contemporary American Theology (Ferm), 73

Cooke, G. A., 70

Cooperation. *See* Synergism

Corruption. *See* Sin

Course of study, 32-36, 40, 42, 47, 51, 55, 58, 59, 67, 68, 69, 71

Cousin, Victor, 50, 74

Creation, 137, 178-79, 180, 189

Creator, 83, 84

Crook, R., 57

Crooks, George R., 56

Culture, impact of, 14, 61, 62-64, 124, 189, 200, 202

Curnock, Nehemiah, *23, 148, 209*

Curry, Daniel, 47, 50, 53, 54, 56, 57, 65, *120*, 199

Curtis, G. L., 70

Curtis, Olin A., 33, 35, 61, 65, 66, 67, 69, 72, *133, 135, 139, 179*

Cushman, Robert E., *81, 83, 118*, 151, *152*, 211

Cyclopedia of Biblical, Theological and Ecclesiastical Literature (Strong and McClintock), 56

Dale, R. W., *146*

Darwin, Charles, 51

Darwinism, 50, 62, 201

Death, 117, 126, 159, 160

Deed of Union, 23

Deism, 28, 40, 41, 145, 201

Demerit. *See* Guilt

Dempster, John, 201

Depravity. *See* Sin

Deschner, John, *25, 27, 31, 78, 79, 145, 146, 155, 156, 157, 158, 210*

Despair, 151-52, 163

Determinism, 45, 138, 140-41, 179

Dewey, John, 74

DeWolf, L. Harold, 64

Dillenberger, John, *51, 63, 189*

Discipline, 24, 25, 32

Discourses (Clarke), 41

Divine-Human, 148, 150, 179-80

Doctrinal interdependence, 28-31, 190-95

Doctrinal standards, 22-26, 47, 55, 57, 59, 70, 71, 77, 184

Doctrine, 22, 26, 100, 101

Doctrine of God, The (Knudson), 35, 72

Doctrine of Original Sin, The (Wesley), 119

Doctrine of Redemption, The (Knudson), 35, 73

Doddridge, Philip, 88

Drew Theological Seminary, 34, 58, 64, 66, 67, 68, 71

Du Bose, H. M., 70
Duncan, W. B., 46
Dunlap, Eldon Dale, 34, 39, 42, 46, 49, 50, 51, 66, 85, 88, 94, 122, 129, 153, 158, 160, 162, 164, 187, 211, 213
Dunn, Samuel, 42
Duvall, S. M., 51, 78

Ecumenical movement, 25, 30, 66
Education, 44, 45, 49, 51, 201
Edwards, Maldwyn, 42
Einleitung (Warren), 55
Election, 134, 160
Elements of Divinity (Ralston), 48
Elements of Theology (Lee), 48
Empiricism, 62, 63, 65, 80, 100, 114, 187, 201
Enthusiasm, 29, 81, 85
Entire sanctification. See Sanctification
Epistemology, 64, 106-9, 114, 182, 188, 201; see also Knowledge, Reason, Revelation
Errors of Hopkinsianism Detected and Exposed, The (Bangs), 44
Eternal death, 117, 120-21, 126, 147
Eternal life, 157, 165, 175, 182
Evangelical liberalism, 65, 68, 69, 73
Evangelical revival. See Wesleyan revival
Evidence, 39, 49, 91, 98, 103, 187-88, 192, 201
    collateral, 91
    external, 76, 85, 89, 98
    internal, 76, 85
    presumptive, 89-90
    rational, 104-14, 186
Evil, 118, 138-39
Evolution, 51, 61
Experience, 23, 27, 42, 43, 48, 119, 187, 190

Experience—cont'd
    confirmation of, 76, 82, 85-86, 91, 101-2, 171
    evangelical, 29, 80-82, 83, 91, 101
    religious, 79-80, 103, 107-8, 113, 114
Explanatory Notes Upon the New Testament (Wesley), 23, 24, 78
Exposition of the Articles of Religion (Comfort), 54

Faith, 27, 49, 98, 152, 155, 186, 189
    act of man, 174, 181, 186
    as assent, 163, 173-74
    as trust, 152, 154, 163
    definition, 154, 163-64, 173, 181, 194
    gift of God, 154, 164, 186
    justification by, 154, 163-64, 173-74
Fall of man. See Man
Faulkner, John A., 51, 63, 71, 199
Federal Representative. See Transmission of Sin
Ferm, Vergilius, 68, 72, 73, 112
Finney, Charles G., 45, 53
Fisk, Wilbur, 34, 45, 61, 127, 170, 199, 201
Fitzgerald, O. P., 56
Fletcher, John, 33, 38, 40, 42, 70, 80, 82, 120, 134, 149, 157
Flew, R. Newton, 123
Flewelling, R. T., 64
Forgiveness of sin, 147, 155, 163-64; see also Justification
Fortney, Edward M., 30
Foster, Frank H., 65
Foster, Randolph S., 52, 53, 56, 58, 65, 90, 120
Free Will. See also Freedom
    natural, 144, 161, 172

Free Will—*cont'd*
supernaturally restored, 149-50, 161-62
Freedom (Free will), 14, 45, 52, 53, 54, 55, 60, 116, *118*, 123, 126, 131, 133, 138, 139-43, 144, 150, 171-72, 186-87
contrary choice, 53, 138, 178, 180
in grace, 138, 162, 171-72, 175, 180, 183, 194
metaphysical, 178-80, 182
of choice, 49, 169-72, *187*
Freedom of the Will, The (Whedon), 35, 52
Frontier, 39, 201
Fruits of the spirit, 82, 100, 156
Fundamental doctrines, 18, 26-32, 185, 200
Fundamentalism, 68, 70, 99

Garrett Biblical Institute, 17, 34, 54, *64*, 66, 68
Garrettson, Freeborn, 42
Garrison, R. Benjamin, *82*, *85*, 86
General Conference, *57*
1745, 144
1770, 144-45
1808, 24
1816, 32
1844, 51
1864, 57, 71
1880, 57
1896, 69-70
1916, 71
1928, 71
General Rules, 24
Genetic transmission. *See* Transmission of sin
God, 29, 38
and evil, 117-18, 125-26, 131, 142
character, 95, 111

God—*cont'd*
existence, 94-95, 98, 110-11
holiness, *146*, 162, 168, *177*
idea of, 93-94, 96, 103
immanence, *176*, 177
justice, 117-18, 146, 159, 167, 168, 173
love, *146*, *150*, 167, *177*, 191
mercy, 146, 167
personality, 178
power, *150*
sovereignty, 144, 157, 187, 190-91, 194, 205-7
wrath, 120, 146, 153, 159, 167
Goudge, H. L., *153*
Grace, 26, 29-32, 38, 190, 204
and depravity, 153, 165, 174
and freedom, 160-63, 199
and guilt, 153, 164, 173-74
as pardon, 153, 155
as power, 153, 155
cooperant, *162*, *163*, *187*
free, 29-31, 144, 148-57, 186-87, 193-94, 205
fullness of, 156-57, 165, 174
irresistible, 149, *152*, 161, 169
justifying, 153-54
optimism of, 30, 206
prevenient, 29, 30, 44, 45, *53*, 54, 60, *85*, 118, 120, 132, 148-53, 160-63, 171-72, 186, 193-94
sanctifying, 154-57
sovereignty of, 31, 152-53, 187
universal, 30, 147, 148, 149, 160, 168-69, 194, 199
Green, J. Brazier, *147*
Gregory, J. R., *47*
Guilt. *See* Sin

Handy, Robert T., *43*, 213
Harnack, Adolf, 68, 72

Haven, Gilbert, 52
Hegel, 63, 64, 201
Hendrix, E. R., 70
Hildebrandt, Franz, 25, 31, 77, 79, 118, 152, 155, 157, 210
Hobbs, R. G., 66
Hodgson, Francis, 44
Holdich, Joseph, 45
Holiness, 21, 27, 155, 156; see also Sanctification, Christian perfection
Holy Spirit, 29, 78-79, 82-84, 89, 149, 153, 155, 162; see also Fruits of Holy Spirit, Witness of Holy Spirit
  deprivation, 128-29
  redemptive work, 131, 154-55, 163, 164, 173-74
Homilies, 84
Hoon, Paul W., 81, 86, 120, 123, 146, 150, 152, 210
Hopkinsianism, 44
Horton, Walter Marshall, 74
Howe, John, 94
Hudson, Winthrop S., 66
Human consciousness, 53, 100, 104
Human depravity. See Sin
Human initiative. See Freedom
Human nature. See Man, Sin
Hume, 90
Huntington, D. W. C., 70
Hurst, John Fletcher, 47, 51, 53, 56

Iliff School of Theology, 68, 72
Immortality. See Eternal life
Imputation of righteousness. See Jesus Christ
Imputation of sin. See Transmission of sin
Incarnation. See Jesus Christ
Infants, 120, 135, 160, 169
Intuitive principles. See Moral intuition

Jackson, Thomas, 21, 46, 48, 148, 209
James, William, 80
Jameson, A. A., 54
Jamison, A. Leland, 50, 64, 213
Jesus Christ, 14, 62
  death, 146-47, 159, 177
  divinity, 27, 176
  imputation of righteousness, 147, 154-55, 159, 164
  incarnation, 173, 176-77, 194
  merit, 145, 146, 154
  prophet, priest, and king, 145-46
  sacrifice for sin, 146, 159, 194
  second Adam, 118, 147
  suffering, 146, 167
  work. See Atonement
Johnson, Paul, 64
Jones, Curtis K., 73, 74, 137, 141, 177, 211
Journal (Wesley), 37, 84
Joy, James R., 33, 59, 67
Judgment. See God
Justification, 27, 122, 151, 186
  and guilt, 154, 164
  as pardon, 154, 164, 173
  by works, 144-45, 150, 155, 165
  Christ's part, 154, 164, 173
  concomitants, 155, 164-65
  forgiveness of sins in, 154, 164, 173
  God's own act, 154, 164, 173
  repentance and, 151-52, 156, 163, 174
Justification of faith, 104-14, 186
Justifying faith. See Faith

Kaftan, J. W., 72
Kant, 106-9
Kelley, William V., 59, 99, 135, 166, 172
Knowledge, 65, 106-9, 175
  of God, 83, 84-85
  religious, 107-8, 175, 192

Knudson, Albert C., 33, 35, 36, 64, 65, 67, 68, 69, 72-75, 104-14, 136-43, 175-83, 185, 186, 188, 189, 192, 193, 201, 211

Law, William, 147
Lee, Luther, 48, 54
Lee, Umphrey, 23, 80, 151, 155
Leger, Augustin, 155
Leibnitz, 64
Letters (Wesley), 76
Lewis, Edwin, 33, 68-69, 74, 200
Liberal evangelicalism, 65
Liberalism, 71-72, 74, 176, 186, 187, 199, 200
Liebhart, H., 57
Lindström, Harald, 85, 118, 119, 120, 122, 146, 147, 148, 151, 155, 210
Literalism, 77-78, 79, 116, 125, 199
Literature, theological, 32, 39, 44-45, 49, 50-51, 56, 61, 66, 209-13
Locke, John, 33, 50, 93, 94, 104
Loetscher, Lefferts A., 43, 213
Lotze, 61, 63, 64
Luther, Martin, 85, 152

Mahomet, 81, 115
Man
    accountability, 124, 127, 131, 161-62, 201
    bondage of. See Sin
    depravity of, 117, 119, 121, 128, 129, 130, 131-34, 172
    fall and its results, 116-17, 123, 125-29
    fall, depravation by deprivation, 124, 128-29, 131, 140-41
    free will. See Freedom
    image of God in, 116, 124, 130
    moral agency, 129, 150, 161, 166, 169, 186, 199

Man—cont'd
    moral responsibility, 53, 60, 134-35, 145, 150, 158, 168, 172, 186, 187, 189, 199
    natural. See Natural man
    nature of, 190, 193, 199
    original perfection (primitive condition), 116-17, 124-25, 126, 128, 130-31, 141
    rational being, 136-38
    trial, 116, 125, 131
    worth of, 136-38, 147, 178, 182
Marvin, E. M., 57, 133
Maurice, J. F. D., 49
McChesney, S., 166
McClintock, John, 47, 50, 52, 56, 88, 91
McConnell, F. J., 64
McCulloh, Gerald O., 33, 212
McCutcheon, William J., 68, 69, 71, 72, 73, 74, 108, 142, 205, 211, 212, 213
Mead, Sidney E., 43
Meland, B. E., 64, 69
Melanchthon, Philipp, 152, 162
Mendenhall, J. W., 59, 70, 132, 199
Merrill, S. M., 53, 56, 134
Metaphysics, 65, 83, 109-11
Methodist Church today, 25, 71, 185, 202-4
Methodist Quarterly Review, 42, 50, 52, 55, 56, 57, 70
Methodist theologians, 32-36
Methodist Theology vs. Methodist Theologians (Wilson), 70
Methodists, 21, 22, 26, 30, 38, 41, 45
Middleton, Conyers, 76
Miley, John, 33, 34, 36, 49, 56, 58-61, 65, 70, 90, 95-104, 108, 114, 120, 127, 129-36, 137, 158, 165-

Miley—*cont'd*
75, 185, 186, 188, 189, 192, 193,
194, 199, 201, 211
Mims, Edwin, *47, 67*
Miracles, 40, 89, 90, *91, 99*
Mitchell, H. G., *70, 72*
Mode, P. G., *43*
Model deed, 23
Modernism and the Christian Faith
(Faulkner), 71
Monergism, 152-53, 171, 174, *180*
Moral ability, 44
Moral government, 159
Moral intuition, *50, 52, 93, 96, 103,*
134, 169, 171, 199
Moral restoration, 138, 177-78, 182
Moralistic revision, 45, 49-54, *173,*
185, 187, 189, 201
Moses, 84
Mossner, E. C., *41*
Motives, 53, 159, 169-73, 178, 196
Muelder, Walter J., 64

Nash, Arnold, *74*
Natural ability, 44, 200
Natural conscience, *148*
Natural man, 117-18, 119, 193
Natural virtues, 132, 148, 160, 169
Neely, Thomas, *47, 57, 70, 71,* 199
Neo-Orthodoxy, 69, 73, 74
Neo-Wesleyanism, 74, *205*
New birth, 27, 155, 156
New Testament, 16, 27
New York Christian Advocate, 59
Niebuhr, H. Richard, 200, *203*
Niebuhr, Reinhold, *182*
Norwood, Frederick A., *25, 42,* 57
Notes, Critical, Explanatory and Prac-
tical (Benson), 41
Notes on the Twenty-Five Articles
(Jimeson), 54

Olin, Stephen, 44
Opinions, 21, 23, 26, 27
Original sin. *See* Sin
Orthodoxy, theological, 16, 48, 61, 93,
176, 200
Outler, Albert C., *25, 122, 158*

Paley, William, *33, 49, 50,* 94, 104
Pardon. *See* Justification
Paul, 91, 118, 153, 161
Peck, George, *50*
Pelagianism, 48, 53, 126, *163*
Personal idealism, 35, 63-65, 67, 72-
75, 104, 108, 109-11, 113-14,
137-38, 139, 176, 182-83, 186
Peters, John L., *25, 30, 57, 67, 70,*
119, 122, 156, 165, 174, 212
Philosophy, 14, 40, 49, 50, 60, 63-65,
71, 72, 74, 85, 94-95, 100, 110,
201
Philosophy of religion, 64, 73
Piette, Maximin, *80, 151, 155,* 211
Pope, William Burt, *33, 34, 42, 53,*
56, 62, 70, 102, 103, 133, 167,
172, 187, 213
Practical reason, 65, 108-9, 114
Pragmatism, 86
Prayer Book, 78
Predestination, 45, 78, 152
Present and Future of Methodism
(Cooke), 70
Prevenient grace. *See* Grace, prevenient
Primitive state. *See* Man, original per-
fection
Prophecy, 40, 89, 90, *91*
Protestantism, 18, 19, 22, 23, 30, 31,
50, 65, 155
Pullman, J., 57
Punishment. *See* Sin

Quaker, 76

Quarterly Review of the Methodist Episcopal Church, South, 50, 55, 56, 59

Rall, Harris Franklin, 33, 35, 65, 68, 69, 71, 74
Ralston, Thomas N., 48, 54, 129, 165
Ramsey, Paul, 140
Randall, John Herman, 41
Rational proof. *See* Evidence
Rational suspension of choice, 170, 172
Rationalism, 40, 41, 81, 93, 95, 97, 102, 113-14, 152, 192, 199
Rattenbury, J. Ernest, 155
Raymond, Miner, 33, 34, 47, 53, 54-55, 61, 102, 103, 120, 133, 134, 165, 166, 199
Reason, 29, 40, 76, 79, 82-84, 86, 92, 186, 192, 194
  divine, 102, 192
  limits, 93, 191
  uses, 92-93, 97, 102-3, 112-13
Reconciliation. *See* Atonement
Recovery of past, 19, 202-4
Redemption. *See* Atonement, Faith, Jesus Christ, Justification, Sanctification
Rediscovery of John Wesley, The (Cell), 69
Reformation, 19, 27, 31, 84, 152
Regeneration, 155, 156, 164-65, 174, 177
Reid, Thomas, 50, 74
Repentance, 27, 151-52, 163, 174, 180-81, 186, 189
Reprobation, 147
Restrictive Rules, 24
Revelation, 26, 28-29, 53, 175, 186, 188
  and reason, 108, 188, 191-93
  interpretation of, 78, 83, 86, 92-93, 96, 102-3, 108, 113

Revelation—*cont'd*
  nature of, 79, 87-88, 96-97, 108, 192
Revivalism, 39, 42, 62, 201
Ritschl, Albrecht, 61, 63, 201
Romanticism, 43, 49, 63
Roy, James, 54
Rupp, Gordon, 30

Salvation, 29-32, 42, 120-21, 153-54, 193-95, 199-200, 206; *see also* Atonement, Faith, Jesus Christ, Justification, Sanctification
Sanctification, 30, 122, 156; *see also* Christian perfection, Holiness
  by faith, 155, 165, 174
  entire, 156, 164, 174
  instantaneous or gradual, 156-57, 165
  moment by moment, 157, 174
  regeneration and, 156, 165, 174
  second blessing, 69
Sanders, S. Paul, 24, 39, 43, 212, 213
Satan, 125
Schilling, Paul, 23, 25, 63, 71, 151, 212
Schilpp, Paul A., 68
Schleiermacher, 49, 61, 63, 79, 80, 201
Schneider, H. N., 64
Scholastic theologians, 39, 40-41
Scholasticism, 39, 43, 49, 78, 95, 124, 152, 185, 187, 189
Science, 14, 40, 49, 50, 61, 62, 65, 71, 97-101, 187, 201
Scott, Leland H., 38, 42, 43, 44, 45, 46, 47, 50, 51, 53, 54, 56, 57, 59, 60, 63, 64, 66, 92, 102, 103, 127, 134, 135, 167, 170, 172, 187, 211, 212-13
Scottish philosophy. *See* Common-sense philosophy

Scripture, 29, 41, 48, 54, 76, 77-79,
  81-92, 112, 160, *187*
  authority of, 89-92
  infallibility, 77-78, 89, 92, 96-97,
  112
  inspiration, 77-79, 88-89, 99-100
  interpretation, 78-79, 86, 92, 99
Scriptural Christianity, 82, 85, 115
Self, 65, 110, 183
Self-knowledge, 151-52
Seminal identity. *See* Transmission
Sensation, 93, 94
Sheldon, Henry C., 33, 35, 47, 59,
  61, 65, 66, 67, 68, 72, 90, *139*,
  166, 167, *179*, 201
Shinn, Asa, 45, 61, *127*, 170
Shipley, David C., *28*, *31*, *40*, 44, 54,
  56, 60, 80, 82, 85, *117*, *120*,
  122, *123*, *134*, *146*, *149*, *152*,
  154, *157*, *187*, 210, 212
Sin, 26, 29, 183, 189
  actual, 121, 133, 173
  Adamic. *See* Original sin
  bondage of will, 119, 123, 126, 129,
  139, 142, 186, 191, 193
  definition of, 121-23, 128, 134-36,
  139-40, 186
  depravity, 29, 53, 57, 60, 117, 118-
  21, 126, 128-29, 131-34, 136,
  153, 170-71, 186, 193
  guilt, 29, 53, 56, 60, 118-21, 133,
  140-41, 153, 189, 199
  inbred. *See* Original sin
  original, 27, 116-18, 121, 193, 199
  original guilt (native demerit), 118-
  21, 127-28, 130, 131-34, 136,
  147-48, 150, 173, 186, 193
  outward, 121
  power of, 165
  punishment of, 116-17, 118-19, 121,
  123, 126, 131, 133, 139, 141,

Sin—*cont'd*
  146-47, 153, 159, 160
  root of, 165
  transmission. *See* Transmission of sin
Sloan, H. P., 71, 199
Smith, H. Shelton, *43*, *45*, *51*, 62, 69,
  70, 213
Smith, Henry B., 53
Smith, J. Weldon, III, *150*
Smith, James Ward, 50, 64, 213
Smith, Timothy L., *31*, 212
Social gospel, 63
Socinianism, 44, 48, *163*
Soper, David W., 69
Soteriology, 45, 188, 189; *see also*
  Salvation
Soul, 136-38
Spellmann, Norman W., *24*
Standard Sermons (Wesley), 23, 24,
  184
Starkey, Lycurgus M., Jr., 29, *78*, *79*,
  82, 85, *118*, *146*, *147*, *150*,
  151, *154*, *155*, *156*, 210
Steele, Daniel, 57, 199
Stevens, Abel, *44*
Stewart, Dugald, 50, 94
Strauss, D. F., 51
Strong, A. H., *103*
Strong, James, 56
Subjectivism, 43, 80-81, 109
Suffering, 120, 138-39
Sugden, E. H., 26, 86, 209
Summers, T. O., 33, 34, 47, 52, 53,
  55-56, 66, 102, 120, *134*, *135*,
  166, 167
Sweet, William Warren, 24, *33*, 69
Synergism, 151, 152, *162*, 171, *174*,
  179-80
System of Christian Doctrine (Shel-
  don), 59

Systematic Theology (Miley), 34, 56
Systematic Theology (Summers), 56

Tappan, H. P., 52
Taylor, John, 115
Taylor, Nathaniel W., 53
Telford, John, 24, 209
Temptation, 116, 125, 131, 141
Terry, Milton, 62, 65, 66, 68
Thelen, Mary Frances, 195
Theodicy (Bledsoe), 52
Theologian, 15-16, 190, 198
Theological Compend (Binney), 48
Theological Institutes (Watson), 33,
    46-48, 54
Theological irrationalism, 108
Theological method, 55, 77, 84-87,
    92-95, 101-4, 111-14, *187*, 188,
    190, 192, 201
Theology
    decline of, 13-15, 25, 49, 190, 191-
        95, 202
    duties, 16, 112, 198-99
    integrity of, 13-15, 55, 58, 198-200
    natural, 39, 41, 49, 84, *85*, 96, 186,
        187, 192-93
    nature of, 16, 28, 62, 185, 198
    relevance of, 13-15, 55, 56, 58,
        198, 200-202
    renewal of, 13-16, 19, 23, 29, 31,
        196-98, 200, 202-4, 205-7
    revealed, 96, 192
    simplification of, 43, 175, 195
    sources of, 96-97, 112, 113
    systematic, 18, 28, 49, 54-56, 72,
        92, 101-4, 186
Thirty-Nine Articles, 24, 146
Tigert, John J., 53, 56, 57, 59, 60,
    134, 166
Tillett, Wilbur F., 33, 65, 66-67, 120
Tillich, Paul, 28, 200

Tipple, Ezra S., 59
Tittle, Ernest Fremont, 68
Total depravity. *See* Sin
Transition, 13-16, 19, 23, 25, 31, 38,
    43, 48-49, 58, 61, 63-64, 65-66,
    68, 74, 87-88, 91-92, 93, 96, 97,
    101, 102-3, 104, 108, 113-14,
    129, 130, 132, 136, 137, 138,
    140-43, 161, 165-66, 168, 171,
    172, 173, 175, 176, 177, 180,
    181-83, 184-207
    dynamics of, 13-16, *187*, 190-95,
        200-202
    inevitability, 196-204
    profile of, 185-88
    sequence, 188-90
Transmission of sin, 29, 117-20, 136,
    142
    physical generation, genetic trans-
        mission, mediate imputation, 117,
        118, 126-27, 132-33
    representative participation, federal
        representation, immediate imputa-
        tion, 117, 118-19, 132
    seminal identity, 127, 132
Trinity, 27
Twenty-Five Articles, 24, 57, 71
Tyerman, Luke, 22, *40*, *145*, *148*

Unitarians, 44
Universal Grace. *See* Grace
Universalists, 44

Vanderbilt University, 55, 56, 66
Van Dusen, Henry P., 63, *74*

Wakefield, Samuel, 48, 54, 129, 166
Ward, Harry F., 63
Warren, William Fairfield, 33, 51, 54,
    55, 56, 65, 66, 67, 70, 99, 166,
    201

Watson, Richard, 33, 36, 39, 42, 46-49, 54, 56, 60, 62, 70, 87-95, 97, 100, 104, 108, 114, 123-29, 132, 134, 137, 158-65, 163, 167, 168, 171, 175, 185, 186, 188, 189, 192, 193, 199, 211, 213
Watts, Isaac, 127
Weisberger, Bernard A., 43
Weiss, Johannes, 72
Welch, Claude, 51, 63, 189
Welch, Herbert, 63
Wellhausen, Julius, 51
Wendt, H. H., 72
Wesley, Charles, 38, 40
Wesley, John, 30, 31, 37, 38, 39, 40, 42, 61, 67, 70, 76, 77-87, 88, 91, 93, 94, 97, 100, 101, 104, 113-14, 115, 116-23, 125, 128, 129, 131, 134, 135, 137, 140, 143, 145-57, 159, 161, 162, 163, 164, 168, 171, 173, 174, 178, 180, 183, 184, 185, 186, 188, 190, 191, 192, 193, 194, 195, 199, 205, 206, 209, 211
Wesleyan preaching, 27, 184
Wesleyan revival, 13, 22, 31, 37, 39, 85, 115, 205
Wesleyan Theology, 17, 19, 22, 25, 26, 27, 28-32, 42, 48, 54, 56, 60, 61, 66, 69, 70, 71, 72, 82,

Wesleyan Theology—cont'd
86, 90, 113-14, 121, 123-24, 129, 136, 137, 140, 143, 144, 158, 161, 162, 163, 168, 172, 175, 180, 183, 185, 188, 190, 194-95, 200, 205
Wesleyana, 54
Wheatley, R., 57
Whedon, Daniel D., 33, 34, 35, 36, 50, 52-54, 56, 59, 61, 65, 67, 94, 103, 129, 134, 135, 166, 169, 170, 199
Wheeler, Henry, 70
Whitchurch, Irl G., 68
Whitefield, George, 149, 191
Whitehead, A. N., 74
Wieman, H. N., 64, 69
Will, James Edward, 64, 73, 74, 114, 137, 211
Williams, Colin, 23, 25, 27, 31, 78, 79, 80, 85, 121, 145, 147, 155, 156, 210
Williams, N. P., 153
Williston, Seth, 44
Wilson, George, 70, 199
Witness of the spirit, 27, 29, 82, 100
Works. See Justification
Wrath. See God

Yates, Arthur S., 29, 211